Stilwell and Mountbatten in Burma

STILWELL AND MOUNTBATTEN IN BURMA

Allies at War, 1943-1944

Jonathan Templin Ritter

Number 3: American Military Studies Series

Denton, Texas

10 9 8 7 6 5 4 3 2 1

Permissions:
University of North Texas Press
1155 Union Circle #311336
Denton, TX 76203-5017

The paper used in this book meets the minimum requirements of the
American National Standard for Permanence of Paper for Printed Library
Materials, z39.48.1984. Binding materials have been chosen for durability.

Library of Congress Cataloging-in-Publication Data

Names: Ritter, Jonathan Templin, 1983- author.
Title: Stilwell and Mountbatten in Burma : Allies at war, 1943-1944 / by
Jonathan Templin Ritter.
Other titles: American military studies ; no. 3.
Description: Denton, Texas : University of North Texas Press, [2017] |
Series: Number 3: American military studies series
Identifiers: LCCN 2016052140| ISBN 9781574416749 (cloth : alk. paper) | ISBN
9781574416862 (ebook)
Subjects: LCSH: World War, 1939-1945--Campaigns--Burma. | Mountbatten of
Burma, Louis Mountbatten, Earl, 1900-1979. | Stilwell, Joseph Warren,
1883-1946. | Allied Forces. Southeast Asia Command.
Classification: LCC D767.6 .R57 2017 | DDC 940.54/25910922--dc23
LC record available at https://lccn.loc.gov/2016052140

Stilwell and Mountbatten in Burma: Allies at War, 1943-1944
is Number 3 in the American Military Studies Series

The electronic edition of this book was made possible
by the support of the Vick Family Foundation.

TABLE OF CONTENTS

LIST OF FIGURES

ACKNOWLEDGMENTS

The author would like to acknowledge and thank the following people who assisted him in the research for and the publication of this book:

Kevin Starr (1940-2017), late University Professor of History, University of Southern California, the Dean of California Historians, for his support and encouragement in the publication of this book. I sincerely regret that he did not live to see it published.

John Easterbrook, General Stilwell's grandson, who provided the author with valuable insights into his grandfather's military career and who graciously allowed the reproduction of documents for use in this book;

Carol Leadenham, Assistant Archivist for Reference, Hoover Institution Archives, for responding to several inquiries about General Stilwell's papers and for putting the author in touch with John Easterbrook;

The staff of the Mountbatten Papers Database, University of Southampton Special Collections, Hartley Library, Southampton, Hampshire, UK, for granting the author online access to the papers of Admiral the Lord Louis Mountbatten (Earl Mountbatten of Burma), especially those concerning the South-East Asia Command; and

Professor Alexander Mendoza, University of North Texas, for drawing the maps.

Finally, this book could not have been written without the benefit of the many fine works by and about Mountbatten and Stilwell, especially their own published diaries and the biographies by Philip Ziegler and the late Barbara Tuchman, respectively. The author is indebted to them all.

Figure 1. Stilwell and Mountbatten in Burma, 1944.

(Courtesy of the Imperial War Museums, London)
Supreme Allied Commander South East Asia: Mountbatten conferring with Lieutenant General J. W. Stilwell Commander-in-Chief US Forces in China, Burma, and India.

Figure 2. Map 1, Southeast Asia, 1943-1944

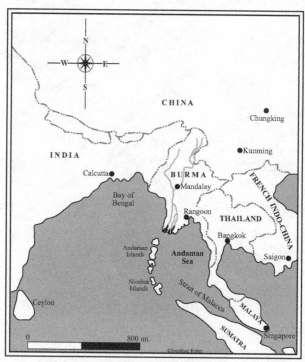

Southeast Asia, 1943-1944

Figure 3. Map 2, Burma and India

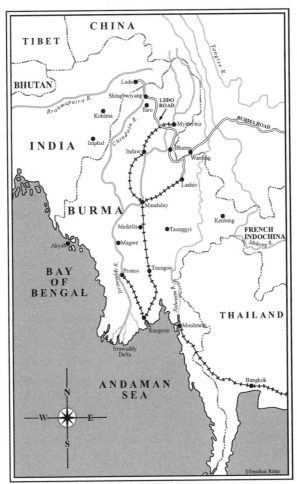

Burma and India

Prologue

A Night at the Movies: New Delhi, October 1943

Shortly after Lord Louis Mountbatten's arrival in India in October 1943, he and General Joseph W. ("Vinegar Joe") Stilwell went to the movies in New Delhi. Although they never became friends and later fell out, especially over Allied strategy in Southeast Asia, they were both avid movie buffs. (Mountbatten had a private movie theater at his Broadlands estate near Southampton.) "Mountbatten and his staff watched a film nearly every night. He was involved in filmmaking and was featured in several productions, including the 1945 documentary *Burma Victory*."[1] In his diary for October 23-29, 1943, Mountbatten wrote, "I find that Vinegar Joe (General Stilwell) is a movie fan like me and so we have been to the pictures together in Delhi."[2] Both Stilwell and Mountbatten used the movies to escape the pressures of their work.

Stilwell also recorded this event in his diary, but all he said was "Louis and I went to movie after dinner. Dumb show. "[3] He did, however, write his wife a letter dated October 24, 1943, saying "Louis [Mountbatten] is a good egg."[4] He also wrote, more ominously, "I will be happy when the real shooting starts: it will be a welcome relief from bickering and recrimination and throat cutting."[5] Soon there would be more of the latter than of nights at the movies.

INTRODUCTION

Two Extraordinary Men

This is the story of two extraordinary men who grew up an ocean apart, were thrown together by the fortunes of war during a twelve-month period, and never saw each other again. These two very different men had to work together under extremely difficult circumstances in a distant and difficult theater of operations in World War II, the China-Burma-India Theater (CBI). This book describes their collaboration and rivalry from October 1943 through October 1944.

It is also the story of how the "special relationship" between the United States and Great Britain was tested in Southeast Asia. That "special relationship" was both strengthened and hampered by the personalities of the leaders involved, of whom U.S. President Franklin Delano Roosevelt (FDR) (1882-1945) and British Prime Minister Winston Churchill (1874-1965) were the foremost. They and their countries shared a common goal of defeating the Axis, but had different national interests, especially postwar goals. Although a general feeling of commonality and shared interests between the U.S. and Britain developed during the late nineteenth and early twentieth centuries, which culminated with America's entry into World War I on the side of Britain and France, the "special relationship" was a wartime alliance between the U.S. and

Britain that began in 1941 with the Atlantic Charter. It extended beyond the personalities of Churchill and FDR.[1]

That wartime "special relationship" grew stronger during the Cold War, was formalized with the North Atlantic Treaty Organization (NATO) in 1949, and has lasted to the present day.[2] In his remarks to the British Cabinet in July 1943, Churchill spoke of establishing a "Fraternal association with [the] U.S.," which was his lifelong dream, and he concluded with these words: "This will be the English speaking century."[3] Upon his retirement as prime minister in 1955, he gave this parting advice to his junior ministers: "Never be separated from the Americans!"[4]

The Burma Campaign was the longest land campaign the British and Americans fought together in World War II. (The Battle of the Atlantic and the Combined Bomber Offensive against Nazi Germany were the two longest Anglo-American campaigns overall.)[5] While the political and diplomatic areas are important, the military aspect is particularly so, because Mountbatten and Stilwell were fighting a hard and brutal "forgotten" war within a world war. The Burma Campaign also marked the transition of the U.S. and Britain as world powers in the 1940s, with the U.S. becoming the dominant partner. Now, seventy-two years after the end of World War II, questions remain concerning the military, political and diplomatic aspects of Anglo-American cooperation, the convergences and divergences of British and American policies regarding the Burma Campaign, and the influence of the personalities involved.

Anglo-American cooperation in the South East Asia Command ("SEAC")[6] was hampered by personality differences between Stilwell and Mountbatten, among others, and by differing views over wartime goals and postwar plans. The U.S wanted to support Nationalist China in the war, not to restore the British Empire in Asia. Britain wanted to restore its empire, perhaps to be followed by some form of self-determination at a later date. Stilwell agreed with America's policy of building up a strong China and encouraging Asian independence movements. Mountbatten was basically a liberal who saw that Britain would have to grant independence or at least dominion status to its Southeast Asian colonies. However, he was hampered by his instructions from Churchill and the British Chiefs of Staff, which emphasized the restoration of the empire after Japan's defeat.

Mountbatten was the Supreme Allied Commander in Southeast Asia. His job was to retake Burma, Malaya, and Singapore after the British defeats there in 1942. His victory in 1945 was the longest and greatest land victory by the Allies in the war against Japan. At one time as well-known as Stilwell, even today many people in both Britain and America vividly remember his assassination in by the I.R.A. in 1979 (but more so in Britain, due to his royal connections). Overall, Stilwell and Mountbatten are less well known today than the more famous American and British commanders in the European or Pacific theaters, such as Eisenhower, Patton, Montgomery, MacArthur, Nimitz, and Halsey.

Stilwell was the American theater commander in China and the Chief of Staff to Chiang Kai-shek (Chiang Chung-cheng or Jiǎng Jièshí) (1887-1975), Nationalist Chinese President and Generalissimo, from 1942 to 1944.[7] During that period, Chiang was the third most important person in the Stilwell-Mountbatten relationship, which would have major consequences in the wartime alliance with the U.S.

Stilwell was also Mountbatten's Deputy Supreme Allied Commander at SEAC from late 1943 to late 1944. His job was to reestablish the land supply routes between India and China, which had been cut by the Japanese when they occupied Burma in 1942. By the time he was recalled in late 1944, he was well on his way to accomplishing his mission, and the "Stilwell Road" from India to China across northern Burma was opened in January 1945.

The geography of Burma[8] was critical to Anglo-American policy differences, with the United States focusing on northern Burma as the link between China and India, and Great Britain focusing on southern Burma and the port of Rangoon, then capital of Burma,[9] as a springboard to recapture Singapore. Here Stilwell the infantryman and Mountbatten the naval officer parted company, with the former favoring a land campaign and the later a sweeping amphibious assault.

Stilwell was a colorful character. He was five-foot nine, with a slim figure, which later became lean and bony, and had a hard-lined, decisive face. He had the appearance of being physically frail, which was decep- tive.[10] Despite being very acerbic (he acquired his nickname "Vinegar Joe" from a cartoon drawn by one of his students when he was an instructor at the U.S. Army's Infantry School at Fort Benning, Georgia, in the 1930s, and it stuck with him for the rest of his life), he initially liked Mountbatten when they first met in 1943 and called him "very cordial and friendly . . . full of enthusiasm and also of disgust with inertia and conservatism."[11] However, despite that initial friendly observation, they were never really close and Stilwell's Anglophobia increasingly led him to dislike Mountbatten by 1944.

At the outset it is important to ask just why Stilwell was so hostile to the British, since that hostility came to poison his relationship with Mountbatten. His best biographer, the late American historian Barbara Tuchman, did not really answer that question, merely referring in passing to unpleasant experiences Stilwell had with the British in Hong Kong in 1911 and in France in 1918 during World War I.[12] His latest biographer, British historian Frank McLynn, suggests that his Anglophobia was simply an "idiom of the time, a relic of the very strong undercurrent of isolationism in the USA," and that Stilwell may have transferred his dislike of his parents' formality to the British.[13] However, that explanation overlooks the fact that most late Victorian parents *were* formal, but their children did not all develop a dislike for the British. Whatever the reason for it, Stilwell's attitude towards the British only seemed to get worse as the war proceeded, and his diary entries make that clear.

Stilwell's Anglophobia was shared by many other senior American military leaders, notably General George S. Patton, Jr. (1885-1945) and Admiral Ernest King (1878-1956).[14] Britain, after all, had been America's traditional rival up to the beginning of World War I, even though the

War of 1812 was the last time the U.S. and Britain had actually fought each other. Moreover, many of the British military leaders, such as Field Marshal Sir Alan "Brookie" Brooke (1883-1963), 1st Viscount Alanbrooke, Chief of the Imperial General Staff (CIGS), General Marshall's British counterpart, were just as anti-American as some Americans were anti-British. Both American Anglophobia and British disdain for America and Americans were widespread up to World War II. In that sense the attitudes that Stilwell and Alanbrooke held towards their respective allies were the rule, not the exception.

Mountbatten was an exception: all his life he seems to have genuinely liked Americans. He was also a larger-than-life figure. After restoring morale in the British 14th Army, dubbed the "Forgotten Army," Mountbatten and his key general, Sir William "Bill" Slim (later Viscount Slim) (1891-1970), stopped the Japanese advance into India at the battles of Kohima and Imphal between March and June 1944. That led to the Allied liberation of Burma by the summer of 1945. Meanwhile, although Stilwell's forces had reopened the land route from India to China, he was recalled to America in October 1944 at the insistence of Chiang, and with at least the tacit approval of Mountbatten. Chiang believed, rightly or wrongly, that Stilwell was ignoring the existential threat to China from the Japanese in East China by focusing on securing a land route from India through Burma to China.

Mountbatten and Stilwell reflected the larger issues that both united and divided the United States and Britain as to how they viewed Southeast Asia. This book will analyze and compare Stilwell's and Mountbatten's personalities and command styles within the larger context of Anglo-American relations in Southeast Asia during the critical period from late 1943 to late 1944, interweaving political, military and diplomatic history as it unfolded over Burma during that time. The British have usually focused on World War II as a "European war," not an imperial one, and have only recently started looking into how and why British Asia ended the way it did. There have been numerous memoirs by British veterans of Southeast Asia, of which Slim's *Defeat into Victory* (1956) was probably the most notable. However, more than thirty years passed between the publication in 1984 of Louis Allen's *Burma: The Longest War, 1941-45* and that in 2005 of *Forgotten Armies: The Fall of British Asia, 1941-1945*. Most of the attention on Southeast Asia in Britain has been given to the story of the British and Allied prisoners of war ("POWs") on the Thailand-Burma "Death Railway," which was immortalized in the 1957 movie *The Bridge on the River Kwai*, and more recently in the British film *The Railway Man*. (It is often forgotten that more Asian laborers died on the railway than did Allied POWs.)

This focus on the plight of Allied POWs to the exclusion of almost anything else that happened in Southeast Asia during World War II was noted in an article in the magazine of the Imperial War Museum in 2010[15] and was also reflected in an exhibit the author attended at the Canadian War Museum in Ottawa in the summer of 2003, which portrayed the plight of Canadian prisoners who had been captured at Hong Kong. The sufferings of the POWs, while both heart-rending and important, have often overshadowed the sacrifices of the Allied soldiers, sailors and aircrew who fought the Japanese in Burma. On this point, British historian Ashley Jackson wrote that "The Second World War, notwithstanding the Eurocentric manner in which it is often remembered [in Britain], was viewed at the time as an imperial struggle, not only by politicians and senior servicemen responsible for grand strategy, but also by ordinary people around the world."[16]

Stilwell and Mountbatten, and the two countries they represented, were key players in that "imperial struggle." Now they are distant images on old black-and-white newsreels and photos. Where they agreed, where they disagreed, and where they fought each other while fighting the Japanese, is a fascinating story.

CHAPTER ONE

STILWELL

In the town of Carmel-by-the-Sea on the Monterey Peninsula, two hours down the coast from San Francisco, near the beach where the Pacific surf crashes, is a two-story house in a quiet residential neighborhood near the famous Carmel Mission, nestled amidst pine and cypress trees. In front of the house there is a plaque which reads:

Stilwell House: Home of Joseph Warren Stilwell "Vinegar Joe"
General, U.S. Army 1883-1946
A soldier without peer who never deviated in his absolute dedication to the United States of America.

Joseph Warren Stilwell was born on March 19, 1883, in Florida, where his father was running a lumber business. Stilwell came from a patrician Northern family—his father was descended from an English colonist who had come to America in 1638. Although his father obtained both a law degree and a medical degree, he never practiced either profession, preferring to be a country gentleman and then vice-president of a public utility. Stilwell grew up in upstate New York. Although he planned to go to Yale, his father encouraged (or rather, ordered) him to go to West Point, to give Stilwell, who had become increasingly rebellious, the discipline to be found there. He was able to get in through family connections with President William McKinley (1843-1901). [1]

During his time at West Point, Stilwell was a good student in languages, especially French, and he is credited with introducing basketball to the academy. He also participated in cross country and varsity football. He graduated in the Class of 1904, where he ranked thirty-second out of 124 students.[2] Later, Stilwell taught English, French, and Spanish at West Point and attended the Infantry Advanced Course and the Command and General Staff College. In 1910 he married Winifred "Winnie" Smith (1889-1972). Together they would have five children. His son, Joseph W. Stilwell, Jr. (1912-1966), graduated in the West Point Class of 1933, and served with the 15th Infantry Regiment, his father's old regiment, in Tientsin, China, in the late 1930s. He became a brigadier general and served in World War II, Korea, and Vietnam.

In the summer of 1912, Stilwell and his family first visited Carmel, a seaside town just south of Monterey, the old Spanish and Mexican capital of California. Stilwell and his wife decided Carmel would be a nice place to live and to have a home for their retirement. However, due to Stilwell's various military postings, he was not able to build his house there until 1934.[3]

Stilwell first visited China during the 1911 Revolution that overthrew the Qing (Manchu) Dynasty and created the Republic of China. He was stationed in the Philippines and took three months' leave to tour Japan and China.[4] There he met his first British military counterparts in Hong Kong, which left a lasting and unfavorable impression. His biographer Barbara Tuchman wrote that Stilwell "admired the English drill sergeants who 'for commands, appearance and results beat our average officer 500%.'"[5] On the other hand, Stilwell said (in what Tuchman called "the first statement of what was to become a historic prejudice") that the English officer "is a mess. At least here in Hong Kong. Untidy, grouchy, sloppy, fooling around with canes, a bad example for the men."[6] Tuchman noted that all his life Stilwell hated "swagger" sticks ("canes"), which were carried by British officers and by some U.S. Army officers, including officers of the 15th Infantry Regiment in which Stilwell served in China during the 1920s.

Stilwell's dislike of the British officers in Hong Kong and their frequently snobbish and racist attitudes would shape his attitudes towards them in World War II, with unfortunate consequences for Anglo-American cooperation.

During World War I Stilwell served in France as the U.S. Army's Fourth Corps intelligence officer, helped plan the St. Mihiel offensive in 1918, and was awarded the Distinguished Service Medal. In France Stilwell's unfavorable view of British officers and the British Army that had started in Hong Kong in 1911 was reconfirmed. When he was assigned to a British division on the Western Front, he wrote that "These English are beyond me—most of them are so very pleasant and some of them are so damn snotty ... too god-damned indifferent and high and mighty to bother about an American officer."[7] In contrast to his feelings for the British, Stilwell liked the French because he thought they were more polite and helpful to him as an American. Tuchman wrote "his command of French opened the way to cordial relations."[8] Stilwell wrote to his wife that "They treated me like a long-lost brother."[9]

During the interwar period the U.S. and Britain formed, or rather reinforced, their opinions of each other based on certain historic national views and stereotypes. According to British historian David Reynolds, most Americans had an "Old World" image of Britain of "class, Crown and colonies" which largely came from Hollywood, while many British, also influenced by Hollywood, saw America as a land of cowboys, gangsters, bandleaders, and Hollywood movie stars.[10] Although the Americans and the British had fought together in World War I, the military and naval leaders in both countries largely went their separate ways between the two world wars, which further reinforced the attitudes that the U.S. and Britain had about each other until World War II.

There were exceptions, such as the Washington Naval Conference in 1921-1922, which was designed to balance naval tonnage. This resulted in the "Five Power Treaty," by which the U.S., Britain, Japan, France, and Italy agreed to limit their ratio of battleships and aircraft carriers to five each for the U.S. and Britain, three for Japan, and 1.75 each for France and Italy.[11] The agreement actually favored the Japanese, even with their lower ratio, because they could concentrate their fleet in the Pacific, while the U.S. had to maintain a "two-ocean navy" and Britain needed to maintain its naval forces around the world. Thus, Japan gained naval superiority in the Pacific. The Japanese only accepted the lower ratio in exchange for an American agreement not to fortify Guam and the Philippines, which the Japanese promised not to attack, a promise that was finally broken on December 7, 1941.[12]

The conference also replaced the Anglo-Japanese alliance with the "Four-Power Treaty" consisting of the U.S., Britain, Japan, and France.[13] However, many Japanese were angry about being considered "inferior" vis-a-vis the U.S. and Britain due to their lower ratio. Over a decade later, at the London Naval Conference in 1934, Japan announced that it planned to terminate the treaty. At the end of 1936, the provisions of the treaty expired and were not renewed.[14]

Moreover, during this period the U.S. and Britain became naval competitors for a while, which strained, rather than improved, relations. Anglo-American historian Kathleen Burk wrote that "During the inter-war period, relations between Britain and the US were often fraught, particularly during the 1920s. They were fighting for their respective positions. Great Britain, still the only global power although no longer financially pre-eminent, wished to remain the strongest. . . The US navy . . . wanted to supplant the Royal Navy."[15] Burk also wrote that back in 1916, before the U.S. entered World War I, President Woodrow Wilson had said to Colonel Edward House, his friend and close advisor, "Let us build a navy bigger than hers [Britain's] and do what we please."[16]

The Washington Naval Conference was actually motivated in part by Canadian fears that, in the event of war between the United States and Japan, Britain, which had been bound by treaty with Japan since 1902, would be forced into a war with the United States, which might then invade Canada. Far-fetched as that prospect seems now, many Canadians had not forgotten that the United States *had* invaded Canada twice, first in the Revolutionary War and then in the War of 1812.[17]

There was almost no contact between American and British military chiefs and senior officers, such as Stilwell and Mountbatten, during the interwar years, as there has been since World War II, *e.g.*, in the North Atlantic Treaty Organization (NATO). British military historian Alistair Horne wrote that "After nearly half a century of NATO, we all tend to take for granted the close proximity of American and British officers' joint headquarters. But in the 1920s and 1930s, for a senior British officer ever to have met his American counterpart was about as unlikely for either one as encountering a Martian in Piccadilly." [18] This lack of contact was a major factor that added to the difficulties of the Americans and the British working together in Europe and in Asia during World War II— the senior officers on either side of the Atlantic did not even know each other. However, the 1939 visit of King George VI (1895-1952) and Queen Elizabeth (1900-2002), who were the first British monarchs to visit the U.S., was a major milestone in Anglo-American relations, and was aimed specifically at establishing closer contact between the two countries. The Atlantic Conference between FDR and Churchill in 1941 was the next major milestone in the development of the Special Relationship.

The interwar period was also a time of transition for the U.S. Army, which changed from continental defense and a small coastal defense force during World War I to the modern U.S. military that emerged in World War II. American military historian Edward F. Coffman wrote about the development of the U.S. Army during that period as follows: "From 1898 to 1941, two momentous developments—the emergence of the United States as a world power and a revolution in warfare—radically changed the Army... Technology precipitated the revolution in warfare. Tanks and trucks replaced horses and wagons, while the airplane came into its own, resulting in the Armored Force and the Air Force."[19] In fact, despite the almost total lack of contact between American and British officers during this period, the 1927 visit of the U.S. Secretary of War to Britain, where he saw the British Experimental Mechanised Force, led to the formation of the first mechanized unit in the U.S. Cavalry.[20]

Stilwell himself was either stateside or in China during the 1920s and 1930's. After World War I, Stilwell wanted another overseas assignment and was sent to China because the postings in Japan—his first choice— were all filled.[21] Stilwell's second visit to China began his deep attachment to the country and its people. He was able to see it beyond the foreign enclaves, such as the Treaty Ports and the missionary compounds, to the vast, real China. He served three tours of duty in China from 1920-1939, where he was the U.S. Army's first Chinese language officer after 1919, became fluent in Chinese, and was the military attaché at the U.S. Legation in Peking (then Peiping, then Beiping from 1928-1949, and now Beijing) from the summer of 1935 to the spring of 1939. In that role he would have had a good deal of contact with British officers serving as military attaches or colonial officers in Shanghai and other "treaty ports." The "treaty ports" were Chinese cities where the British and later other countries could maintain their own compounds, carry on trade under a fixed tariff, and have extraterritorial jurisdiction, *i.e.*, try their nationals under their own and not Chinese law. (Until 1943 there was even a United States District Court for China.) Stilwell's extensive service in China gave him an unusual amount of exposure to his British counterparts, given Britain's leading role among the powers there. Military attachés were the exception to the general lack of contact American officers had with their British counterparts during the interwar period, and an American officer stationed in China would have had at least some exposure to his British colleagues, in Peking or Shanghai.

In 1935 Stilwell wrote a short paper that expressed his own attitudes and prejudices about the British and their role in the world, simply titled "The British." A little over two typewritten pages, it expresses what he did not like about British "superiority" during the interwar period and how they could make themselves better liked by Americans. After criticizing the British Empire and British arrogance, he concluded as follows: "If Great Britain had sense enough to send around a few people who were modest, had a sense of humor, and could see just a little good in someone else, what a hit she would make in the United States. And what a lot of concrete good it would do her." [22]

Although Stilwell's paper was written in May 1935, just before he returned to China as military attaché that summer, it reflects his earlier exposure to the British, both there and elsewhere. He obviously felt he knew them sufficiently well to offer such a critique.

At the same time, we know that he shared information with his British counterparts in China, because Tuchman wrote that "A note from the British Embassy in February 1936 thanked him for 'a most interesting brochure on the Chinese Communist situation.' "[23] His comments about the British seem to have been directed toward British colonial attitudes and not the British people. Moreover, this paper was written before the Battle of Britain and the Blitz in 1940-1941, which helped to change American perceptions of the British people, as opposed to the British Empire, for the better. In 1940 Britain became the heroic island that stood up to Hitler and the Nazis after the fall of France.

When the Japanese invaded China in July 1937, starting the Second Sino-Japanese War, which later became the Pacific War and the largest Asian war in the twentieth century, Stilwell and other American officers in China witnessed Japanese brutality firsthand and were frustrated with the initial unwillingness of the U.S. to become actively involved there. During Stilwell's last two years in Japanese-occupied Peking from 1938-1939, he encountered the Japanese on a regular basis and wrote about what he saw as their good and bad qualities.[24] (He tallied up six good qualities, including courage, and twenty-six bad ones!)

After World War II began in Europe in 1939, Stilwell believed the U.S. would go to war with Japan in the near future and felt that the FDR Administration was focusing more on the war in Europe than on the war in China.[25] In fact, FDR was more concerned with the Nazis, whom he saw as a bigger threat to the U.S. than the Japanese.

By 1939 Stilwell was stateside commanding a brigade and in July 1940 was promoted to major general.[26] He organized and trained the 7th Infantry Division at Fort Ord, near Monterey, California. During this period he "rapidly gained a reputation as one of the best and most aggressive commanders in corps and army exercises." [27] Chiang's biographer Jay Taylor, who is generally critical of Stilwell, wrote that "By Pearl Harbor . . . he [Stilwell] had been named the best corps leader in the U.S. Army."[28] Stilwell succeeded brilliantly during the summer peacetime maneuvers in California in 1941, which caused General Marshall, by then the U.S. Army's Chief of Staff, to promote him to command the IIIrd Corps. [29] (In the early 1930s when Stilwell was at Fort Benning, Georgia, and Marshall was his commanding officer, Marshall had called him "qualified for any command in peace or war." [30])

Stilwell went to the top of the army list due to his drive and hard work (he had gone to both the Infantry School at Fort Benning and the Command and General Staff School at Fort Leavenworth in the 1920s), but perhaps more than any other reason, because Marshall supported him and refused to relieve or reprimand him when he ruffled feathers, which he frequently did. His was one of the names in Marshal's "Black Book," officers who would be promoted when war came. Still wiry and physically fit in his late fifties, despite having lost an eye in World War I, Stilwell roughed it with his men and became known as a "soldier's general."

On Sunday, December 7, 1941, Stilwell was at his home in Carmel, hosting a party for junior officers from Fort Ord, when news came of the Japanese attack on Pearl Harbor. He described that day vividly in his diary, as follows:

> Japs attack Hawaii. [Plan] Rainbow 5 in effect... Jap fleet 20 miles south, 10 miles out [of Monterey, which was not true]. Sent [Major Frank] Dorn [Stilwell's personal aide, who later became Brigadier General Dorn, and was closer to Stilwell than anyone else in the Army in CBI] to [Ft.] Ord to call off show and alert garrison. Phoned [Colonel Thomas] Hearn [chief of staff of III corps, who later became Major General Hearn, chief of staff of the CBI Theater]... White [at Fort Ord] to send reconnaissance troop down High No. 1... Guam being attacked.[31]

A few days later he wrote in his diary about the total unpreparedness of the West Coast for defense: "We have two battalions along the coast ... two battalions in reserve = 175 miles of coast... six tanks coming from Fort Ord. (The others won't run) .... Had the Japs only known, they could have landed anywhere on the coast, and after our handful of ammunition had gone, they could have shot us like pigs in a pen." [32]

In late December 1941 Stilwell was ordered to report to Washington, D.C. The late British military historian Sir John Keegan wrote the following poetic, poignant words:

> The call to Washington meant not only separation from his family but farewell to their beloved Carmel on the Monterey Peninsula, where he and his wife had come to settle before the First World War and where the headquarters of the III Corps had later been fixed. Its dark cypress groves and operatic crags, the Steinbeckian charm of the waterfront and the rag, tag and bobtail of the crowd which peopled it... made it an unlikely setting for a military headquarters.[33]

The "Europe First" or "Germany First" strategy had been adopted in 1941.[34] After Stilwell was called to Washington, he was initially selected to command the Allied invasion of North Africa at the end of 1942. Instead, after rejecting other possible choices, including Lieutenant

General Hugh Drum (1879-1951), the U.S. Army's senior ranking officer, Marshall sent Stilwell back to Asia to command the new China-Burma-India (CBI) Theater. [35]

Stilwell was an old China hand, spoke the language well, and both Marshall and Secretary of War Henry Stimson wanted him to go there.[36] So, old soldier that he was, in February 1942 he went off to China. In addition to commanding whatever American forces there would be in that theater, Stilwell would be Chief of Staff to Generalissimo Chiang Kai-shek, China's Nationalist leader since 1925, and would also be the commander of the Chinese forces in Burma. Stilwell knew that China was militarily weak compared to the other Allied powers, a weakness he believed came from the Chinese tradition of winning by outlasting the enemy (which was similar to the Russian strategy of trading space for time during foreign invasions, such as on the Eastern Front after the German invasion in 1941 and 1942).

This was the beginning of Stilwell's wearing several hats, a role for which his old soldier's temperament and single-minded devotion to a task did not particularly suit him. It was also the beginning of Stilwell's contentious relationship with Chiang Kai-shek. After the Japanese invaded China, Chiang was seen by the Allies as a symbol of China's resistance to the Japanese. Stilwell, on the other hand, came to have a real loathing for Chiang. Almost the only thing they had in common, apart from the war against Japan, was their dislike of the British. Stilwell's dislike of the British appears to have been personal, and based upon his earlier experiences with some of them, while Chiang's was political. After all, Britain was the great western imperial power that had seized Hong Kong in 1841 during the Opium Wars, demanded and received trade concessions from China, including extraterritorial privileges in cities such as Shanghai, and generally humiliated the Chinese for over 100 years.

Stilwell believed that Chiang's Nationalist regime was venal and corrupt. While this may well have been true up to a point, Stilwell ignored

Chiang's genuine military successes, including his "Northern Campaign" against the Communists in the late 1920s. Stilwell also bemoaned what he saw as Chiang's lack of preparedness. Stilwell had criticized Chiang's generalship in 1936 and wrote that "He can have no intention of doing a thing or else he is utterly ignorant of what it means to get ready for a fight with a first class power [Japan]."[37] However, that was before the Japanese attacked in China in 1937, when Chiang formed an uneasy alliance with the Communists to fight the Japanese for the duration. Japan did not begin all-out war until the Japan-China Incident in 1937, but it had already begun to take over part of China with the invasion of Manchuria in 1931.

Chinese strategy in the war before Pearl Harbor fell into two periods: the first during 1937 and the second from 1938-1941. During the war, there were twenty-two major battles between China and Japan (involving more than 100,000 troops on both sides).

A recent (and very pro-Chiang) American historian, Jay Taylor, put it this way:

> Stilwell saw Chiang Kai-shek as a cruel and unthinking dictator who "changed nothing" ... In Stilwell's mind, Chiang had no values; no skills in government or generalship; no real interest in the modernization and welfare of China except to the extent it increased his power; no human qualities worth noting such as patriotism, bravery, loyalty, or a sense of duty and honor; and no valid intellectual or cultural interests. For Stilwell, life was categorical, nuances nonexistent.[38]

Taylor also wrote that Stilwell and other Americans in China were influenced by Edgar Snow and other writers who were sympathetic to the Communists, who reinforced their negative views of Chiang and the Nationalists both during and after the war. According to Taylor, and contrary to Stilwell's belief, Chiang had actually started modernizing China's armed forces and defense industry even before the Japanese invasion.[39]

Part of the problem was that Stilwell and Chiang were polar opposites in temperament and attitude. Another recent historian, also pro-Chiang, said that "The general and the Generalissimo were about as different as it was possible to be. Stilwell wanted to build a modern, professional army. Chiang saw military units as chess pieces to be manipulated for his benefit."[40]

However, at the same time Stilwell doubted the ability of their leaders, he did have confidence in the fighting ability of the Chinese soldiers whom he commanded in Burma after March 1942.[41] The Chinese had troops in Burma to stop the Japanese from taking the old Burma Road, which would cut off China completely. To that end at least two Chinese armies were in Burma. Stilwell believed that Chiang had given him command of the Chinese armies in Burma and he proceeded to exercise that command.[42] While some accepted his command, other local Chinese commanders believed that Stilwell's role was merely advisory.[43] Stilwell would be bedeviled throughout his time in CBI because it was unclear how much authority he actually had over the Chinese forces that were at least nominally under his command.

The late American historian Eric Larrabee wrote that, in contrast to Eisenhower, who was working with allies who had similar traditions, "Stilwell was not ... His story as theater commander is therefore one of continuous conflict between the unpleasant truth and a roseate distortion of it, and the task fell to him of pointing out the contrast."[44] This comment shows how great were the contrasts between operations in the European theater and CBI, all of which colored Stilwell's relations with both Chiang and the British after 1942. The Australian historian Alan Warren wrote that the British were not sure what to make of Stilwell as a general since he did not have any American troops under his command in Burma.[45] A journalist described Stilwell this way: "He did not look like a General, but like a tramp or a character actor on the films or a dissenting parson or even somebody out of Alice in Wonderland."[46]

A sample from Stilwell's diary entry for January 24, 1942, sums up the rancor between the British and their Chinese "allies":

> The British have one brigade east of Rangoon and one more on the way. That's what they thought sufficient to hold Burma. And the SUPREME COMMANDER, Wavell, refused Chiang K'ai-shek's offer of two corps. [He] didn't want the dirty Chinese in Burma.[47] (capitalization in original.)

The next day he wrote, "It seems the reason Wavell refused Chinese help for Burma was that the British are afraid of the Burmese civil government. . . The Burmese hate the Chinese and the British: maybe they are pretty right."[48] He was putting it mildly. A British possession since 1885, Burma was governed first as part of the Indian Empire, then separately after 1937, with limited self-government. It had a Chinese and an Indian merchant class, native Burmese ("Burmans"), and several ethnic minorities, including Shans, Kachins, and Karens, who were loyal to the British for a variety of reasons dating back to the British conquest of Burma. [49]

In 1942 U Saw, the Burmese Prime Minister, contacted Japanese agents after Churchill refused his request for dominion status. British Intelligence found out, arrested U Saw, and interned him in Uganda for the duration of the war.[50] Other Asian nationalists, including Subhas Chandra Bose in India and Manuel Quezon in the Philippines, also made overtures to the Japanese before the war. However, the Philippines were already a self-governing U.S. Commonwealth as of 1935, and Quezon's secret trip to Tokyo in 1938 was part of an unsuccessful attempt to preserve Philippine neutrality in the event of a war between Japan and the United States. In November 1941, just before Pearl Harbor, Quezon won an unprecedented second partial term as president of the Philippines in a landslide in the Philippine presidential election. After the Japanese invasion, Quezon led the Philippine government-in-exile in the U.S. until his death in 1944, just before MacArthur's famous return to the Philippines.

Many Burmese nationalists were trained and armed by the Japanese, including Aung San (1915-1947), also called "Bogyoke" (General), and his "Thirty Comrades," who formed the Burmese Independence Army (BIA), which in 1943 became the Burma National Army (BNA) or Burma Defence Army (BDA). They welcomed the Japanese and fought alongside them. [51] Even the normally anti-colonialist FDR sympathized with the British on this issue; he wrote to Churchill "I have never liked the Burmese [FDR had probably never met a Burmese in his life] and you people must have had a terrible time with them for the last fifty years. Thank the Lord you have He-Saw, We-Saw, You-Saw [sic] under lock and key."[52]

The first half of 1942 was disastrous for the Anglo-American Allies in Southeast Asia and the Pacific, as the Japanese won victory after victory. The Philippines, Hong Kong, and the Dutch East Indies all fell to them. The crowning indignity to the Allies came in February 1942 with the fall of Singapore, which was the greatest defeat in British military history. It ended the myth of British military supremacy, from which they never fully recovered, even after their comeback in 1944 and 1945. The Japanese attacked the weak British forces and drove them out of Burma by May 1942. The First Burma Campaign (December 1941-May 1942), as it came to be called, with the BIA fighting alongside the Japanese, was the longest retreat in British military history. The invasion of Burma was also one of the last major Japanese military successes in Asia.

In *Why the Allies Won*, British historian Richard Overy wrote that Japanese victories, along with German victories in Europe and North Africa in the first half of 1942, made an Allied victory seem impossible, which is hard to understand in hindsight over seventy years later. It is difficult to realize today just how desperate the Allied situation looked at the time. As Overy wrote, "[T]he conflict was poised on a knife-edge in the middle years of the war. This period must surely rank as the most significant turning-point in the history of the modern age."[53]

General William "Bill" Slim (1891-1970), who led the main British retreat from Burma, wrote in his memoir, *Defeat into Victory,* how badly things were going for the Allies at the time:

> [T]he most distressing aspect of the whole disastrous campaign had been the contrast between our generalship and the enemy's. The Japanese leadership was confident, bold to the point of foolhardiness, and so aggressive that never for one day did they lose the initiative . . . Tactically we had been completely outclassed. The Japanese could—and did—do many things that we could not.[54]

By the time Stilwell got to Burma in March 1942, Rangoon had fallen (March 8) and the Allied front was collapsing. Although Stilwell personally led Chinese forces in a counterattack for which he was awarded the Distinguished Service Cross,[55] the Japanese pushed Stilwell's Chinese forces past Mandalay and Myitkyina (whose airfield was crucial) and up toward China. They destroyed two of Chiang's armies, along with its heavy equipment and his only motorized heavy artillery.[56] Most of these vital supplies were lost as the Chinese armies fled back into China. The Japanese also captured Lend Lease supplies of fuel and vehicles, which speeded up their advance into Burma. The Chinese Fifth Army's 200th Division—China's only mechanized unit—at first followed Stilwell's orders to protect the Allied flank, but then continued its drive eastward and crossed the Salween River, effectively leaving the campaign.[57] The retreat turned into a rout in which the Chinese forces suffered heavily. Compared to the information available as to the Allied losses in the First Burma Campaign, the losses of the Chinese armies in Burma are unknown.[58]

The Japanese were now closing in. Stilwell and his staff made for Myitkyina, but the Japanese got there first.[59] His army having disintegrated after the defeat of the Chinese armies, Stilwell (who at the time was in poor health with jaundice, as well as being blind in his left eye and having a weak right eye) led a small group out of Burma into India, covering 140 miles in fourteen days, reaching Imphal in northeast

India on May 20. He did this without losing a single man, a remarkable achievement at the end of a disastrous campaign. During his march out of Burma he turned fifty-nine. He could have flown out of Burma himself (he flew out most of his staff to India), but it was not his way to fly out when his men were forced to walk.[60] When he reached New Delhi, he said about the Allied defeat in Burma (which could also sum up all the Allied defeats by the Japanese after Pearl Harbor):

> In the first place, no military commander in history made a voluntary retreat. And there's no such thing as a glorious retreat. All retreats are as ignominious as hell. I claim we got a hell of a beating. We got run out of Burma and it is humiliating as hell. I think we ought to find out what caused it, go back and retake it.[61]

This was Stilwell's first direct report about the retreat from Burma, which the American newspapers reported on May 25, 1942. The Associated Press dispatch reported "Still full of fight after a 'hell of a beating' in Burma and a weary march of 140 miles through wild Burmese jungles, Lieutenant General Joseph W. Stilwell declared today that Burma could be—and must be—retaken from the Japanese."[62]

On Stilwell's retreat and the disastrous situation he faced in Burma, Slim wrote,

> His difficulties were greater than mine, and he met them with dogged courage beyond praise, but his Chinese armies were, as yet, not equal to the Japanese. He was constantly on the look-out for an aggressive counter-stroke, but his means could not match his spirit. He could not enforce his orders nor could his inadequate staff and communications keep touch with his troops. When he saw his formations disintegrate under his eyes, no man could have done more than and very few as much as Stilwell, by personal leadership and example to hold the Chinese together, but once the rot had set in the task was impossible.[63]

Stilwell's and Slim's comments reflected the serious situation the Allies faced in CBI in 1942. The Japanese had won the first battles of the war, and when they halted that summer, the Japanese Empire was at its peak. At this point, the Allies were still on the defensive and had to wait until they had the resources and skills for going on the offensive. During the rest of 1942 and the first half of 1943, Stilwell spent most of his time planning for the next offensive in northern Burma to reopen the Burma Road—China's only remaining supply route with the outside world, which the Japanese had cut off in 1942. To that end he and his fellow American officers trained Chinese troops in India for the invasion of Burma.[64] In fact, Chiang demanded that three American divisions be sent to Burma to reopen the Burma Road.[65]

Whether Stilwell should have stayed with the retreating Chinese forces, which were at least nominally under his command, or flown to China instead of to India, has been hotly debated ever since. The front was collapsing all around him and his orders were being ignored. As one modern historian put it, "General Stilwell's task as commander of Chinese forces in Burma was badly undermined by political interference; his thankless role in China would have confounded the most skillful of diplomats."[66] There was a parallel to General Douglas MacArthur's (1880-1964) desire to return to the Philippines after being forced to retreat and leave his men behind at Bataan and Corregidor in March 1942, at the same time Stilwell was fighting in Burma. MacArthur famously said "I shall return!" Stilwell was far less grandiloquent than MacArthur, but like him, Stilwell *would* return.

In 1942, the two main U.S. goals in the Pacific and East Asia were to begin the first major offensive of the Pacific War at Guadalcanal, which resulted in the first major Japanese land defeat in the war, and to keep China in the war through India. It is often forgotten that despite the "Germany First" or "Europe First" strategy, the U.S. did not get to Europe through Sicily until after defeating the Germans in North Africa in 1943, which was the first major land victory of the U.S. against Germany.

Meanwhile, the British, having lost both Malaya and Burma, remained on the defensive. They had suffered two major defeats, at Singapore and at Tobruk in Libya, in the first half of 1942. During the last half of 1942 Britain punched back, winning its first major land victory of the war, at El Alamein in Egypt, in November. With American and Canadian aid Britain was also on its way to winning the critical Battle of the Atlantic, which hung in the balance during most of 1942, and which was won in 1943.[67] Britain had to keep open its lifeline to the U.S. and Canada, while the U.S. had to keep open its lifeline to Australia. America also wanted to reopen the lifeline from India to China through North Burma.

That reopening would become Stilwell's obsession.

CHAPTER TWO

MOUNTBATTEN

In the City of Westminster, on the Horse Guards Parade in Whitehall, near No. 10 Downing Street, close to the Churchill War Rooms and the Churchill Museum, there is a bronze statue that was dedicated by Queen Elizabeth II in 1983 (and behind a small security fence since 2001). A tall man in a naval uniform is holding a pair of binoculars and looking outward with confidence. On the front of the base is inscribed, "Admiral of the Fleet / the Earl Mountbatten of Burma / KG PC GCB OM GCSI GCIE GCVO DSO FRS / 1900-1979," and on the west side, "Chief of Combined Operations / 1941-1943 / Supreme Allied Commander / South East Asia / 1943-1946."[1]

The Horse Guards Parade, where the Trooping of the Colour for the Queen's official birthday is held every June, was also the site of one of the 2012 Olympic venues in London. When the statue was dedicated, his eldest daughter Patricia, the Countess Mountbatten, said, "I can't help thinking how much he would have enjoyed today."[2]

In contrast to Stilwell's relatively modest American background, the baby who was to become Admiral of the Fleet the Earl Mountbatten of Burma was born into the heart of the British monarchy at Windsor

Castle on June 25, 1900. He was Queen Victoria's great-grandson and was known as *His Serene Highness Prince Louis of Battenberg,* a title he kept until 1917. His father, also named Prince Louis of Battenberg, was an admiral in the Royal Navy and was First Sea Lord at the Admiralty— the equivalent of the Chief of Naval Operations in the U.S. Navy—until October 1914, when he was forced to resign his post due to growing anti-German sentiment in Britain at the start of World War I.[3] Later the family name was changed from the German "Battenberg" to the more English "Mountbatten." In 1917 the official name of the British Royal Family was also changed, from the German "House of Saxe-Coburg-Gotha" to the English "House of Windsor." When he learned of the name change, Kaiser Wilhelm II (not generally known for his sense of humor), quipped that he was going to the Berlin Royal Opera to see a performance of "*The Merry Wives of Saxe-Coburg-Gotha.*"[4]

Lord Louis, as he then became, and his older brother went to the Naval Cadet School at Dartmouth (the British version of Annapolis). During World War I he served as a midshipman and junior officer. After the war, he attended Cambridge, where he studied engineering. In 1922 he married Edwina Ashley, later Countess Mountbatten of Burma (1901-1960), one of the richest heiresses in Britain, who later became famous for her humanitarian work during and after World War II. They had two daughters, one of whom is now the Countess Mountbatten of Burma.[5] In marked contrast to Stilwell's Anglophobia, Mountbatten genuinely appeared to like America and Americans, starting with his first visit in 1922. He and Edwina honeymooned in the United States, where they met, among others, Jerome Kern, Douglas Fairbanks, and Charlie Chaplin. The American press lionized Mountbatten and his wife, since he was a close relation of King George V. The *Washington Herald* said that they "were both attractive ... and quite human, and natural and likable."[6] One of his biographers, British naval historian Richard Hough, referred to that trip as the beginning of "the long and ardent love affair between the Mountbattens and America."[7] There is a remarkable similarity between the Mountbattens' favorable treatment by the American media and that given to Prince William and his wife Catherine, the Duchess of Cambridge, who visited Canada and the United States in 2012.

Although Mountbatten did not work with Americans until World War II, this early encounter probably shaped his attitudes that would be essential during the war. His favorable attitude towards America (and Americans) was a huge contrast to the attitudes that many British had that time, which went from general ignorance to outright hostility. (Churchill was a notable exception—his mother was American.) David Reynolds wrote that "Conservative elements in Britain had . . . been persistently anxious about America as a subversive force, whether political, economic, or cultural."[8] The anti-American views during this period were also shared by many on the British left. Mountbatten was a member of the British Royal Family, yet his political views were essentially democratic and even socialist, which often put him at odds with British policies, particularly in Southeast Asia during and after the war.[9]

Mountbatten earned the reputation of a playboy in his youth, especially due to his dashing movie star good looks, but he later showed himself to be a thorough professional and a good naval officer. Brave to the point of recklessness, Mountbatten drove both cars and destroyers at high speeds, with equal gusto, albeit sometimes with disastrous results. During the 1920s and 1930s he studied electronics and the use of radio in the Navy. He got his first command at sea in 1934. In 1936 he was appointed to the Admiralty as a member of the Fleet Air Arm. When war broke out in 1939 he was the captain of a destroyer, and in 1940 he fought in the Norwegian campaign.[10] Norway was the first British defeat and retreat in the war. The German *Kriegsmarine* (*War Navy*) lost half its destroyer fleet—which later hindered Hitler's plan of invading Britain in 1940—but not their U-boats or their battleships. The campaign was certainly "ill-fated" for Prime Minister Neville Chamberlain, because it was the direct cause of bringing down his government.

In July 1940 Mountbatten had his two daughters evacuated to the U.S. when Britain was bracing for invasion after the fall of France. Not only were they members of the Royal Family, but Edwina's grandfather was Jewish. He carried on a lively correspondence with his daughters, writing "How I envy you being in New York. It is the most thrilling city in the world, isn't it?"[11] In a letter written to his daughter Patricia on December 13, 1940, he mentioned the similarities and differences between the Americans and the British, saying "Don't get too snuffy about the Americans . . . because it only makes one unhappy to look down too much on the land that is giving one hospitality. It is true that they are different from us, but who is to say who is the better? We like to think and hope we are, but what do you suppose they think? So I am glad that you conceal your thoughts from them."[12] Later on, in 1943 and 1944, Mountbatten's generally positive regard for Americans and his enlightened views on colonial policy should have enabled him to overcome, or at least soften, Stilwell's Anglophobia and his belief that the "Limeys" were simply out to reestablish their empire after the war. In a sense, Mountbatten personified the type of Briton whom Stilwell had praised in his 1935 paper: "modest, had a sense of humor, and could see just a little good in someone else."[13]

Mountbatten was first noticed by Churchill for his heroism when his ship HMS *Kelly* was sunk off Crete during the German invasion in May 1941.[14] From August to October 1941, Mountbatten made an inspection visit to the U.S., which was still officially neutral. It was a neutrality in name only: Mountbatten was supposed to take command of the British aircraft carrier HMS *Illustrious*, which was being refitted in the Norfolk, Virginia, navy yard.[15] In 1941 the U.S. was actually more of a non-belligerent than a true neutral, especially after Lend Lease was passed. The U.S. Navy was escorting British convoys as far as Iceland (which the U.S. occupied in May 1941, relieving the British garrison), and was fighting an undeclared naval war in the North Atlantic against German U-boats six months before Pearl Harbor.[16] Between April and December 1941, the U.S. reverted to what in the eighteenth century had been called "armed neutrality," supplying Britain with war materiel and training British aircrews in the U.S. Mountbatten met with FDR at the

White House; FDR liked him from the start.[17] Mountbatten also visited Pearl Harbor, where he commented on the poor state of the defenses.[18]

From October 1941 to August 1943 Mountbatten was Chief of Combined Operations (CCO) in London, where he began the planning for D-Day, and was promoted by Churchill from commodore to vice-admiral. By the spring of 1942, Churchill's admiration for Mountbatten had grown so high that he briefly considered making him First Sea Lord. That may have not been a serious idea and in any case did not happen.[19] Perhaps Churchill saw something of himself in Mountbatten: they were very similar, recklessly brave, energetic men in a hurry, Churchill in politics and Mountbatten in the navy. Both were the younger sons of British aristocrats and neither would inherit their family titles. Each of them had to make a name for himself.

Admiral Sir Roger Keyes (1872-1945), the hero of the 1918 Zeebrugge raid against German U-boat bases during World War I, and since 1940 the first Chief of Combined Operations, wrote to Churchill that "Dickie Mountbatten is a splendid fellow, and a live wire with lots of drive."[20] Ziegler wrote that in contrast to the seventy-year old Keyes, Mountbatten at forty-one in 1941 "had youth, panache and, glamour."[21]

In April 1942 General Marshall went to London to oversee the U.S. buildup in Britain. When Marshall met Mountbatten, he was impressed with his energy. Mountbatten later said Marshall was "The most important man in the American military machine throughout the war."[22] When Marshall asked Mountbatten how army, navy, and air force personnel at Mountbatten's CCO headquarters could work together, unlike in the U.S., where inter-service rivalry was fierce, Mountbatten said, "It's quite simple, sir. They all speak English, you see. . . So why don't you send over some soldiers and airmen and sailors and join us here at headquarters? And so, quite early on, we got the first integrated Allied Headquarters operating in London."[23]

In May 1942, when Eisenhower first went to London (a month before he officially became the U.S. commander in Europe), he only knew

Mountbatten by reputation. At a meeting with the British Chiefs of Staff, after Eisenhower was asked who should lead an amphibious operation, he recommended Mountbatten:

> In America, I have heard much of a man who has been intensively studying amphibious operations for many months. I understand that his position is Chief of Combined Operations, and I think his name is Admiral Mountbatten . . . I have heard that Admiral Mountbatten is vigorous, intelligent, and courageous, and if the operation is to be staged initially with British forces predominating, I assume he could do the job.[24]

Mountbatten was at the meeting—in fact, he was sitting across the table from Eisenhower, who had never met him—and Eisenhower later wrote that "from then on Admiral Mountbatten was my warm and firm friend."[25] This warm friendship contrasted sharply with the relationship that developed between Mountbatten and Stilwell.

As Chief of Combined Operations, Mountbatten planned and oversaw the disastrous Dieppe Raid in August 1942, which made him a controversial figure in Canada for the rest of his life, because most of the troops—and the casualties—in the operation were Canadian. Dieppe was a large-scale commando raid designed to capture and hold a port that could be used by the Allies in the final invasion of northwest Europe. Everything went wrong and almost the entire landing force was either killed or taken prisoner.[26] In 1973, Mountbatten tried to justify his role in the attack on Dieppe, telling Canadian veterans that "the successful landing in Normandy [D-Day] was won on the beaches of Dieppe."[27] This was not exactly true, as most historians have pointed out. At the same time, many of Dieppe's lessons were learned and used successfully on D-Day two years later, including the futility of attacking a fortified port city. To be fair to Mountbatten, and contrary to the views of some Canadians and Mountbatten critics, then and now, the Dieppe Raid was hardly the madcap idea of one man. The Canadians had been in Britain since 1939 and were itching for action by 1942; the Allies wanted to stage a major raid on occupied Europe when the Germans were advancing on Stalingrad; and Stalin had been demanding a "Second Front" since Hitler invaded the Soviet Union in June 1941. All of those factors contributed to what happened at Dieppe. David Reynolds wrote that the Canadian experience in Britain was carefully studied by the Americans during the buildup to D-Day.[28] There were more Canadian than American troops in Britain before mid-1943.

Although Churchill did not explicitly say so in his war memoirs, it is likely that he did not want Mountbatten to suffer the same fate he had suffered after the disastrous Gallipoli expedition during World War I in 1915, which had almost destroyed his political career. On the Dieppe disaster and Mountbatten's responsibility for it, Reynolds wrote that:

> Mountbatten's failures—which were appalling—were, however those of a man who had been absurdly overpromoted by Churchill. The prime minister was desperate for action, and Mountbatten's energy and verve contrasted refreshingly with the negativism of the senior [British] military.[29]

One of Mountbatten's other biographers, Sir Ian McGeoch, himself a retired admiral, defended Mountbatten's actions at Dieppe as follows: "The decision to employ Canadian troops was political-military and not made by the Chief of Combined Operations." [30] Despite Dieppe, in August 1943 Mountbatten was appointed Supreme Allied Commander of the newly created South East Asia Command, for reasons that had as much to do with Anglo-American relations as with his own abilities.[31]

The overall British strategy in Southeast Asia in 1943 was to get back to Singapore by amphibious operations once they had built up their forces. British historian Frank McLynn wrote "Churchill's only real interest in the East was Singapore, regaining which he viewed as vital for the prestige of the British Empire. He was broadly in favour of bypassing Burma, which he saw as being of advantage only to China."[32] However, the overall U.S. strategy was to support China through India, which required retaking at least North Burma in order to re-establish a land route. The Pacific War was a U.S. theater of operations, so the British did not have any major focus there, although the British Pacific Fleet later joined with the U.S. Navy during the Battle of Okinawa in 1945. As a result, Southeast Asia, apart from the defense of India, was a low priority for British strategy, which was focused on Europe, North Africa, and the Middle East in 1942 and into 1943.

These different strategies were reflected in the personalities of Stilwell and Mountbatten. Stilwell was an old-line infantry officer who had come of age in the rapidly changing U.S. Army between the two world wars. Mountbatten came from a naval family within the Royal Family, which shaped his attitudes about the role of the Royal Navy and seaborne operations. Stilwell cared little about his appearance, while Mountbatten always looked smart, even when he was visiting the troops. Finally, Stilwell had survived the grueling retreat from Burma in 1942, and had been the American commander in China for a year and a half, when Mountbatten—the new boy—arrived on the scene in 1943. That was the year these two very different men began to work together in one of the toughest theaters of operations in World War II.

CHAPTER THREE

ANGLO-AMERICAN RELATIONS IN SOUTHEAST ASIA

Stilwell and Mountbatten were not only different in temperament, but they also reflected the very different American and British ways of looking at the world at war. During the war, there were contradictory attitudes among Americans, supporting Britain against the Germans in Europe but often failing to understand the contribution to the British war effort from the Commonwealth and the Empire, especially in Southeast Asia. Apart from defeating the Axis powers, British and American geopolitical and strategic goals were very different.

American-born historian Kathleen Burk, professor of Modern and Contemporary History at University College London, who specializes in Anglo-American relations, wrote, "The Anglo-American relationship during the war, whilst by general agreement the closest and most successful in history, was nevertheless bedeviled by widespread and apparently irradicable American suspicions of British motives."[1] The U.S. did not want to fight the war to preserve the British Empire, while the British, especially Churchill, were fighting both to protect Britain and to preserve the British Empire, especially in India and Southeast Asia. The

British goal was to move its colonies and overseas possessions toward gradual independence within the British sphere of influence, a goal that Mountbatten favored. (The so-called "White Dominions"—Canada, Australia, New Zealand and South Africa—were all effectively independent after 1931.) At the same time, the U.S. was becoming the dominant power in the bilateral relationship, which made wartime Britain's contributions, important as they were, increasingly secondary. Burk wrote that "The Second World War saw the destruction of Great Britain's global predominance and the United States' assumption of that role."[2] On the contrast between the material wealth of the U.S. and the growing weakness of Britain during the war, David Reynolds wrote that for the first American forces that came to Britain in 1942, "The GIs left a country that was growing richer. They arrived in a country that was getting poorer. Such was the alchemy of war."[3]

Although FDR and Churchill agreed on most of the Allied war goals, what divided them were the imperial and colonial issues. FDR, like Woodrow Wilson, admired the British and their democratic traditions, but he did not like the British Empire, ostensibly because it was not based on the American concept of self-rule and independence, which was so much a part of the legacy of the American Revolution. The exception to this democratic belief was U.S. expansion in the Pacific and U.S. spheres of influence in Latin America in the late nineteenth and early twentieth centuries. Ironically, many Americans who were critical of the British Empire accepted U.S. expansion into the Pacific as a legitimate extension of America's westward expansion.

At a dinner in Washington in December 1941, with Churchill present, FDR expressed not only his own anti-imperialist attitudes, but also the American people's disdain for both the British Empire and British Imperialism:

> You know my friend [Churchill] over there—doesn't understand how our people feel about Britain and her role in the life of other peoples ... it's in the American tradition, this dislike, this

dislike and even hatred of Britain—the Revolution you know and 1812; and India and the Boer War and all that. There are many kinds of Americans of course, but as a country, we're opposed to imperialism—we can't stomach it.[4]

The American attitude was summed up in an editorial in *Life* magazine on October 12, 1942, entitled an "Open Letter" to the "People of England." It said that while there was no consensus in the U.S. on its war aims, the Americans agreed that "[O]ne thing we are sure we are not fighting for is to hold the British Empire together. We don't like to put the matter so bluntly, but we don't want you to have any illusions. If your strategists are planning a war to hold the British Empire together they will sooner or later find themselves strategizing all alone."[5]

On November 10, 1942, Churchill made his famous speech at the Mansion House in London about the turning of the Allied tide in 1942, saying "I have not become the King's First Minister in order to preside over the liquidation of the British Empire."[6] This speech was also called "the end of the beginning" speech about the end of the first phase of World War II for the Allies and the road to victory in late 1942. Churchill also said, "Now this is not the end. It is not even the beginning of the end. But it is, perhaps, the end of the beginning."[7] Churchill's statement of support for the British Empire was a direct rebuttal to the U.S. anti-colonial position that the editorial in *Life* had expressed. Churchill's twin wartime goals were to preserve Britain *and Britain's imperial power,* to which he had devoted his life. The British writer, broadcaster and film-maker Jonathan Dimbleby (the son of BBC war correspondent Richard Dimbleby) writing in *Destiny in the Desert* (2012) about the North African campaign from 1940-1943, said that "Churchill fought the Second World War as much to save the global reach of the British Empire as to destroy Nazism."[8] For his part, FDR thought that Britain, the U.S., the Soviet Union, and China would be "the four policemen" of the world after the war, but that Britain would not be as important a major power as it had been. This belief may explain why he distanced himself from Churchill on key issues during their later wartime conferences, from Tehran in 1943 to Yalta in 1945. This was another area of change that Churchill neither understood nor accepted, along with his general views on imperial policy. Britain's status as the senior partner, which had been strong from 1940 to 1942, diminished after 1943.

At the same time, FDR's effort to distance himself from Churchill had as much or more to do with trying to convince Stalin that he was not up against united opposition from the Anglo-Americans, than with any conscious disregard for Britain's postwar role.

The differences between the U.S. and Britain over strategy and postwar goals did not hinder the overall cooperation between the two countries in Europe and the Mediterranean as much as they did in Southeast Asia. Eisenhower was able to work well with his British allies, (except for Field-Marshal Bernard Montgomery "Monty"[9]) before and after D-Day, because they all shared the common goal of defeating Nazi Germany. In the Mediterranean, especially in Italy, the major American criticism of the British was that the Italian theater was a diversion from the main theater in northwest Europe. Another major difference in Europe was that the British were fighting to restore the sovereignty of the Nazi-occupied countries, none of which had been British colonies or possessions, as opposed to their regaining their Eastern Empire.

Moreover, many Americans did not fully understand the importance of the British Empire and the British Dominions in the war effort. On the imperial and global nature of the war for the U.S. and Britain, British historian Ashley Jackson wrote:

> In 1939 America was not a global power in terms of military strength, international diplomacy, reputation and overseas pres-ence in the way that Britain was, despite the republic's phenom-enal wealth and potential. The fact that America had risen to global pre-eminence by 1945, and Britain had been eclipsed, is a measure of the war's impact on the world order ... Given the huge importance of imperial forces, resources and bases for the British war effort, the wartime alliance that defeated the dictators needs

to be better understood. The ubiquitous term "the Allies" has come to stand as a short-hand for Britain and America's deservedly celebrated war-time partnership, with France and Russia somewhat uncomfortably tagged on as well.[10]

What many Americans forgot was that most of the soldiers who were fighting in Southeast Asia against the Japanese were neither American nor British: they were Chinese and Indian, African and Burmese, including several ethnic minorities from the hill peoples of the north.[11] The Karens and Kachins in North Burma strongly supported the British. The Karens inflicted very heavy casualties on the Japanese, while the U.S. Office of Strategic Services (OSS) trained and equipped the Kachin Rangers. Paradoxically, it was the much-maligned British Empire that provided most of the manpower to defeat the Japanese in Burma. The Indian Army was the largest single source of manpower for the British 14th Army.[12]

In 1942, the British Cabinet had been concerned about Britain's imperial image, especially in the U.S. Sir Ronald Campbell (1883-1953), a British diplomat, said Britain needed "to educate [American] opinion on the real facts of our stewardship and the nature of our Empire and our Commonwealth."[13] Sir Reginald Dorman-Smith (1899-1977), the British Governor of Burma from 1941 to 1946, was convinced the Atlantic Charter would mean "the end of the British Empire"[14] because it at least implied, along with the defeat of the Axis powers, the independence of the British and European colonial possessions after the war. In fact, it did not. The Atlantic Charter was vague as to what extent it applied to the British and the other colonial empires in Southeast Asia. It merely stated that "[The U.S and the U.K.] respect the rights of all peoples to choose the form of government under which they will live; and they wish to see sovereign rights and self-government restored to those who had been forcibly deprived of them."[15]

The Atlantic Charter was proclaimed in August 1941, two years into the war in Europe, but before Pearl Harbor, when both Churchill's and FDR's focus was on Europe and not Asia. In many ways, it was FDR's updated version of Wilson's Fourteen Points in 1918. Churchill supported its main goal of destroying Nazi Germany and restoring freedom in Europe, but he expressed reservations about extending it to the British Empire. Churchill expressed especially strong reservations when his Deputy Prime Minister, the Labor Leader Clement Atlee, told an audience of West African students in London that the Atlantic Charter "applied to all peoples of the world."[16] Thorne wrote that Churchill chose to interpret the references to the restoration of "sovereign rights and self-government" mainly in terms of Europe and not to what Churchill called the "progressive evolution of self-governing institutions" in the British Empire.[17]

The official British wartime policy about the importance of the British Empire was reflected in the 1987 British film *Hope and Glory,* in the scene where a British schoolteacher asks her class about the importance of the colors on the map of the world:

Teacher: Pink, Pink. What are all the pink bits?

Rowan (student): They're ours, Miss.

Teacher: Yes. The British Empire. What part of the world's surface is British?

Jennifer (student): Two-fifths, Miss.

Teacher: Yes. Two-fifths—ours. That's what this war is all about. Men are fighting and dying to save the pink bits for you ungrateful little twerps.[18]

The war for the U.S. and Britain was not just about defeating the Axis powers. Different British and American postwar goals changed the global power structure that was to last until the end of the Cold War. Britain had been the great power of the nineteenth century, just as the U.S. became the great power of the twentieth century. That was the new reality that FDR realized before his death in 1945, but which Churchill tried to ignore or resist well into the 1950s.

During the 1943 Cairo Conference, John Paton Davies, Jr. (1908-1999), a U.S. State Department Officer and Stilwell's chief political advisor in China, wrote to Clarence Gauss (1887-1960), the U.S. ambassador to China, that U.S. and British war aims in the Far East and Southeast Asia were fundamentally different: "The British will wish to throw their main weight southward for the repossession of colonial empire. Our main interest in Asia will lie to the East from whence can strike directly and in coordination with other American offensives against Japan's new Empire."[19]

The following year, in a memorandum titled "American Policy in Asia," Davies wrote:

> The British Empire in Asia and its Dutch satellite system cannot survive because the people in the United Kingdom, Mr. Churchill notwithstanding, have lost their will to empire and because the historical dynamics of nationalism throughout Asia will sooner or later bring about the downfall of colonial imperialism. . . Temporarily the British imperial system may be regarded as a stabilizing influence in Asia. We shall, therefore, not now wish to take positive action which would weaken it. On the other hand, we must avoid steps which will commit us to the maintenance of British imperialism in Asia.[20]

Davies also wrote a memorandum for Secretary of State Cordell Hull (1871-1955), saying in part that "General Stilwell's mission is to open through North Burma a land route . . . into China. For reasons of political policy the British have consistently obstructed the opening of a land route across North Burma."[21] According to Davies, the British were also afraid that American influence meant Chinese influence. On November 15, 1943, he wrote in a memorandum titled "Anglo-American Cooperation in East Asia" as follows: "American impatience to assume the offensive in Burma is vexatious to the British. This is due primarily to their realization that American plans call for the use of Chinese troops. The British are frankly afraid that the Chinese will retain or claim any section of Burma which they recapture."[22]

In his book, *Dragon by the Tail*, Davies described the Stilwell-Mount-batten relationship and the different strategic goals in SEAC and CBI as follows: "While Stilwell made private fun of Mountbatten's lordly station in life and his splendid tailoring, this was no more than traditional republican parochialism. What did incense Stilwell was something for which Lord Louis was not, fundamentally, responsible. That was Churchill's strategy of bypassing Burma, to which SACSEA [Mountbatten] was bound."[23] For his part, Mountbatten noted in his diary in May 1944 that he had hosted a small luncheon party which included Davies, "whom my spies tell me is reputed to have been responsible for the notorious article in *Time* saying that Stilwell and I had had a disagreement."[24] Mountbatten's biographer Philip Ziegler, who also edited his diary, noted after that entry that "Davies was energetically opposed to imperialism and fueled Stilwell's suspicions that the main object of British policy was to restore the British Empire."[25]

According to American historian E. Bruce Reynolds, "[W]hile Stilwell had been initially impressed with Mountbatten, the Admiral subsequently had enraged him by supporting Churchill in focusing SEAC's efforts on an amphibious invasion of Sumatra instead of Stilwell's cherished ground campaign in Burma to open up an overland supply route to China."[26] Stilwell put it this way in a hand-written entry in his "Black Book," or secret diary: "The 'feud' between Louis and me is the really the conflict of Br. and U.S. policy. That's all. And when I stand up, I am non-cooperative, and my own people smack me down."[27]

The differences in Anglo-American strategic aims in Burma were noted in a letter from Major Fred Eldridge, U.S. public relations officer for the India-Burma sector, to the deputy director of the Army's Bureau of Public Relations. He wrote in part: "To go back into history again, there has always been a clash of national policy on this question of support of the Chinese. The United States has been committed to that support while the British have been against it.[28] At the heart of Anglo-American differences were differing views over the role of China. The main U.S. postwar goal in East Asia was to have a sphere of military, political, and economic influence, with a strong China.[29] The overall American postwar regional goal was for a stable, non-communist Asia, composed of independent states (as opposed to colonial possessions). American leaders believed China to be essential to fill the role formerly held by Japan, not through military conquest, but rather through commercial and cultural influence.

British and American public relations officers also fought their own war over who would get the credit for defeating the Japanese in Burma. On March 19, 1944, Eldridge wrote a memorandum to Stilwell describing a conversation with Charles Eade, Mountbatten's political and press advisor, who was also the "Personal Representative of the Prime Minister."

> He agreed this North Burma clam bake is a one-man show and that man is Stilwell ... I told him that we were not being petty about these things but, what with the clash of national policies out here, the British had always been either against this operation or only passively cooperative . . . He then discussed the differences in national policies of Britain and America and confirmed practically all of the things you and I have talked about and John Davies has told me.[30]

Eldridge also noted that Eade had told him, in effect, that "We recognize that our two governments differ as to policy out here, but let's get along as best we can in spite of that."[31]

The different strategies of the war in Burma were also discussed by correspondent Hanson W. Baldwin in a *New York Times* article in April 1944, as follows:

> The British Empire, the United States and China are trying to work in harness in the Burma campaign, with increasing but, so far, with distinctly limited success. One of the fundamental problems concerns the attitude of Britain and the United States toward China ... A patronizing attitude on the part of some of

the British in India toward the Chinese, an attitude that too often characterizes the British colonial system.[32]

In *Richer by Asia,* journalist and former OSS officer Edmond Taylor (1908-1993) also expressed the American view of CBI's objectives, as follows:

> In the American strategic view Southeast Asia was a minor theater of war where no decisive result could be accomplished while China was relatively important . . .The British discounted the Chinese army as a major factor and wanted the greatest possible amount of American help to strike a blow at the pivot of Japanese military power in the theater—Singapore.

> [C]ontrary to a widespread belief in the theater there was no personal animosity between him [Stilwell] and his nominal chief, Lord Louis. Yet the characters and viewpoints of these two men both expressed and determined to some degree the pattern of Anglo-American misunderstanding in the theater... His [Mountbatten's] goal was to restore the white man's prestige in Asia, the foundation-stone of the empire, and to achieve it he had to use the blunted and discredited tools of empire. Stilwell's point of view was almost exactly the opposite. He did not believe in the goal of empire and he did not believe that the British military forces in Southeast Asia, impregnated with the toxins of decaying imperialism, were capable of achieving the kind of spectacular military success which might restore the white man's prestige. I do not think he particularly desired the restoration of the white man's prestige.[33]

Besides dealing with the Americans, Mountbatten had to contend with his own people who believed the British Empire in Asia would go back to where it had left off in 1941.[34] Like most Americans, but unlike many Britons, he knew it could not. After Rangoon had been retaken in May 1945, Mountbatten told British officials in Burma who said he was too "soft" on the Burmese that "[M]y policy would make them wish to remain a member of the British Commonwealth once they had Dominion Status, but that their [the British officials'] policy would ensure that they voted themselves out of the British Empire the moment they were given the chance."[35] That is just what happened when Burma became independent in 1948. Mountbatten was a royalist, but he was also a realist, who knew that later victories could not overcome the psychological effect of British defeats in 1942, especially the loss of Singapore.

Mountbatten was often more American than British in his attitudes, as this passage from Ronald H. Spector's *In the Ruins of Empire: The Japanese Surrender and the Battle for Postwar Asia*, illustrates:

> Beneath Mountbatten's charm and flamboyance was an unsentimental realism. The supreme commander saw more clearly than most of the British ruling class, more clearly than most of his own subordinates, that the world before Pearl Harbor and the fall of Singapore was gone forever. His Southeast Asia Command (SEAC) could not restore the old colonial empires, even if it had the forces to try.[36]

In *The Road Past Mandalay*, Lieutenant-Colonel John Masters of the Indian Army (1914-1983) gave the British perspective on SEAC and CBI, where he wrote about his admiration for Mountbatten and his dislike of Stilwell, in contrast to the attitude of many American observers:

> Lord Louis Mountbatten was popular, capable and shrewd. He exuded confidence and charm, and his reputation as a fighting sailor, who had had numerous ships shot from under him, did him no harm either ... Stilwell was an unmitigated disaster for inter-Allied relations ... He had an extraordinarily difficult task as President Roosevelt's military representative in China, . . . In his dealings with America's other principal ally, though—Great Britain —he was animated chiefly by a desire to "burn up the Limeys" ... With Slim he got on comparatively well, and Slim liked him.[37]

These debates reflected the different strategic and geopolitical aims of America and Britain. Although, as Thorne put it, "Mountbatten himself worked hard to bring about inter-allied harmony,"[38] all the good will in the world could not erase the basic differences between Britain and America over policy in Southeast Asia.

CHAPTER FOUR

THE CREATION OF SEAC

During 1943 the Anglo-American Allies built up their forces for the campaigns in Europe, the Pacific, and in CBI. From mid-1942 to early 1943, the Allies had defeated the Axis Powers at Midway, Guadalcanal, El Alamein, and Stalingrad, turning the tide of the war in the Pacific, North Africa, and Europe. At this point, the U.S. was becoming the major Western Allied nation upon which the war depended, both financially and militarily.

During the first half of 1943, CBI was a theater in stalemate after the Allied defeat in 1942. In December 1942, the British Eastern Army had fought its first offensive on the Arakan Peninsula (in Rakhine State), but it was pushed back by the Japanese in March 1943. The British were still learning to fight jungle warfare, as the famous "Chindits" under Brigadier General Orde Wingate (1903-1944), a brilliant tactician but an eccentric and erratic personality, demonstrated when they conducted a long-range raid into Burma between February and May 1943. Although the Chindits took heavy losses, they did prove that the British could beat the Japanese in jungle warfare, just as the Americans learned to fight jungle warfare in the Pacific. The British at this stage did not have an overall plan to retake Burma, especially when they were stretched elsewhere. Although General

Archibald Wavell (1883-1950) was the Commander-in-Chief, India, and later the Viceroy of India, there was no overall commander in Southeast Asia during the first half of 1943. This lack of overall command in Asia contrasted unfavorably with the situation in the Pacific Theater, where General Douglas MacArthur and Admiral Chester Nimitz (1885-1966) were the two supreme commanders, in what were American theaters with Australian support (along with New Zealand army units until later in Pacific War). In Europe, General Eisenhower, who became Supreme Allied Commander in December 1943, was in charge of U.S. forces in Britain and was already planning D-Day while he commanded the U.S. forces in North Africa and later in Sicily and Italy.

Eisenhower, unlike Stilwell, liked the British, even if he did not always agree with them on strategy.[1] Also unlike Stilwell, Eisenhower was a natural diplomat who had the benefit of a clearly defined organizational structure between American and British forces in Europe. The Eisenhower model from 1942 onward was that of running an inter-allied command that could successfully conduct Anglo-American operations. Eisenhower's command became the model of how the supreme command could be organized effectively and was the model of command that would shape how the war in Southeast Asia would be waged after 1943. For Churchill and the British, the Atlantic, Europe and North Africa were the main theaters of operation, not CBI. Also, FDR and Churchill had similar goals in those other theaters, unlike CBI, which was not considered as important as the others. Despite the British defeats in 1942, there was as yet no burning urge on the part of the Allies to launch a major offensive there.

Stilwell, however, was determined to regain northern Burma as the way to reopen the link with China. In 1943 the first major goal of the U.S. mission there was to defend the air routes to China (a hazardous, 500-mile flight over rugged mountains, known simply as "the Hump") before establishing a land route to China. However, at the beginning of 1943, Stilwell did not have the resources for carrying out any major operations. In early 1943 his Chinese forces were being trained in India, but they had not seen any major action since 1942. Although CBI as a theater was only a year old, it was already apparent that a single command structure could not successfully conduct the war there, since China and India-Burma were really two separate theaters. CBI was also the farthest U.S. theater of war from the American mainland. Supplies from America had to go around either Australia or Africa, which took two months, with the distances up to 12,000-14,000 miles.[2]

A new plan was needed to end the stalemate in CBI, with a more organized command structure, providing resources and rebuilding morale, especially for the British forces there. The first major plan for Allied strategy in CBI was formulated at the meeting of the Chiefs of Staff Committee, India Command, American-British Conference, in Delhi in February 1943. There Wavell and Stilwell outlined the plan for the Allied offensive in Burma for the end of 1943, as follows:

Re-conquest of Burma—Winter 1943/44 Outline of Operations

General Conception of Operations—Upper Burma-Lower Burma

The timetable for operations is:

(a) November 1943—Advance into Upper Burma [which did not happen until late 1944]

(b) December 1943—Operations on Arakan Coast including capture of Bassein

(c) January 1944—Attack on Rangoon [which did not happen until May 1945][3]

This plan was also based on the Allied war effort in India, which had three components: (1) The British sought to defend India against a Japanese invasion; (2) The Americans wanted to use India as a supply base for the air route to China; and (3) Both the British and the Americans wanted to use India as the launching point for the liberation of Burma.

The other major Allied conference that specifically included a discussion of CBI was the Third Washington Conference (TRIDENT) between FDR,

Churchill, and the Allied Chiefs of Staff in May 1943. They finalized the plans for the Italian Campaign, the bombing campaign against Nazi Germany, and the Pacific War. They agreed the U.S. and Britain would coordinate their land and air forces, which had been under separate command. They decided "not to attempt the re-conquest of all Burma in the near future but rather to reoccupy North Burma only." [4] The Allied Chiefs of Staff also made the following proposals to Chiang on future operations in CBI: (a) Intensifying air operations against the Japanese in Burma; (b) Maintaining increased American Air Forces in China; (c) Maintaining the flow of airborne supplies to China; (d) Securing naval command of the Bay of Bengal; and (e) Relieving the siege of China, which did not happen until the completion of the Ledo Road (also called the Stilwell Road) in 1945 [5]

Stilwell was in Washington for TRIDENT. As usual, he was very unhappy at what he saw as Churchill's lack of interest in the Pacific (which he and the British saw as a distraction from the war in Europe) and his undue influence over FDR. "The Limeys are not interested in the war in the Pacific, and with the President hypnotized they are sitting pretty." "Roosevelt wouldn't let me speak my piece. I interrupted twice, but Churchill kept pulling away from the subject, and it was impossible."[6] Stilwell, never good at keeping his feelings to himself, made an unfavorable impression on Churchill's personal physician, Lord Moran (1882-1977), who later made the following remark in his memoirs: "I sat next to General Stilwell, a sour, dried-up little man whom they call Vinegar Joe. He complained bitterly that Winston wasn't interested in the Pacific . . . He is pretty critical of the British."[7]

The next major decisions on CBI came at the First Quebec Conference (QUADRANT) between FDR, Churchill, and Canadian Prime Minister Mackenzie King, in August 1943. There they agreed to launch D-Day in 1944, build up the U.S. forces in Britain, increase the bombing campaign against Germany, advance the Italian Campaign, and coordinate nuclear research between the U.S. and Britain. QUADRANT also reaffirmed the basic mission of U.S. forces in CBI as follows: (1) Keep China in the war; (2) intensify operations against the Japanese; and (3) maintain increased U.S. and Chinese Air Forces in China.

Finally, QUADRANT set up a new command structure to be called South East Asia Command (SEAC) to better coordinate offensive operations against Japan. The purpose of SEAC was as follows: "The vigorous and effective prosecution of large scale operations against Japan in South East Asia, and the rapid deployment of the air route through Burma to China." SEAC's authority would cover Burma, Malaya, Sumatra, Ceylon, and Thailand.[8] China was expressly excluded.

The last major decision was who was going to command SEAC. Churchill decided that Mountbatten, despite the fiasco at Dieppe in 1942, was ideal to lead this new command because of his experience in combined operations and his perceived ability to work with Americans.[9] According to McLynn, Churchill saw Mountbatten as "the one British officer who could get on easily with Americans. . . ."[10] Adrian Smith discusses Mountbatten's appointment to command SEAC in great detail in the last chapter of *Mountbatten: Apprentice War Lord*, writing that "[F]rom the White House down he had both administration and military on board."[11]

On August 22, 1943, Churchill telegraphed the news of Mountbatten's selection at Quebec to Clement Atlee, the British Deputy Prime Minister, as follows:

1. The President and General Marshall are very keen on Mountbatten's appointment, which it is certain the United States Government will cordially accept. Our Chiefs of Staff concur. There is no doubt of the need for a young and vigorous mind in this lethargic and stagnant Indian scene.

2. We have also cleared up to our satisfaction the difficulties about the Southeast Asia Command. Broad strategic plans and major assignments of forces and supplies will be decided by the Combined Chiefs of Staff subject to the approval of their respective Governments. But all operational

control will be vested in the British Chiefs of Staff acting under His Majesty's Government, and all orders will go through them. [12]

Churchill wanted to reassure Atlee both that Mountbatten would be a *British* Supreme Commander and that he would take his orders from the British Chiefs of Staff in London and would not be subordinate either to the Americans in CBI or to overall U.S. policy in East Asia. In other words, the young, impetuous, and possibly pro-American Mountbatten would not have total control.

The SEAC command structure was designed to unify the theater of operations in Southeast Asia in a way that the CBI structure had been unable to do. However, this structure also created its own problems, especially by 1944. Mountbatten was in Southeast Asia to achieve the British objectives, especially the grand design of retaking Singapore in a seaborne assault, while Stilwell was there to achieve the U.S. goals, especially that of keeping China supplied by land through India in the war against Japan.

Mountbatten made his objective clear in a lecture to the Royal United Service Institution in London on October 9, 1946, shortly after his return from SEAC, when he said, "I should like to stress that my object in South-East Asia was always to recapture Singapore *before* the Japanese were forced to surrender."[13] (italics supplied) The "before" is significant because the British wanted to return to Singapore on their own, and not after America had defeated the Japanese.

Mountbatten never said so, but his desire for amphibious operations in SEAC may also have reflected his desire to wipe out of the memory of Dieppe.

The conference outlined the following organization and responsibilities for SEAC:

(a) The Command and the Staff to be a combined British and American one, on the lines of the North African Command [*i.e.*, Eisenhower's command];

(b) The Supreme Commander to be British with an American Deputy. He should have under him Naval, Army, and Air Commanders-in-Chief, and also a Principal Administrative Officer to coordinate the administrative planning of all three services and of the Allied forces;

(c) The Deputy Supreme Allied Commander and the Commanders of the three services mentioned above, acting under the orders of the Supreme Allied Commander, to control all operations and have under their command such naval, military and air forces as might be assigned to the South-East Asia theater from time to time. [14]

Although this predated Eisenhower becoming Supreme Allied Commander in Europe in 1944, Eisenhower's North African Command was by 1943 the model of how to run an Allied command, with the "supreme commander" as the chairman of the committee. The American journalist Edmond Taylor, who served on the SEAC staff and so could observe what was going on first-hand, referred to "[T]he Southeast Asia Command, an integrated inter-Allied general staff, modeled after Eisenhower's but with the emphasis reversed—that is to say, with a British head and an American deputy at each staff level. . ."[15] The other model was the MacArthur model in the Southwest Pacific, with one person being in almost total command.[16]

Mountbatten wanted to emulate Eisenhower, but Churchill wanted him to adopt the MacArthur model.[17] In fact, he became a little of both, with consequences down the line for himself and his other commanders, especially Stilwell. At a meeting on New Year's Day, 1944, Mountbatten told Stilwell "I should like to place on record that I am the Supreme Commander out here and that what I say goes." At which Stilwell laughed and replied, "We none of us dispute that."[18]

The American Joint Chiefs welcomed Mountbatten's appointment, while the British Chiefs were less enthusiastic, because they viewed Mountbatten as a royal upstart who had been over-promoted by Churchill.[19] According to British historian Max Hastings, "Mountbatten's many critics, who included Britain's service chiefs, regarded him as a

poseur with a streak of vulgarity, promoted far beyond his talents on
the strength of fluency, film-star good looks, and his relationship to the
royal family."[20] However, Hastings added that he "possessed two virtues
which justified his appointment. First, he was a considerable diplomat.
He liked Americans, as so many British officers did not, and had a sincere
respect for Asians and their aspirations. And the glamour of his presence,
in a theatre where so many British soldiers felt neglected by their own
nation, did wonders for morale."[21]

The First Sea Lord, Admiral Sir Dudley Pound (1877-1943), damned the
appointment with faint praise, saying that Mountbatten was "as likely
to make a success of the job as any junior officer."[22] Field Marshal Sir
Alan Brooke, Chief of the Imperial General Staff, said "What he lacked in
experience he made up in self-confidence. He had boundless energy and
drive, but would require a steadying influence in the nature of a very
carefully selected Chief of Staff."[23] Like FDR, Brooke knew that "Dickie"
Mountbatten was at heart an "impulsive kid."

In his book on SEAC after World War II, Australian historian Peter
Dennis summed up how Mountbatten was received when he was made
Supreme Commander:

> The choice of Mountbatten as Supreme Allied Commander in
> SEAC was initially welcomed by the Americans, who saw in his
> energy and youth some chance of reversing the sorry British
> record in Malaya, Singapore and Burma. But it did not take long
> before Mountbatten's appointment was dismissed as a public
> relations exercise. Stilwell spoke contemptuously of him as the
> "glamour boy", and SEAC became known to some Americans as
> "Save England's Asian Colonies."[24]

On the larger importance of SEAC in Mountbatten's life and career,
British historian and Mountbatten's latest biographer Adrian Smith
wrote that:

> From the autumn of 1943 Mountbatten found himself a pro-consul,
> charged with hurling the barbarians back and reclaiming the

territories of a great yet fading empire. A trusted general [Slim] rebuilt the legions and recaptured the eagles, but final victory relied upon the military might of a new and increasingly assertive ally —an emergent imperial power still stubbornly refusing to accept itself as such ... Providentially, SEAC offered him a rare opportunity to display great leadership; in even the fiercest conflagration theatre commanders are few and far between. Many of course had their doubts. Mountbatten had served a 30-year apprenticeship.[25]

The SEAC command structure created endless problems, especially for Stilwell, who held a number of positions simultaneously. He was all of the following: Chief of Staff to Chiang; U.S. military representative to China; Commanding General, U.S. Forces, CBI; Deputy Supreme Allied Commander, Southeast Asia; and U.S. Lend-Lease Administrator. Unlike Eisenhower, who reported directly to General Marshall and then to FDR, Stilwell reported to Chiang, Marshall, and Mountbatten, all at the same time, depending upon which hat he was wearing at the time. [26]

Another potential cause of problems was India, which was not included within the boundaries of SEAC. This would result in some interesting chain-of-command issues, as the official U.S.A.A.F History of World War II noted: "Although SEAC did not include India, the major part of its assigned forces would have to be based there. Mountbatten's command did not include the large Indian Army."[27] It was ironic that the largest Allied force in India, the huge, multicultural Indian Army, pride of the British Raj, was not under Mountbatten's command, but under that of the Commander-in-Chief of the Indian Army. Both the Viceroy of India, Lord Wavell (after 1943), and the Commander-in-Chief of the Indian Army, General Auchinleck, were veteran combat soldiers—like Stilwell— with far more experience than had Mountbatten.

Although Churchill was interested in the Allied operations in CBI, he did not consider them as important as Europe in the larger context of the war in 1943. He wanted to keep and restore Britain's Indian and Southeast Asian Empire after the war, but he had no recent first-hand knowledge of conditions there. He had not visited India since the 1890s, when he was a young officer and war correspondent, and he had never been to either Burma or Singapore. India, or the Indian Empire, was an empire within the British Empire from 1858-1947. The only connection Churchill had with Burma was that his father, Lord Randolph Churchill, had annexed Burma into the Indian Empire when he was Secretary of State for India in the 1880s.

In his memoirs Churchill stated his criticisms of the Allied strategy in CBI, as follows:

> We of course wanted to recapture Burma, but we did not want to have to do it by land advances from slender communications and across the most forbidding fighting country imaginable. The south of Burma, with its port of Rangoon, was far more valuable than the north. But all of it was remote from Japan, and for our forces to become side-tracked and entangled there would deny us *our rightful share in a Far Eastern victory*. I wished, on the contrary, to contain the Japanese in Burma, and break into or through the great arc of islands forming the outer fringe of the Dutch East Indies. Our whole British-Indian Imperial Front would thus advance across the Bay of Bengal into close contact with the enemy, by using amphibious power at every stage.[28] [italics supplied]

Churchill also expressed dismay that the Americans were focusing so much on China when the British focus was on Malaya and Singapore. He believed the American focus on the land route to China was a diversion. Churchill and the British never had the same feelings for China as did FDR, Stilwell, and the American public in general during the 1930s and throughout World War II. Veneration of China had become almost a religion among many Americans, fueled by the novels of Pearl Buck, two of which were made into popular films;[29] magazines such as *Time* and *Life;* Protestant and Catholic missionary societies; the China Lobby; and the "China Clipper" flying boats across the Pacific from San Francisco to Hong Kong after 1935,[30] which recalled the historic trading link so dear to FDR. From 1939-1944, the Clippers took off from Treasure Island in San Francisco Bay, which was the site of the 1939-1940 World's Fair, the Golden Gate International Exposition (GGIE), and then a U.S. Navy base from 1941-1997. Ironically, the pre-Pearl Harbor theme of the Fair was "Pageant of the Pacific" and "Pacific unity." In fact, the Japanese pavilion, complete with gardens and a Japanese restaurant, which was a propaganda exercise by Japan, was the largest of the Pacific and foreign pavilions at the Fair. The local Chinese community represented China at the Fair, because the Chinese government could not participate due to the war with Japan.

At the same time, Churchill's dismissal of the U.S. China policy as a peripheral diversion was ironic because, in both world wars, Churchill wanted to win the war through the backdoor in Europe and the Mediterranean. At heart, perhaps the best explanation for Churchill's aversion to a strong China policy was his belief that a strong China would threaten British commercial interests in the Far East after Japan's defeat. Hong Kong was the most obvious concern, since Britain had occupied it during the Opium Wars and China wanted it back.

In 1946 Mountbatten wrote that although Hong Kong was "logically and obviously part of SEAC" it was not included under his control because the British Admiralty "wanted it as a base for the British Pacific Fleet." He also wrote that "All the richer Chinese, including the Government itself, are most anxious that Hong Kong should remain British." Ironically, the British remained in Hong Kong until 1997.[31]

Churchill also criticized a campaign that centered on the relief of China, in the following words:

> Certainly we favoured keeping China in the war and operating air forces from her territory, but a sense of proportion and the study of alternatives were needed. I disliked intensely the prospect of a large-scale campaign in Northern Burma. One could not choose a worse place for fighting the Japanese. Making a road from Ledo to China was also an immense, laborious task, unlikely to be finished until the need for it had passed. Even if it were done in time to replenish the Chinese armies while they were still

engaged, it would make little difference to their fighting capacity. The need to strengthen the American air bases in China would also, in our view, diminish as Allied advances in the Pacific and from Australia gained us airfields closer to Japan. [Which is what actually happened in 1944] [32]

This statement also reflected Churchill's view that China would not play as important a role in the war as the Americans wanted it to do in 1943. Events may well have proved him to be correct.

British historian Christopher Thorne wrote that "[T]he question of China's potential role in the war continued in 1943 to create considerable strain between the British and Americans over Southeast Asia." [33] British historian Philip Ziegler, Mountbatten's official biographer, wrote that "Mountbatten's responsibilities were to defend India, to drive the Japanese from Burma, Malaya and the rest of South-East Asia and to reopen land communications with China across the north of Burma." [34] When Mountbatten became Supreme Commander, CBI was still stalemated, but the British forces, after a year of defeat and reorganization, were on their way to becoming the fighting force that would eventually defeat the Japanese in Burma.

The timetable for the Allied offensive during the coming "dry" season (i.e., not the monsoon season) was outlined in a series of conferences between August and November 1943. The purpose of the coming offensive in North Burma was to reopen the link to China from Ledo near the Indian border. British historian Eric Morris wrote, "The scene was set for one of the truly remarkable turnarounds—a military metamorphosis—not just of World War II but in the annals of military history." [35] The plan was as follows:

1. Strategic air offensive to be intensified as weather permits against bases and LOC [Lines of Communication] in Burma.

2. Possible amphibious operations against the Andaman Islands and Ramree off Akyab.

3. Preparation for a full-scale operation against the Arakan, using two and two-thirds divisions with one additional division in reserve, to be completed by early January. If the amphibious operations against Akyab are not carried out, the Arakan offensive would be limited to securing the line Indin-Rathedaunhg-Kyauktaw. It would start in mid-January 1944.

4. Three divisions of the British IV Corps to seize Kalemyo and Kalewa. An all-weather road to be pushed to the Chindwin. The offensive was to start in mid-February 1944.

5. Continued offensive on IV Corps front to seize bridgehead on Chindwin in Kalewa area, and advance to Yeu. Yeu to be retained during the monsoon with a force of three divisions and one in reserve which could come from the Arakan front in late April 1944.

6. One Chinese division to move forward in the Chindwin in October 1943 to cover the advance of the Ledo Road eastward. Another Chinese division to move forward to Shaduzup area in mid-January, while one regiment from another Chinese division, flown from Fort Hertz, moves south to the Bumrang area. These two divisions, with one in reserve, to move on Kamaign and Myitkyina in March, and continue against the Katha-Bhamo area in May. Chinese armies in Yunnan to move on the Bhamo-Lashio line in February.

7. In mid-January, one LRPG (Long Range Penetration Group) to operate from Homalin toward Katha to assist the Chinese advance.

8. One LRPG to begin operations in February and another in March from Chittagong area toward Haka-Gangaw-Pakokku.[36]

This in a rather large nutshell was the basic Allied plan for retaking North Burma in 1944. It was a tall order, given the lack of Allied resources and the difficult topography of Burma. The plan required the coordination of American, British, Chinese, Imperial, and Commonwealth forces across the entire width of North Burma, from the Arakan region in the west to the Chinese border in the northeast. What is remarkable about this plan is that apart from a reference to "Possible amphibious operations against the Andaman Islands," all the other items involved a land campaign, which is exactly what Churchill did not want. The plan meant that the Americans and Chinese could concentrate on North Burma and the British could focus on defending the Indian-Burmese border region before going back into Burma down through the Arakan and then on to Rangoon. By this time the U.S. was providing most of the money and materiel, so, as the old adage goes, whoever pays the piper calls the tune.

The plan called for a heavy emphasis on Chinese troops, both those whom Stilwell was training in India and the Yunnan Force that was being assembled in China. Yet here the British and the Americans also saw things differently. Stilwell's Chinese forces were reviewed from the British perspective in a letter dated August 17, 1943, written by Major General G.E. Grimsdale, the British military attaché in Chungking, China's wartime capital. That letter was both highly critical of Stilwell and very complimentary towards his arch-rival, U.S. Army Air Force General Claire Chennault (1893-1958), who had led the famous "Flying Tigers" against the Japanese from 1941 to 1942 and who thereafter commanded the 14th Air Force of the U.S. Army Air Forces (USAAF). The letter also expressed the British disdain, bordering on contempt, for the Chinese Army. Here are some relevant portions:

> Stilwell's army is in no better condition than other parts of the Chinese army. Many of the troops are malnourished and others incapable of walking. Furthermore the Chinese are not by nature an aggressive nation and might be reluctant to recapture Burma for the British. Stilwell's son [Lt. Col. Joseph W. Stilwell, Jr.] has also expressed doubts about the feasibility of the expedition.[37]

> Furthermore there is the "scurrilous campaign conducted by Stilwell to the effect that he would have taken Burma long ago had it not been for the obstinacy of the British."

> *With regard to the influence of the USA in China Chennault, in contrast to Stilwell and other Americans, is a first class officer. He*

appreciates that the USA's strong position is largely due to British efforts.

Chennault is encountering difficulties in trying to get essential equipment from Kunming to his forward operational bases in South East China. The Chinese are proving very uncooperative. *Chennault has a better attitude towards the British than Stilwell. Chennault has proved quite outstanding.*

With regard to the USAF in China *Stilwell has not supplied Chennault with essential equipment.* He has insufficient ground staff, workshops, spare parts and gas. Bomber planes have been forced to go to Assam several times to fetch stores before an operational flight. He has therefore not been able to carry out much offensive work. *This should change since Chennault has been given priority on air transport supply by presidential directive. He has extensive plans.*[38] [italics supplied]

Why was Grimsdale so partial to Chennault? If anything, Chennault was as pro-Chinese as was Stilwell (Chennault's second wife was Chinese) and definitely much more pro-Chiang. He was a gregarious southerner who "saw an air offensive from China as the key to victory over the Japanese."[39] Grimsdale's analysis may have been due in part to the fact that Chennault, unlike Stilwell, knew how to flatter his allies, as well as to the desire to keep American counsels divided by siding with one American general against another. Most important of all, Chennault's plan for "victory through air power" did not involve major land operations in North Burma,[40] which the British did not want, but instead called for supplying China by air from British India. In order to increase the flow of supplies to China, FDR directed that air tonnage to China over the "Hump" should increase to 10,000 tons in the fall of 1943, and he had so informed Chiang.[41]

The paper "British Attitude Towards Chinese Troops" in Burma, dated January 28, 1944, by Raymond P. Ludden, a U.S. Foreign Service officer and one of Stilwell's political advisors in India, discusses this topic in detail; it concludes that the British were motivated more by political concerns for their empire in South Asia and Southeast Asia rather than by sound military judgment regarding Chinese troops. [42] In fact, Stilwell told Mountbatten bluntly that "Chinese troops can stand up under conditions that would stop white troops."[43]

While Stilwell was planning his campaign in North Burma, the British were also working on their strategic plans. They wanted to bypass Burma with an amphibious attack on Sumatra and Malaya, which was in the JPS (Joint Planning Staff) Paper No 81 in September 1943.[44] This did not happen because the Combined Chiefs of Staff issued directions for other priorities. Stilwell had hoped that such an amphibious operation would persuade Chiang to bring the Chinese Sixth Army or Y-Force troops into northern Burma.[45] The plan was for the Y-Force in China and the X-Force in India, which was made up of Chinese soldiers who had retreated to Burma in 1942, and which was being retrained under American auspices at Ramgarh in India, to attack from both China and India and link up with the British after Rangoon had been retaken.[46]

Another important decision at the Quebec Conference was the dispatch of three battalions of the 5307 Composite Unit (Provisional), under Brigadier General Frank Merrill (1903-1955), a West Point graduate, at the end of October 1943. They were the first American infantry in CBI. They would be known thereafter as "Merrill's Marauders." This is an often forgotten part of the story of CBI and SEAC, since the vast majority of Allied troops who fought in Burma were British, Indian, African, Chinese, and Burmese. The Marauders were the first American troops to see active combat on the mainland of Asia since the Boxer Rebellion in 1900.[47]

FDR was more interested in keeping China in the war than in any operations in Burma. He believed himself to be an expert on China because of his historic family links there,[48] even though he had never been there. The late American historian Eric Larrabee wrote, "The China Stilwell knew was unknown to the President and, having confidence in his own 'background,' Roosevelt did not know what it was he did not know."[49] Larrabee also wrote that "Roosevelt wanted postwar China to be a 'great power' and he believed, quite properly, that the first step in making it one was to treat it like one. Japan's 'Asia-for-the Asians' propaganda would be counteracted by our having this massive Asian ally, drawn into the alliance and then strengthened after the war was over by the promised return of Formosa [Taiwan] and Manchuria."[50]

Such was the atmosphere in October 1943 when Admiral the Lord Louis Mountbatten assumed supreme command in SEAC.

CHAPTER FIVE

ENTER THE SUPREMO

On October 7, 1943, Mountbatten arrived in India to take up his new position as Supreme Commander. Although Mountbatten's initial aim was to help rebuild morale, his main priority was planning a series of amphibious operations, which were still being considered. Meanwhile, British General Slim was building up the new 14th Army. Slim had been in the First Burma Campaign and he knew how the Japanese had won and how they could be defeated. Together Slim and Mountbatten would make a formidable team.

Mountbatten's arrival was the beginning of his complex relationship with Stilwell. At first Stilwell liked Mountbatten and wrote in his diary that "Louis is a good egg ... full of enthusiasm and also of disgust with inertia and conservatism ... Louis is hot for the 'one happy family' idea and is very cordial and friendly."[1] According to Theodore White, the phrase "one happy family" referred to Mountbatten's desire to establish an Allied High Command, with British, Americans and Chinese: "such a staff would parallel Eisenhower's staff in the Mediterranean."[2]

Mountbatten's arrival also coincided with Chiang's first attempt to remove Stilwell both as the commander of U.S. Forces in China and as his own chief of staff. When Mountbatten met with Chiang in Chungking, China's wartime capital, in mid-October 1943, he wrote that:

> [T]he Generalissimo [Chiang] had made up his mind absolutely to remove Stilwell and indeed I had heard from [U.S. Lieutenant] General Somervell that the Generalissimo had made it quite clear that Stilwell no longer had his confidence or the confidence of any of the Chinese he was working with ... I then went to call on General Stilwell at his house and was photographed with him afterwards, which gave him great pleasure for certain special reasons.[3]

Stilwell wrote in his diary for the same day, October 17, 1943, that "Mountbatten called and we had a long talk. He is burned up. Feels the double-cross himself, because he'll have to work with a brand-new man. Wants me to wait over and break him in."[4] On the same day, Mountbatten wrote in his diary that General Somervell had told him, "Would you believe it? After the Gissimo [Chiang] had told me categorically that Stilwell was out he sent for Stilwell this evening, kissed him on both cheeks and said he loved him more than ever and said he was right in again."[5] On October 21, 1943, Stilwell wrote in his diary: "The Peanut [Chiang][6] is now affable again. Impressed by my presentation [at Mountbatten-Somervell conference] of Chinese participation [in projected Burma attack]!!"[7]

In his *Report to the Combined Chiefs of Staff,* Mountbatten said he told General Somervell to tell Chiang that he (Mountbatten) "did not wish to proceed with plans for using Chinese forces if the man who had commanded most of them for nearly two years was to be removed just before the operations. . ." [8] However, Mountbatten's later recollection of what happened (as recounted by one of his biographers, the British naval historian Richard Hough), was that he asked Stilwell whether he wanted his job back (to which Stilwell replied "you bet"), after which Mountbatten told T.V. Soong, China's Foreign Minister (and Chiang's brother-in-law), to tell Chiang "Not one Chinese soldier will be moved one yard nearer to the enemy except on the orders of General Stilwell. They can rot as far as I'm concerned. You tell him that."[9]

October 1943 was the same month that Stilwell began the campaign in North Burma, which would become a major offensive in 1944. When Mountbatten visited Chiang in Chungking, he may well have argued for keeping Stilwell, the most seasoned American commander of Chinese troops, as the Commanding General in the CBI Theater. At the time Stilwell believed this was the reason Chiang retained him, a retention that lasted for a year.[10] This may also have been the main reason why Stilwell was initially favorable to Mountbatten. However, one year later, after Stilwell's recall from China, when Mountbatten wrote him that "Last year I was fortunate enough to be with you in Chungking and to be able to join forces . . . in insisting upon you being retained," Stilwell would write in a margin note to the letter that "he [Mountbatten] had nothing whatever to do with it."[11]

Biographers and historians are divided over whether Mountbatten "saved" Stilwell's job in 1943. Tuchman wrote that Mountbatten sent word that "he could not proceed with plans for using the Chinese forces if the man who had commanded them for nearly two years was to be removed,"[12] which tallies with Hough's account. Ziegler wrote that Mountbatten's only contribution may have been a message to Chiang that he would be sorry to see Stilwell leave at a critical period of the war.[13] Hough, as noted above, gave Mountbatten credit, but this was based upon conversations with him some thirty years after the event.[14] Whether Mountbatten "saved" Stilwell's job by interceding with Chiang is open to question. More likely the decision was the result of Chinese internal politics in late 1943, when Chiang was having problems with his brother-in-law T.V. Soong. According to both Stilwell and Tuchman, Soong overplayed his hand by pushing too hard for Stilwell's removal in 1943, thereby causing Chiang to become suspicious of Soong and supportive of Stilwell.[15] According to the modern British historian Jonathan Fenby, both Madame Chiang and her sister supported Stilwell against Soong (their own brother—to say that Chinese politics were Byzantine is putting it mildly), but Stilwell did not really know what was going on in the inner circle around Chiang. "Vinegar Joe had no idea what was really going on. His diary shows him to have been an innocent caught in the middle of a feud which he read the wrong way . . ."[16] Whatever the reason, Stilwell stayed.

In any event, at the end of 1943 Mountbatten thought that he had established a good relationship with Stilwell. (This was when he and Stilwell went to the movies together in Delhi.) However, Stilwell's letters and diary entries during this period are contradictory, first expressing admiration for Mountbatten and then shifting almost immediately to expressing distrust of him and his motives. In early October 1943 Stilwell wrote the U.S. Army Adjutant General in the War Department that "[W]e need fresh air and Mountbatten will be welcome."[17] Stilwell also wrote that "Admiral [Mountbatten] is really out to fight."[18] In early November 1943 Stilwell sent a message to Marshall in Washington, which read in part as follows: "Relations with Mountbatten and staff excellent. He is reasonable and open-minded, but there is [an] obvious tendency on [the] part of [the] British to muscle in on us in China, and in general to submerge and absorb all American effort and participation in this area."[19] Mountbatten had already said that CBI should be split up into separate commands.[20]

However, at the same time Stilwell also distrusted Mountbatten, writing in his diary on November 10, 1943, "Louis is after my scalp," was playing the "Empah [Empire] game," and was "working up" the "controversy" between Stilwell and Chennault.[21] Around this time Stilwell sent a memorandum to U.S. Major General Thomas B. Hearn, Chief of Staff of U.S. Army Forces in CBI, in which he wrote that "Mountbatten is dogging on the Burma job . . . the limies have now shown their hand [by wanting to do as little as possible in Burma and by including Hong Kong in SEAC] . . They are determined to keep China blockaded and powerless. They aim to go to Singapore, but that is the limit of their contribution."[22]

WEDEMEYER

After Stilwell, the most important American in the SEAC chain of command was Lieut.-General Albert C. Wedemeyer, Mountbatten's deputy chief of staff, who later succeeded Stilwell as Commanding General of U.S Forces in China (until 1946). Wedemeyer was born in 1897 and graduated from West Point in 1919. Between the two world wars, he served in Stilwell's old regiment in China. He and Stilwell knew each other, as most officers did in the interwar army, but they did not get on, largely because of their different temperaments. Stilwell, who was often self-doubting, summed up their differences when he wrote that Wedemeyer "thinks well of himself, that young man"[23] and "the young man sure does appreciate himself." [24] These comments, especially the repetition of the phrase "young man," also suggest that Stilwell, who was fourteen years older than Wedemeyer and seventeen years older than Mountbatten, resented what he saw as their relative youth and inexperience and their rapid advancement.

From 1936 to 1938, Wedemeyer had studied at the *Kriegsakademie*, the German war college in Berlin, which had a major influence on him. He became the foremost U.S. military expert on German military thinking. Between 1938 and 1941 he laid the plans for mobilizing and reforming the U.S. military for fighting World War II. Entitled the "Victory Program," it was sent to FDR in September 1941. It outlined how the U.S. Army would be organized to fight a land war on a scale similar to Nazi Germany while fighting the Japanese in the Pacific with large amphibious task forces. When the *Chicago Tribune*, a notoriously anti-New Deal and anti-FDR newspaper, broke the story of the "secret" Victory Program on December 4, 1941, Wedemeyer, still only a major, was suspected of having leaked the story and was investigated by the FBI. However, three days later the Japanese bombed Pearl Harbor, and on December 11, 1941, Hitler declared war on the United States, doing what FDR had never been able to do—bring America into the war on the side of the British against Nazi Germany. Wedemeyer was cleared of any wrongdoing and became a rising star in the U.S. Army's War Plans Division, reporting directly to General Marshall.[25] Because it was overshadowed by Pearl Harbor, this incident—"The Big Leak"—has been largely overlooked in the American historiography of World War II.[26]

In 1942 Wedemeyer, by now a full colonel, went to London with General Marshall and first met Mountbatten. In a 1983 interview, Wedemeyer remembered their first meeting:

> He was handsome and personable, as everyone knew, and seemed to be caught up in his work and very much on top of it. I knew of his connections with the Royal Family, and of Churchill's high regard for him, so I confess that I kept an open mind as to whether he had "made it" on his own. But my doubts proved unfounded. Mountbatten was first-rate in every respect. He did a remarkable job of holding together all the various forces that were resisting the Japanese in that part of the world. There were tensions among the Allies, problems with the natives, inter-service rivalries, prima donnas—to say nothing of the fact that we were operating almost at the end of the global pipeline, under conditions of terrain and climate that were extremely difficult, against an ingenious and ruthless enemy. Surmounting all of this, the "Supremo"—as the admiral came to be known by all ranks—brought a sense of common purpose to the command. He was fair-minded and diplomatic and had a flair for leadership.[27]

In fact, this was all in hindsight. According to both Ziegler and Smith, Wedemeyer certainly liked Mountbatten—almost everybody did—but did not quite trust him at first, since he was seen correctly as being Churchill's protégé, emissary and fixer vis-a-vis the Americans.[28] Mountbatten's goal was to convince FDR to delay the cross-channel invasion in favor of attacking the Germans in North Africa, which Wedemeyer considered to be a side show. Mountbatten played his role perfectly and FDR approved Operation Torch, the Anglo-American invasion of French North Africa, which took place in November 1942.

In 1943 Wedemeyer, by now a major general, was "eased out to Asia," as he put it, as Mountbatten's deputy chief of staff.[29] He was more of a background figure until well into 1944, but he was to play a more important role towards the end of the war. Up to now his experience had been in "grand strategy," with an emphasis on Europe. He wrote in his memoirs that he was sent out to SEAC because his strong support for an earlier date for D-Day angered Churchill.[30] Also, he arrived with a reputation for being anti-British, writing in his memoirs:

> My own reputation for being anti-British didn't help him [Mountbatten] much at the start. This drawback was somewhat alleviated, however, when it became known that Stilwell thought I was extremely pro-British. Lord Louis's troubles with Stilwell remained; for Vinegar Joe was constantly making wisecracks to the effect that the British had no intention of fighting, that they would do everything possible to avoid getting involved themselves but would push the Americans and Chinese into doing the job against Japan.[31]

In his memoirs Wedemeyer wrote that Eisenhower had highly recommended Mountbatten to him as a man he could trust:

> You will have a most interesting job in the Far East. Lord Louis is occasionally belittled by people who think they know more about war than he does, but in my honest opinion he has a lot on the ball and you will find that you are under a man you can respect in every way. Moreover, he is a man who will listen to advice and soak it up.[32]

In his 1983 interview, Wedemeyer also wrote the following:

> I can't really recall any [disagreements] during my year in SEAC. We were on the same team, working toward the same goals, under the same instructions from the Combined Chiefs of Staff. I understand that a few of the Americans serving with General Stilwell in India thought I was too "pro-British."

Later, when I was transferred to China, I found myself working for a radically different Allied commander —Generalissimo Chiang Kai-shek—under a different set of instructions from Washington. Frictions inevitably developed under these circumstances between the two geographically contiguous commands—SEAC and the China theater (which included French Indo-china). I continued, nonetheless, to find Admiral Mountbatten a cooperative ally and an understanding friend.

Several recent historians and biographers have blown out of all proportion the issues that arose between our respective commands. It has even been suggested that my personal friendship with Mountbatten was strained by suspicions of double-dealing, but all I know is that our friendship survived in all its warmth until his tragic death in 1979.[33]

Wedemeyer was the most senior American officer on Mountbatten's staff and might have bridged the personal, strategic, and geopolitical differences between Mountbatten and Stilwell. Instead, he became Stilwell's nemesis and one of his strongest critics. Perhaps the reason is obvious: both Mountbatten and Wedemeyer were young, polished, and very ambitious officers who knew how to work hard and to play politics when necessary.[34] Smith described Wedemeyer as a "well-groomed young colonel whose style, respect for European ways . . . and clarity of thought appealed strongly to Mountbatten." For his part, Wedemeyer described Mountbatten as "charming, tactful, a conscious gallant knight in shining armor . . ."[35] A comment like that would have made Stilwell laugh. This does not mean that they were not capable, only that they understood, far better than Stilwell, that World War II was a political as well as a military war. Also, to be fair to Wedemeyer, by all accounts he really believed (and his vision of grand strategy certainly supported his belief) that the way back for the Anglo-American Allies in Southeast Asia was by sea to Malaya and Singapore and not by land through Burma. Since that was Mountbatten's view as well, the two got along perfectly.

Wedemeyer's recollections of his time with Mountbatten, both in his memoirs (1958) and in his *American Heritage* interview (1983), reflected how his relationship with Mountbatten was the opposite of Stilwell's during the critical year from October 1943 to October 1944. As already noted, most Americans, with the exception of Stilwell, liked and got on well with Mountbatten. In early 1944 Mountbatten wrote to Lord Beaverbrook (1879-1964), the Anglo-Canadian press baron, that when he arrived at SEAC Anglo-American relations were the worst he had encountered in the war, and that Stilwell hated the British and still distrusted them, despite having become friends with Mountbatten. But then he added that, thanks to Wedemeyer, relations had improved dramatically and the integrated British and U.S. air forces "have achieved notable results."[36]

Although the Stilwell-Mountbatten relationship never developed the way Mountbatten wished, at least it never got to the kind of open disagreements over strategy that existed between Eisenhower and British General Bernard "Monty" Montgomery in Europe, both before and after D-Day. Moreover, as noted above, Mountbatten grew to like and rely upon Wedemeyer. So, to that extent at least, Mountbatten had his "one happy family."

Then they all went off to Cairo for the big conference.

CHAPTER SIX

CAIRO, CHIANG AND CBI

The final Allied conference which dealt specifically with CBI and SEAC was the Cairo Conference (SEXTANT) between FDR, Churchill, and Chiang at the end of November and early December 1943. Cairo was the first and only major Allied conference that Chiang attended, because he was the leader of the fourth major Allied power (the other three being the U.S., Britain, and the Soviet Union.)[1] Mountbatten, Stilwell, and the Combined British and U.S. Chiefs of Staff also attended. Although Stilwell and Mountbatten appeared to have had very little interaction at Cairo, apart from attending meetings together, the conference was important because it attempted to set forth Allied strategic policy goals in CBI and SEAC. In fact, before leaving for Cairo, together they had drafted plans to be submitted to FDR, Churchill, and the Combined Chiefs of Staff, which called for "serious" amphibious operations in southern Burma, which in turn would "encourage" Chiang to send Chinese troops in force across the border into northern Burma.[2]

At the November 23 session Stilwell was going to make China's case but was told not to do so by Chiang, who was on his way to Cairo, which was followed by Chiang's canceling and then resuming his plans.[3] On November 26, Stilwell wrote in his diary that Mountbatten "is fed up on Peanut. As who is not?"[4] Mountbatten, only a month or so into his new job, found Chiang increasingly difficult to deal with. In his diary, Mountbatten wrote that "I may say that he [Chiang] made several more illogical suggestions and I cannot help wondering how much he knows about soldiering."[5] Mountbatten also wrote that the Cairo Conference was badly organized because the opening session included FDR, Churchill, and Chiang, and their staffs. Mountbatten had hoped the staffs would meet first and then present their conclusions to the three Allied leaders. Apparently, this "putting the cart before the horse" was done in order for Chiang not to be kept waiting.[6] Stilwell complained of waging "War by Committee" and got in another dig at Wedemeyer (who was also at Cairo), writing in his diary "I'm getting tired of that important young man."[7]

At Cairo the main issues were the Asian-Pacific War strategy, the defeat of Japan, and plans for postwar Asia. Churchill, however, was not interested in Chiang or China's war, which he later described as being "lengthy, complicated and minor."[8] As at Quebec, he was more interested in strategic plans for Europe in 1944. Cairo also reconfirmed what had been decided at Quebec on the strategic goals for 1944 in SEAC, as follows: "Operations for the capture of Upper Burma in order to improve the air route and establish overland communications with China ... Continuance of operations during autumn 1944 within the limits of forces available to extend the position held in Upper Burma ... Should the means be available, additional ground offensive forces." [9] The U.S Joint Chiefs of Staff (JCS) estimated that: "It may be expected that Japan will initiate local offensive operations to forestall operations by the United Nations in Burma and to prevent the establishment of air bases by the United Nations in China."[10]

The JCS were also critical of the British strategy in Southeast Asia and the effect it would have on China in the war, as follows:

> The British determination to by-pass Burma, deflecting offensive efforts southward, cannot be expected to encourage the General-issimo [Chiang-Kai-shek] to adopt a more aggressive attitude

toward the Japanese. It is quite evident to informed Chinese that, if land communications to China are not opened, they cannot be reasonably asked to mount any significant offensive against the Japanese.[11]

After talking with FDR during the Cairo Conference, Stilwell wrote dismissively that FDR's policy toward China was "Policy: 'we want to help China.' —Period."[12] Stilwell was critical of the U.S.'s uncritical support of Chiang, whom Stilwell thought was not doing enough to fight the Japanese. Stilwell also believed FDR knew next to nothing about modern China and that he viewed China through the lens of his family history going back to the mid-nineteenth century.[13]

Stilwell's relationship with FDR, which went back to 1942, was complex. Larrabee wrote that Stilwell and many other Army officers thought that FDR "was a rank amateur in military matters and that he was vacillating, impulsive, too easily influenced by the last person to see him, especially if that person was British, or, worst of all, Churchill."[14] Stilwell also disliked FDR's partiality for the Navy over the Army, writing, "The Navy is the apple of his eye and the Army is the stepchild." [15] Stilwell was not alone in this view. During the war, Marshall once humorously asked FDR if he would stop referring to the navy as "us" and the army as "them." [16] FDR was not a military genius or thinker, but he was a good Commander-in-Chief despite his faults, just as Churchill was a better politician than a tactician.

FDR for his part had nothing against Stilwell personally, but because FDR thought he was a China "expert," he kept meddling in CBI, which he did not do with his commanders in the other theaters of war. Admittedly, FDR saw China's importance in diplomatic as well as military terms, but he interfered with the Stilwell-Chiang relationship far more than he ever did with Eisenhower, Nimitz, or MacArthur.[17] As already noted, FDR and many Americans overstated China's importance in the war. Perhaps this was the reason why he continued to send a stream of "special envoys" out to China, including Wendell Willkie (1892-1944), the unsuccessful

Republican presidential candidate in 1940, Vice-President Henry Wallace (1888-1965), and former Secretary of War Patrick Hurley (1883-1963).

The Cairo Conference and the Tehran Conference that immediately followed (which Chiang did not attend, but which Stalin did) changed the plans for the Allied offensive in Burma for 1944 because of the requirements for equipment and personnel in the Mediterranean and European theaters, especially for D-Day. This was an official concession to Stalin, who had been demanding a second front in Europe since the Nazi invasion in 1941, and it was probably the only time in which Stalin directly influenced what was happening in Southeast Asia. This upset Chiang because there were not going to be any amphibious operations in Burma or the Andaman Islands, which Chiang had wanted so that he could move his forces under Stilwell into North Burma, and which he thought he had been promised at Cairo.[18] In fact, after Tehran both FDR and Churchill made it clear to Chiang they did not have the landing craft necessary for an amphibious operation in the Bay of Bengal.[19]

Stilwell wrote in his diary after Cairo that, as far as Chiang was concerned, "Nothing is possible without a big amphibious operation. He [Chiang] doesn't know what a big amphibious operation is, but unfortunately Mountbatten was honest about it. So now that it is on a reduced scale, he [Chiang] screams. It is fatal to promise anything."[20] Exactly what was "promised" to Chiang at Cairo remains unclear. Nationalist Chinese historian Chin-tung Liang referred to a "breach of promise," claiming FDR had "assured [Chiang] of an amphibious operation in South Burma." Despite this disappointment, both FDR and Chiang agreed on postwar decolonization and the future United Nations organization.[21]

However, the main result of the conference was the Cairo Declaration, which was signed on November 27 and announced on December 1, 1943. It called for the return "of all territories Japan has stolen from the Chinese" and for Japan's unconditional surrender.[22] The Western Allies (at the Casablanca Conference in January 1943) had already called for Germany's unconditional surrender, and Italy had gone over to the Allies in September 1943 (as a co-belligerent after Mussolini's overthrow in July), so Cairo made it clear there would be no negotiated peace with Japan. On December 3, Chiang wrote that "the whole world treated Cairo as a great victory for China"[23] because a Chinese leader was treated as an equal with the Western leaders for the first time in a hundred years.

On the results of the Cairo Conference for the Chinese, American, and British strategic goals, the authors of *Stilwell's Personal File* wrote as follows:

> The viewpoints of the three nations involved varied widely. The Chinese wanted a land route opened, and had already expressed willingness to consider a reduction in Hump tonnage if necessary to achieve this goal. The Americans were definitely committed to north Burma operations, and their plans all pointed east toward China. British wishes, on the other hand, lay to the south. Consequently, a meeting of the international minds and agreement to commit "on hand" resources for a united, limited operation poised certain obstacles that had not yet been cleared.[24]

While the U.S. goal was to aid and keep China as a major ally in the war, Chiang wanted to win the war against Japan first and defeat the Communists after the war. To that end he was saving his best troops for a postwar showdown with the Communists, which is what happened.[25] Despite differences in the strategic goals during and after Cairo, the three objectives for the 1944 campaign in Burma were still the following:

1. Defending India by protecting the Assam borders from invasion;

2. Establishing a line from Silchar through Mogaung and Myitkyina [in North Burma] to the Chinese border; and

3. Inflicting heavy damage on the Japanese. [26]

While SEAC was an important strategic theater for the Allies in the Asian-Pacific War, it was not the road to Tokyo, which was the overall goal of the U.S. in the Pacific War. At the time of the Cairo Conference, the U.S. Navy under Admiral Nimitz had just launched the Central Pacific drive at the bloody Battle of Tarawa in the Gilbert (Kiribati) Islands (November 20-23, 1943), which was the beginning of the island-hopping campaign in the Pacific. The U.S. invasion force in the Gilberts was the largest assembled for a single amphibious operation in the Pacific War before the Marianas in 1944 and Okinawa in 1945, along with General MacArthur's advance up the coast of New Guinea toward the Philippines. The British opposed the U.S. offensive in the Pacific because they thought it took important shipping away from Eisenhower in Europe, especially for the D-Day buildup.

Stilwell was becoming increasingly exasperated by the conflicting demands upon him, requiring him to be in both Delhi and Chungking, while he desperately wanted to take the field. In a radio message he sent on December 31, 1943, Stilwell wrote, "Do they expect us to fight the Japs or drink tea in Delhi?"[27]

This was the strategic situation that would shape how the 1944 offensives in CBI and SEAC would be conducted in the land war in Burma against Japan. In the end most of the decisions of 1943 regarding SEAC and CBI did not materialize because of the strategic priorities given to Europe and to the Pacific theaters. What did materialize was a land campaign in North Burma, led by Stilwell and Slim, which turned the tide of the war in Southeast Asia. For Stilwell, the decisions of 1943 would put him back in active field command.

But now let us pause in the narrative to consider some of the issues Mountbatten had to address before the British, Indians, Africans, Americans, and Chinese could begin the liberation of Burma. In handling those issues he really began to take supreme command, but at the same time he and Stilwell began to grow increasingly at odds with each other.

Figure 4. Stilwell and Mountbatten in Chungking, 1943

Courtesy of the Imperial War Museums, London
Vice Admiral Lord Louis Mountbatten (left), new Allied Commander in Asia and Lt Gen
Joseph Stilwell, Commander of US Forces in China, India and Burma, are shown in
Chung-King following a conference.

Figure 5. Bill Slim in Burma, 1944

Courtesy of the Imperial War Museums, London

Field Marshal Sir William Slim (1891-1970): Portrait of the 14th Army Commander.

Figure 6. Stilwell, Chiang Kai-shek, and Madame Chiang in Burma, April 1942

Courtesy of the National Archives, Washington, D.C.
Generalissimo and Madame Chiang Kai Shek and Lieutenant General Joseph W.
Stilwell, Commanding General, China Expeditionary Forces, on the day following
Japanese bombing attack. Maymy; 4/19/1942.

Figure 7. The Cairo Conference, November 25, 1943.

Courtesy of the Franklin D. Roosevelt Presidential Library & Museum, Hyde Park, New York.

The Cairo Conference, November 1943. Seated in the picture (from left to right) are Chiang Kai-shek, FDR, Winston Churchill, and Madame Chiang Kai-shek. Stilwell and Mountbatten are standing in the back row.

Figure 8. Mountbatten Statue, Horse Guards Parade, London.

Courtesy of Alamy.com, London.
The statue of the Earl Mountbatten is an outdoor bronze statue of Admiral of the Fleet Louis Mountbatten, 1st Earl Mountbatten.

Chapter Seven

Lord Louis Takes Charge

Mountbatten and the Three "M's": Monsoon, Malaria, Morale

The main problems that Mountbatten faced when he took over SEAC were known as "The Three M's": monsoon, malaria, and morale. For five months, from May to October, the monsoon shut the war down until operations could be conducted in the "dry "season, which lasted from October to May. Mountbatten had a simple solution: just fight through the monsoon. He proposed to do that through amphibious operations on the Bay of Bengal, while Slim's forces fought through the jungles to the Irrawaddy Valley in central Burma. Mountbatten ordered the Royal Air Force (RAF) and the U.S. Army Air Forces (USAAF) to fly in bad weather, so that troops on the ground could be re-supplied from the air. This was to prove essential for the British forces in their 1944 Burma Campaign.

Airpower was also important in destroying Japanese positions in Burma, especially "bridge-busting" by the U.S. Tenth Air Force, with constant attacks, and follow-up attacks after air reconnaissance revealed repair work.[1] However, Stilwell and Chennault hotly debated the effectiveness of air power in China, which was part of the larger debate in the war between the U.S. Army and the USAAF over bombing strategy, especially in Europe. Stilwell argued that it would take American-trained Chinese divisions as well as Chennault's fighter planes to defend the USAAF's planned bomber attack bases for the new B-29 Superfortresses in the area of southeastern China around Kweilin from a Japanese ground assault.[2] The first B-29s arrived in India in April 1944 after leaving Kansas in March, taking one month to make the trip. Most of the B-29 bases in India were operational by April 1944.

Malaria was another major problem in fighting a war in Burma. Sir Ronald Adam (1885-1982), the British Adjutant-General, told Mountbatten that malaria "is almost a greater enemy than the Japanese in the fighting zones of the East,"[3] which was not an exaggeration. In 1943, most of the men in the British forces had malaria, along with dysentery and other tropical diseases. Mountbatten did not want a sick army for the 1944 campaign, so he toured the military hospitals to make sure they were providing adequate medical help. Because of his efforts, the number of men ill with malaria fell dramatically, from 84 percent to 13 percent between 1943 and 1945. The main weapon used against malaria was DDT (which was relatively new in 1943), sprayed over the swamps that bred the mosquitoes that spread malaria.[4]

In his memoirs Slim described the efforts to combat malaria in the field. After noting the importance of DDT, penicillin, and sulfa drugs, he wrote, "It was, however, forward treatment that brought the first visible results. Up to now, when a man contracted malaria, he had been transported, while his disease was at its height, in great discomfort hundreds of miles by road, rail and boat to a hospital in India . . . To avoid all this we organized M.F.T.U.s, Malaria Forward Treatment Units. They were, in effect, field hospitals."[5]

Morale was the third major problem. Most of the men in the British Army in SEAC did not know why they were fighting there, especially after the debacles of 1942. The phrase "the Forgotten Army," which later became a term of pride for the new 14th Army, was probably coined by a correspondent for the *News Chronicle* in Britain in the summer of 1943, even though that feeling had existed in the Army for some time.[6] In Britain, the Ministry of Information, which was similar to the Office of War Information (OWI) in the U.S., said the British public was ignorant of the war in CBI and SEAC. Mountbatten began a series of morale boosting tours with the 14th Army, where he emphasized the importance of the British war effort in SEAC, why the men there were not "forgotten," and that victory would come after a hard fight back into Burma. This was all welcome news at the end of 1943.

INDIA

India was also another problem, because all Mountbatten's supplies came through there. After the "Quit India" campaign in 1942, the British arrested Mohandas K. "Mahatma" Gandhi (1869-1948), Jawaharlal Nehru (1889-1964), and other Indian Congress Party leaders. During the Bengal Famine of 1943, millions of Indians died because of the loss of rice shipments from Burma and bureaucratic incompetence in Bengal.[7]

The Indian National Army (INA) or *Azad Hind Fauj* (1942-1945) was the renegade[8] army led by General Subhas Chandra Bose (1897-1945), also called the *Netaji* (Hindi/Bengali for "Respected Leader"). Bose was an Indian nationalist and fascist who collaborated first with the Germans and then with the Japanese, trying to exploit the divisions of the subcontinent.[9] Bose had proclaimed a "Government of Free India" in Japanese-occupied Singapore in 1943 and had made radio broadcasts from Germany in 1942 urging Indians to support the Japanese. In fact, Japan never intended to create an independent India, but rather a vassal state under Japan or Germany. There is a brief mention of the INA in a letter from Lieutenant General A.F.P. Christianson to Mountbatten on the Allied victory in the Arakan on February 26, 1944, as follows: "[T]he results of the recent battle should prevent the Japanese sending the INA into eastern Bengal, so upsetting conditions in India and reducing its value as a military base. The troops did splendidly, and many officers and men have said that

Mountbatten's visit to the Arakan was important in keeping morale and the fighting spirit high in the critical three week period." [10]

A search of the wartime records at the Mountbatten Archives does not reveal anything specific about Mountbatten's views on Bose during this period. However, Mountbatten, along with most of the British military, almost certainly thought of Bose as a traitor both to the British *and to the Indians* for fighting alongside the Japanese. In July 1945, just before Japan's surrender and his death, Bose laid the foundation of an INA War Memorial in Singapore, which the Japanese hastily completed. When the British retook Singapore later that summer, Mountbatten ordered the memorial to be destroyed.[11] In fact, Mountbatten was very aware of the situation in India, which influenced him when he became the last Viceroy of India in 1947.

THE MOVE TO CEYLON

When Mountbatten arrived in SEAC, he was first based in Delhi, the headquarters of the Indian Army Command. Because he had come to fight a naval war as well as a land war, he decided that Kandy in Ceylon (now Sri Lanka) would be a better base from which to conduct amphibious operations, and he moved there in April 1944. Although he has been criticized by some historians for doing this, moving to Ceylon made sense to him, because it was much closer to Burma than was Delhi. In his report to the Combined Chiefs of Staff after the war, Mountbatten justified the move:

> I favoured moving to Ceylon, not only because it was the nearest point opposite the centre of the Japanese perimeter, and therefore the best from which to control amphibious operations; but also because it already provided the main base and shore headquarters of the Eastern Fleet. . .[12]

The move to Ceylon was thus part of the larger imperial military strategy of the British in Southeast Asia of using the Royal Navy to get back to Singapore. This was common knowledge at the time. Bill Henry, a columnist for the *Los Angeles Times*, wrote in April 1944 on the war in CBI and Mountbatten's move: "[T]he only offensive operation in the Burma-India theater is Uncle Joe Stilwell's drive toward the Burma Road. Mountbatten's move to Ceylon for his headquarters indicates the British goal is, as mentioned here previously, Singapore."[13]

Mountbatten was first and foremost a navy man, who liked planning large-scale amphibious operations. Also, he had been in charge of Combined Operations, which involved by their very nature the coordination of naval, air, and land forces. On a personal level, his one foray into a large-scale combined operation, the Dieppe Raid in August 1942, had turned into a full-blown disaster. With all of this in mind, it is entirely understandable that Mountbatten saw the sea route from Ceylon to Singapore as not only the path to restore Britain's imperial prestige, but also the path to wipe out the memory of Dieppe. However, preference for the sea route was based on more than Mountbatten's personal feelings. An amphibious operation would avoid British and Commonwealth forces becoming bogged down in the "mud and blood" of Burma, which to British commanders at the time, Churchill most of all, was eerily reminiscent of the Western Front in World War I, and which they feared could evolve into a stalemate.[14]

Above all, the seaborne strategy fit in perfectly with Britain's history of sea power, which is how the British had built their empire in the first place. After Napoleon lost the Battle of Waterloo in 1815, he fled south, finally surrendering to the Royal Navy at Rochefort on the Atlantic coast of France. At the time he was reported to have said, "Wherever wood can swim, there I am sure to find this flag of England." [15] The British had lost Singapore to the Japanese in 1942 because, among other reasons, their heavy guns had faced seaward and the Japanese had come by land.[16] Now, in 1944, if Mountbatten and Churchill had their way, the British would retake Singapore from the sea and wipe out the shame of 1942.

Historians are divided over the wisdom of the move to Ceylon. Ziegler wrote that "The move was a manifestation of his [Mountbatten's] wish to adopt a maritime strategy and not allow his forces to be bogged down in the Burmese jungle." [17] Bayly and Harper wrote that Mountbatten's decision to move his headquarters to Kandy was also taken because "His aim was to counter the 'forgotten army' feeling that particularly affected British troops immobilized for months in the dust or the rains of India or stuck in the mud and malaria of Assam."[18] Just how moving his headquarters to a botanical garden in the cool highlands of Ceylon would make the average soldier feel less "forgotten" is something that Mountbatten never really explained. Moving Mountbatten's staff to Ceylon did not improve the living conditions of ordinary British and Commonwealth soldiers. If he had just wanted to move closer to the Burma front, Calcutta would have been a more logical choice, since it was the major port and the southern terminus of the Bengal-Assam Railway, the vital rail link for supplies going to China and the Burma front. McLynn was very critical of the move, calling it "a criminal waste of resources" and writing how it became a "byword for luxury and elegance."[19] He also wrote that "Mountbatten compounded the problem of being too far from the war and thus being unable to engender any sense of urgency in his personnel by the most grotesque overstaffing." [20] There were at first some 7,000 and later 10,000 men and women on the SEAC staff, including many attractive WRENS.[21]

Mountbatten described his headquarters in detail in his diary entry for April 16, 1944. He noted that his staff had requisitioned the botanical gardens and part of the golf course.[22] The botanical gardens at Kandy were shown in a scene from the 1957 film *The Bridge on the River Kwai*, with a sign reading "Headquarters, South East Asia Command."

On December 6, 1943, Mountbatten sent a letter to General Alan Brooke, the Chief of the Imperial General Staff, asking for high-level representation in Delhi after his proposed move to Ceylon by that coming April 15, 1944, due to "the lack of resources" in his theater, as follows: (a)

For his and Stilwell's staff; (b) For Peirse's air staff; and (c) For Giffard's Army Group staff. The letter stated "A reasonably large rear HQ will be needed in Delhi and the three CINCs will also have to leave staffs there." It is summarized as follows in the Mountbatten Archives:

> Mountbatten asks for a permanent and high level representative in Delhi, to speak for him in inter-command meetings with Auchinleck and the Viceroy. All his senior officers are too busy . . . He needs a soldier with prestige and personality, as there are two Generals, two Lieutenant Generals and several Major Generals in GHQ India. Pownall and Mountbatten would prefer someone of the rank of Lieutenant General.

> *When [HQ SACSEA] moves to Rangoon, Bangkok or Singapore, whilst India is its main base, it will still need a rear HQ at Delhi. This organisation will therefore last until Japan is defeated.* [23] (italics supplied)

The reference to moving SEAC's headquarters to "Rangoon, Bangkok or Singapore" emphasized the southward, seaward thrust of the British plans. This is significant because it highlighted the evolving nature of SEAC's command structure in 1944 and how it would shape the British offensive strategy against Japan until the end of the war. The British would fight the land war in Burma and then make an amphibious landing in Malaya to liberate Singapore.

Kandy also symbolized the two very different living styles of Mountbatten and Stilwell. Two American war correspondents wrote a satirical song about Kandy, which included these lines: "Oh, we fight in botanical gardens, In the lush botanical gardens, Our sailors maneuver in whisky and tea." The song concluded: "The Limeys make policy, Yanks fight the Jap, And one gets its Empire, and one takes the rap."[24] Mountbatten did not rough it even when he was visiting the frontline troops, while Stilwell wanted to be seen as a field commander sharing the experiences of his troops. He was in the field most of the time between December 1943 and July 1944, living in conditions far more Spartan than those of Mountbatten. Stilwell's "leading from the front" and rough style of living was criticized by the British and even by some Americans, who found it unnecessarily ascetic.[25]

THE MEDIA WAR

Like everywhere else in World War II, the media—newspapers, magazines, radio, films, and newsreels—that were used by the Americans and the British played a major role in how CBI and SEAC were perceived by the public. Their use of media during the war is a good example of how both politicians and generals use self-promotion to spin and justify their versions of events at the time and afterward. A good example of famous self-promotion is Winston Churchill's six-volume *The Second World War* (1948-1953), where he refought World War II. It was largely responsible for Churchill being awarded the Nobel Prize for Literature in 1953. None of the other wartime leaders, such as FDR, Stalin, Mussolini, or Hitler (three of whom had died by May 1945), published firsthand accounts of the war. De Gaulle wrote his memoirs in French, of course, so they were not available to English-speaking readers until they were translated in 1955.

Both Stilwell and Mountbatten were media-savvy four-star flag officers who knew how to handle the media images of the Burma Campaign, even with most of the media attention focused on Europe and the Pacific. Wherever they went, friendly reporters were not far away. Stilwell in particular benefited from his friendship with Theodore ("Teddy") White of *Time Magazine,* who later edited Stilwell's diary for publication and who enshrined the legend of "Vinegar Joe." When Stilwell took Myitkyina in August 1944, he brought the press to cover the event.

In the U.S. media, CBI was portrayed as keeping China in the war and promoting Chiang's "democratic" regime against the Japanese (which was similar to the favorable U.S. portrayal of Stalin and the Soviet Union). For example, Frank Capra's *The Battle of China* or *War in the East* (1944), the sixth film of the *Why We Fight* series (1942-1945), focused on Japan's aggression in China as a springboard to conquer Asia and the heroic Chinese resistance under Chiang and Nationalist leadership.[26] Because of political problems with the film, it was not released to the public.

Although John Wayne starred in *Flying Tigers* (1942), a fictionalized account of Chennault's American Volunteer Group (AVG) battling the Japanese in China before the U.S. entered the war, the only major American film about CBI that was made during the war was *Objective Burma!* When it was released in February 1945, Stilwell wrote in his diary: "'Objective: Burma.' Good film. Scare-crow to take my part."[27] However, the film angered the British, since it portrayed the liberation of Burma from the Japanese as a mostly American affair. Several years later a tactful prologue was added to the film that featured Mountbatten, Slim, Wingate, and the 14th Army.[28]

The main media outlet in CBI was the *CBI Roundup* (changed to *India-Burma Theater Roundup* and the *China Lantern* in China in 1945), the oldest overseas GI paper and the CBI newspaper from 1942 to 1946. It was published by the *Statesman* newspaper in New Delhi and Calcutta. In the second issue of *CBI Roundup*, Stilwell described its purpose as follows:

> The main purpose of this paper is to keep the command informed of what is going on at home and in the other theaters of war. We are a long way out, the mail is slow, and all censors are crabs, so *Roundup* should help materially to fill in the gaps. It's your paper, so feel free to contribute to it. If you have a gripe, write a letter to the editor. If you can run the paper better than he can, tell him so, but watch out that he doesn't put you on the staff and make you prove it. He is looking for ideas and if he can't find them, the *Roundup* won't be quite what we want it to be—the most readable sheet in the Far East.[29]

In 1946, just before his death, Stilwell wrote in *Roundup's* last issue: "Congratulations on your record as the best soldier paper of them all. *Roundup* has accomplished its mission and can fold up with a feeling of satisfaction that it never missed a chance to crack down on injustice or laugh at stuffed shirts. And that is the chief reason that all through its existence it was one of the biggest morale factors in the Theater. A bouquet to all who labored to make it so."[30]

For the British, SEAC had to deal with not only the British defeat in Burma and Malaya in 1942, but also the image problem of why the British were fighting there, which will be discussed in more detail in the next chapter. Up to 1943, most of the British coverage of the war focused on North Africa, the Battle of the Atlantic, and the war in Europe. Although Burma received some attention in 1942 and 1943, media attention started to decline after early 1944 with the Allied advances in Europe and the Pacific, as David Hogan Jr. said in the new introduction to the 2000 edition of Slim's 1956 memoir *Defeat into Victory*. In Burma, the only major British general who became famous was the colorful Orde Wingate. Slim was also overlooked because of Montgomery, who became the most famous British general of the war after El Alamein.

While *CBI Roundup* was the newspaper for the American forces, the main British news outlet in SEAC was the *Seac Souvenir: The Services' Newspaper of South East Asia Command*, which was the SEAC newspaper for the British 14th Army in 1944 and 1945. In his memoir, Slim wrote that "An innovation [for the troops in SEAC] was to be the publication of a theatre newspaper—*Seac*."[31] Just before the end of the war in 1945, *Seac* became the main source for urging the return of British troops home to Britain after their long service in Southeast Asia.

Mountbatten said he "wanted to have a joint Anglo-American publication so as to bring the American and British forces closer together in this theatre. [He] thought a weekly picture magazine, on the *Life-Picture Post* model, would be the best. Everyone, even General Stilwell, agreed."[32] However, the Americans and the British could not work out their schedules, so as of January 1945 there was still no joint publication.

Mountbatten also suggested that there should be a joint Anglo-American film about the Burma Campaign, but "when it was found impossible to reach agreement on the script," he agreed with Marshall to have an American film, titled *Stilwell Road,* and a British film, titled *Jungle Victory.*[33] The U.S. Army in fact produced a documentary titled *The Stilwell Road* (1945), which is now at the National Archives. (The film was narrated by Ronald Reagan.) Mountbatten noted that both he and Marshall "pledged each other that we would be fair about the share of the other nation, and I must say Marshall has kept his word, for this film is excellent."[34]

The British view of the Burma Campaign was the documentary *Burma Victory* (1945), which was released just after the war and highlighted the British and Commonwealth forces' victory in Burma. The November 30, 1945, issue of the *Monthly Film Bulletin* stated that "This is a masterly survey of a vast and complex campaign, presented with vivid realism," and the November 1, 1945, issue of *Kinematograph Weekly* wrote that it was an "Outstanding documentary." [35] Ian Kikuchi, a historian at the Imperial War Museum in London, wrote that

> [T]he Ministry of Information's [which was similar to the Office of War Information (OWI) in the U.S.] superb and remarkably even-handed *Burma Victory* languishes forgotten, outgunned in its own day by Errol Flynn's ludicrous *Objective Burma!* Flynn's "meretricious hodgepodge" (an American airman's opinion) had British troops burning down cinemas in disgust, but crucially made it to the big screen before the Japanese surrender and several months before *Burma Victory.*"[36]

Despite this extensive media coverage, the Burma Campaign was largely forgotten in Britain in the years after 1945. It was only with the passage of time, and the formation of the Burma Star Association, under the sponsorship of Mountbatten and Slim, that the troops of the "Forgotten Army" began to receive the recognition they deserved. That recognition was due in large part to the bravery of British, Indian, and African troops in the Second Arakan Campaign of 1944, which became the first British land victory against the Japanese. The following chapters describe that campaign and the series of often overlapping Allied and Japanese campaigns and battles in CBI from the winter through the summer of 1944.

CHAPTER EIGHT

RETURN TO BURMA

China was the main theater of war for the Japanese, but it had become a stalemate for the Japanese Army there after 1938. After Pearl Harbor, the Pacific became the main theater of war for the Japanese Navy, because of the strategically important islands in the Central Pacific. The U.S. needed those islands as bases to attack Japan directly, while the Japanese needed them to access raw materials, especially oil in the Dutch East Indies (Indonesia), and the other islands of maritime Southeast Asia. So why fight in Burma at all? Because it was the gateway to both China and India.

If the relief of China was America's obsession, and the defense of India was Britain's, then Burma—the "B" in CBI—was the stepchild, the land-in-between, of importance to the Americans only because it contained the most direct land route from India to China, and to the British because it either protected (or threatened) the eastern flank of the Raj, the Indian Empire (the official name of British India from 1876-1947), the "Jewel in the Crown." [1]

At the end of 1943, the Japanese were holding a defensive position in Burma, planning to delay the Allied advance they expected in 1944. There were about 350,000 Japanese troops in Southeast Asia, about half of them in Burma, where they had five divisions. [2] Burma, which was a separate British colony after 1937, had the misfortune to be located between the warring powers, and next to Thailand, which was officially a Japanese ally, similar to Hungary, Romania and Bulgaria, German Axis allies in the Balkans. India was an empire within the British Empire and its largest possession, not a "colony," as some books mistakenly claim. India was also a founding member of both the League of Nations and the United Nations.

Both the British and the Japanese considered Burma a very important theater, for different reasons. *The World at War*, the outstanding British documentary series of World War II, put it this way: "For the British, Burma was a shield and barrier protecting their Indian Empire. The Japanese saw they could use Burma to screen their new territorial gains in Southeast Asia, to cut the Allied supply route to China, and to secure new sources of oil and rice."[3] Hideki Tojo (1884-1948), Japanese Prime Minister from 1941 to 1944 and Chief of the Imperial Japanese Army General Staff in 1944, told the Prime Minister of Thailand that Burma was "a bulwark of the defense for us in the Indian area."[4]

The Japanese planned to occupy Burma and then destabilize British rule in India. Before the war, Britain's defense of India had been focused on the Northwest Frontier near Afghanistan, in what is now Pakistan. The war changed all that, so that the Assam-Burma-China border became all-important from 1942-1944. The Indian Army was asked to defend India for the first time after fighting largely outside India in British imperial campaigns for almost a century. In August 1943 the Japanese gave Burma sham independence to reinforce the illusion of the Japanese Empire as the "Greater East Asia Co-Prosperity Sphere."[5] In November 1943, the Japanese held the Greater East Asia Conference in Tokyo, which was the only major conference of an Axis Power and its satellites during the war.[6] Germany was not at this conference, since it was staged by Tokyo to demonstrate a show of Asian support for Japanese war aims. The Germans never held a pan-European conference for Nazi-occupied Europe.

Burma is divided by three great rivers: the Chindwin in the west, the Irrawaddy in the center, and the Salween in the east. In the west, near India and present-day Bangladesh, are the Chin Hills and the Arakan Yoma mountain range along the Bay of Bengal. In the north near China are the Paktai and Kumon Ranges. In the center are the Irrawaddy Valley and the Bago Yoma range. To the south are the Gulf of Martaban and the Rangoon Delta.[7] Then and now, all of Burma's lines of communications run north and south along the three great river valleys that separate the country's mountain ranges. [8]

In 1942 the Japanese had advanced rapidly up the Irrawaddy Valley and had chased the British and the Chinese out of most of Burma. Now, at the end of 1943 and the beginning of 1944, the British under Slim and the Chinese and Americans under Stilwell were coming back. Stilwell wrote in his diary for December 20, 1943: "Off for Burma again. Under better auspices than last time. CAN WE PUT IT OVER?"[9] (The capitalization of the last sentence is in the original.)

Meanwhile, however, the Japanese were already planning their own counter-offensives, one into eastern India through Burma, and the other against Chennault's airfields in eastern China. The Japanese position in Burma at the end of 1943 was a strong one: "The enemy facing the NCAC [Northern Combat Area Command] was the renowned 18th Division, veteran of the first Burma campaign and the conquest of Singapore, considered one of the ablest and best-trained divisions in the Japanese Army." [10] This assessment was echoed by Frank McLynn, who referred to "the crack Japanese 18th Division . . . commanded by one of its ace generals, Shinichi Tanaka."[11] It had taken part in the triumphant capture of Singapore.[12] The Japanese, battle-hardened and confident, would not be easy to dislodge. However, that is exactly what Stilwell and Slim intended to do.

THE SECOND ARAKAN CAMPAIGN

In December 1943, while Stilwell was leading his campaign in North Burma, Slim began the second Arakan offensive with better trained and equipped British forces. By January 1944 there were three Allied fronts in Burma: the North Burma front (Stilwell), the Chindwin River front (Slim's XV Corps), and the Arakan front (Slim's IV Corps).[13]

The Arakan is the western coastal region of Burma, which includes the island of Akyab, whose airfield in British hands would not only protect Calcutta but would allow the RAF to support Allied operations in southern Burma.[14] This approach was consistent with the British "sea" strategy, as opposed to the American "land" strategy, by which British naval, air, and ground forces would sweep around the Japanese in Burma and retake Rangoon. That would be the springboard for retaking the greatest prize of all, Singapore, whose re-conquest would wipe out the shame of its surrender to the Japanese in 1942. The British under Slim had tried (and failed) to penetrate the Arakan and seize Akyab in late 1942 and early 1943. They tried again a year later, with somewhat better results.

On January 4, 1944, at the beginning of the second Arakan operation, Mountbatten had expressed the British view of SEAC's strategy in Burma when he told his staff that Stilwell's campaign to build the Ledo Road (later the Stilwell Road) to connect the Burma Road to China did not fit into the "global" strategy, and that SEAC should hold its forces for a "major" drive instead of using them piecemeal in Burma, as the British had done in 1943.[15] The British reluctance to undertake a major Burmese offensive because of their situation in the Arakan and later at Imphal and Kohima also gave Chiang a good excuse to delay his promised attack on Lungling (a walled fortress city in southwestern China, terminus of the old Burma Road), and to not coordinate his strategy with Stilwell's drive on Myitkyina in North Burma, which had an important airfield the Allies needed. [16] Chiang's reluctance to conduct a major offensive there was to cause more friction in his already estranged relationship with Stilwell. Although the British, especially Mountbatten, did not want to fight a land war in Burma, they could not conduct the amphibious operations they had planned at Cairo because the landing craft were needed for D-Day in Europe. Mountbatten, like it or not, was stuck with a ground war in Burma.

In February 1944, the Japanese 28th Army in Burma commanded by Lieutenant General Shozo Sakurai (1889-1985) counterattacked and cut off one of the British divisions in the Arakan at Ngakyedauk Pass (or Okedoke Pass). Unlike the year before, the British did not retreat and were able to hold their positions, particularly in the Administration or "Admin Box," because of air supplies that were dropped to them by USAAF transport planes. RAF fighters cleared the skies of Japanese aircraft.[17] The Japanese failed to understand that the British and Indian Divisions could be supported and resupplied from the air, and they paid the price.[18] All RAF and USAAF air supply was coordinated under one command, which delivered more than a thousand tons of supplies by air, so that the end of February 1944 the British and Indian troops had been resupplied and the Japanese beaten back.[19]

Another difference between the two offensives in the Arakan was that the morale of the Allied troops was higher the second time. British, Indian, and African troops were becoming more confident and more adept at jungle warfare. Using armor and artillery, and with continued air support, they held out and decimated the Japanese.[20] At the end of February, Sakurai retreated. The Japanese had lost their first battle against the British. For the first time they realized they were not the masters of the jungle.

However, the British once again failed to take Akyab, which would not be captured until January 1945, when Royal Marines landed under cover of the Royal Navy's Far Eastern Fleet.[21] In that sense the Second Arakan Campaign also failed, because it did not achieve its objective. But in beating the Japanese at their own game in jungle warfare, the campaign was a success. Both Slim and the "forgotten" 14th Army had bounced back from the defeats of 1942 and 1943.

The campaign also vindicated Mountbatten's insistence on mastering two of the "Three M's": Morale and Malaria. British and Indian morale was much higher than it had been before, in part because of improved sanitation and other measures to combat malaria. Mountbatten wrote in his diary of the improved morale: "This battle, which is now at its height, is of the utmost importance to us in South-East Asia, as it is a battle of morale...The same troops that ran before [Japanese General] Tanabashi last year have stood firm to the last man this year and I feel confident of ultimate victory."[22] In that sense the Second Arakan Campaign, although it was Slim's victory foremost, was also when Mountbatten began to emerge as a resourceful and successful supreme commander.

In his memoir on the Burma Campaign, *Defeat into Victory*, Slim wrote on why the Second Arakan was the first major turning point of the Burma Campaign in 1944:

> This Arakan battle, judged by the size of the forces engaged, was not of great magnitude, but it was, nevertheless, one of the historic successes of British arms. It was the turning-point of the Burma campaign. For the first time a British force had met, held, and decisively defeated a major Japanese attack, and followed this up by driving the enemy out of the strongest possible natural positions that they had been preparing for months and were determined to hold at all costs. British and Indian soldiers had proved themselves, man for man, the masters of the best the Japanese could bring against them... The legend of Japanese invincibility in the jungle, so long fostered by so many who should have known better, was smashed.[23]

Although it is true that by the end of the campaign Slim and the men of the 14th Army were fighting Japanese soldiers who were on the verge of starvation, because they had outrun their supply lines, that does not take away from the importance of the Allied victory in the Arakan. The British mastered the art of logistics, re-supplying their troops by air, while the Japanese did not. Never good at logistics, their retreat became a rout. Starving or not, they still fought fiercely, and full credit is due to the soldiers of Slim's 14th Army.

CHAPTER NINE

TROUBLE BREWING
MORE THAN TEA

While Slim's forces held out in the Arakan and began to beat the Japanese at jungle warfare, Stilwell's Chinese forces began advancing in North Burma. Their strategic objective was the airfield at Myitkyina, which was very important as a base for Allied air operations in North Burma for 1944. The Chindits under their colorful and controversial leader Orde Wingate were planning to launch a major offensive code-named "Operation Thursday," where they would cut Japanese supply lines to support operations by conventional forces, seize the airfield at Indaw, and attack the "White City," unlike the year before when they had gone into Burma as long-range raiders.

In March 1944 Wingate was killed in an air crash during the operation. After his death control of the Chindits formally passed to Stilwell's command in May 1944. Stilwell's leadership of the Chindits in 1944, especially the way he used them in North Burma, would become controversial during that period and after the war, because he used them as regular infantry and not as a guerrilla force behind the Japanese lines. His treatment of them and of Merrill's Marauders during the siege of Myitkyina, where he pushed them beyond their limits and so incurred their hatred, would be the most controversial episode of his military career.

Meanwhile, the Stilwell–Mountbatten relationship, which had looked promising in late 1943, was rapidly deteriorating, especially on Stilwell's part. Stilwell and Mountbatten were never friends and Stilwell's Anglophobia was still very strong. Stilwell wrote in his diary on January 8, 1944: "Louis [Mountbatten] welches on entire program. . . Limey program: (1) Stop road at Ledo. (2) Do not attack Burma. (3) Go to Sumatra. (4) Include Hongkong in SEAC!" [1]

By the spring of 1944 Stilwell was calling Mountbatten "The Glamour Boy" in his diary.[2] While this was true up to a point, and Mountbatten certainly dressed for the part, he was not just a dashing naval officer as already noted. What Stilwell overlooked, or perhaps did not know, was that Mountbatten had worked his way up through the Royal Navy, had taken a signals course in 1927 because he wanted to learn about radio, and had always driven himself, his ships, and his men very hard— perhaps too hard—throughout his career. Although Mountbatten never fully understood Stilwell's animosity then or later, he knew Stilwell was not easy to work with, especially given the pressures he was facing in Burma and his difficulties with Chiang. Mountbatten's diary entries about Stilwell, though often frank, were never as vituperative as Stilwell's comments about Mountbatten. When Mountbatten badly injured his eye in a jeep accident while visiting Stilwell's headquarters in March 1944, and had to be sent to a U.S. Army hospital (where fortunately there was an expert eye doctor), he noted in his diary that "I was much touched that old Joe Stilwell should have flown up from the Front on Sunday to come and pay me a visit in hospital. He and I always get along very well personally."[3] In June 1944 Mountbatten wrote in his diary that:

> Stilwell has always shown himself as quite remarkably friendly to me ... If only I could see him every day there would never be any difficulties in this Command between the Americans and

ourselves. Not that we do have many difficulties, as our relations on the whole are now quite good.[4]

Mountbatten as Supreme Commander was in overall charge of the British operations in the Arakan and in Bengal-Assam, while Stilwell as U.S. Commanding General in CBI was in charge of the Chinese forces in North Burma. Mountbatten did not have direct operational control over Stilwell's forces, but Stilwell was supposed to keep Mountbatten informed, which he was not doing by January 1944. In contrast, Slim was General Officer Commanding (G.O.C.) of the 14th Army, and reported to Mountbatten and the British Chiefs of Staff.

Mountbatten and Stilwell had a clash on New Year's Day 1944 over the question of command and control. Mountbatten recorded this incident in his diary, where he wrote:

> I had a typical passage of arms with General Stilwell at a meeting on New Year's Day. We were arguing about when certain American Units, which were attached to and training with British forces, should be moved into Burma. General Stilwell said, "I should like it placed on record that I am responsible for the training of all American forces in this theatre and I am the person to decide when they are adequately trained and can move forward."

> I replied: "I accept that in principle, but would remind you that these troops are being trained under British officers. I am responsible for operations and will decide when Units move into the fighting lines. In other words, General, I should like to place on record that I am the Supreme Commander out here and that what I say goes." He took it very good-naturedly and laughed and said "We none of us dispute that."[5]

In contrast to Mountbatten's detailed account, Stilwell's diary entry for January 1, 1944, said simply: "Saw Louis [Mountbatten] at 2:00. Walla-walla. He won't take command; doesn't know where he is."[6] This dismissive comment reflects Stilwell's frustration at what he saw as Mountbatten's lack of leadership. Stilwell, never good in staff meetings,

simply wanted to get on with fighting the war. Mountbatten understand-
ably wanted to show him who was boss.

At this point, SEAC's unwieldy command structure caused more
problems. Stilwell was not only U.S. forces commander in CBI, *and*
Chiang's chief of staff commanding Chinese forces, *and* Mountbatten's
deputy supreme commander, but by now he was also the commanding
general of the newly created "Northern Combat Area Command." Thus,
when he began his offensive against Myitkyina in North Burma with both
Chinese and American troops, it was unclear who would be his superior
officer. Technically, it should have been British General Sir George
Giffard (1886-1964), Commander-in-Chief of Allied Land Forces in SEAC.
However, as SEAC Deputy Supreme Commander, Stilwell outranked
Giffard. Moreover, Stilwell did not like Giffard, believing he was not
aggressive enough. Stilwell put it more bluntly: "That old buzzard Giffard
is not going to command or coordinate me." [7] Finally, Stilwell agreed to
serve under one British commander and one only: Bill Slim! Since he was
junior in rank to both Giffard and Stilwell, this made no sense from an
organizational viewpoint, but it was a practical solution to the problem. [8]
Mountbatten noted that at Cairo in November 1943, Churchill, FDR,
and Chiang had already approved the "temporary solution" that Stilwell
would be under Slim's command until Stilwell's forces reached the town
of Kamaing in North Burma. Thus, Stilwell's insistence that he not serve
under Giffard should have come as no surprise to anyone at the meeting.

Stilwell asked Slim: "Sir, as 14th Army commander, do you have any
orders for me?" Slim said, "No, sir. And, as deputy commander, do you
have any orders for me?" Stilwell grinned and said, "Not on your life." [9]

On January 31, 1944, Mountbatten had another meeting with Stilwell
and the SEAC Commanders-in-Chief in New Delhi. Mountbatten wrote
in his diary the meeting was to discuss a "very important paper," which,
according to Philp Ziegler, was "almost certainly the revised CULVERIN,
a plan for an attack on Sumatra." [10] Mountbatten later wrote that "Lieut.-
General Stilwell did not accept my view that the route of advance to a

port on the China coast was shorter via Sumatra than via Burma and Yunnan."[11] This was putting it mildly: Stilwell did not agree with the "sea" strategy, and Mountbatten did not agree with the "land" strategy.

Here is Stilwell's account of what happened at the meeting on January 31:

> The Limeys take me more seriously now. But *they* won't fight if they can help it. Blew off my head about "the plan" that "we global strategy" experts have evolved. [12] Fancy charts, false figures, and dirty intentions. Got nowhere, of course. Told them "To hell with logistics." And mentioned Clive and his 123 soldiers. Dead silence.[13] [italics in original]

Here is Wedemeyer's account of the meeting:

> Comments were favorable as to the soundness of our strategy from all sources except General Stilwell. He said that the way to defeat the Japanese in this area was to build a strong Chinese Army and drive to the sea. I agreed with him but added, "*if* it were logistically possible," "Clive wasn't worried about logistics," he said. "No," I answered, "but Clive did not have airplanes, either. We just can't do it unless we can install and maintain lines of communication to the interior of China. Our technical experts tell us that we cannot do that for at least two years" ... Stilwell went back to China frustrated and furious.[14]

McLynn summarized the meeting as follows:

> Once again, the personality clashes reflected differential Anglo-American global perceptions. Almost all British politicians and generals by now regarded Burma as an expensive waste of time and Chiang as a waste of space. Churchill himself intensely disliked the idea of a campaign in north Burma . . . Meanwhile FDR remained adamant in his support for Chiang and had no interest in diversions to Singapore and Hong Kong, which he saw merely as Churchill's attempts to regain the British Empire.[15]

Along with the British, American, and Chinese offensives in the first half of 1944, another important development in the strategic operations of CBI and SEAC was the AXIOM Mission in the winter and spring of 1944. Originally code-named CULVERIN, AXIOM was part of Mountbatten's desire for a seaborne strategy that would land in Sumatra, as opposed to Stilwell's road strategy in Burma.[16] Mountbatten wanted AXIOM to begin in the winter of 1944-1945 when he could have the landing craft that would no longer be needed in Europe after D-Day. Mountbatten's timetable angered Stilwell, along with Mountbatten's telling him to not take Myitkyina and advance only to the Moguang valley before the monsoon season.[17] So, to break the deadlock, both Mountbatten and Stilwell each sent their own respective missions to London and Washington.

As already noted, Stilwell's obsession with the overland route to China was part of the larger U.S. mission of supplying China through Burma. Stilwell also mistrusted British motives, always seeing them through the lens of imperial designs. *The Stilwell Papers* make this very clear, explaining the two different strategies in CBI.[18] When Stilwell learned that Mountbatten was sending Wedemeyer, who was a major advocate of AXIOM, [19] to London and Washington to discuss the plan, Stilwell sent his own mission five days ahead of Wedemeyer, without telling Mountbatten. Stilwell explained that he wanted to "checkmate the Limies." [20] He need not have bothered. The Combined Chiefs of Staff opposed Mountbatten's plan because they needed all of the landing craft for D-Day and in the Pacific. (D-Day was actually postponed a month due to the shortage of landing craft and the need for more preparation.) The U.S. Joint Chiefs also opposed the plan and FDR vetoed it, seeing it as a colonialist enterprise. Finally, they opposed the plan because the U.S. Pacific strategy was based on the Luzon-Formosa-Canton triangle and the capture of Myitkyina would provide an important airbase for long-range bombers.[21]

Churchill, who had said "I liked Mountbatten's new plan,"[22] opposed the American decision to reject AXIOM, but the Japanese attacks on India at Kohima and Imphal in early 1944 resolved the issue of the North Burma campaign in favor of Stilwell. All this meant that Mountbatten could not launch a seaborne offensive in 1944 and Slim would lead the land offensive into Burma. By late 1944 it was clear that the European war would not be over in the winter of 1944–1945, which meant that amphibious operations in SEAC would not go ahead as planned. It is ironic that after the war Mountbatten would become Earl Mountbatten of Burma, although he had never wanted to fight a land war in Burma in the first place.

Stilwell's going behind Mountbatten's back, which verged on insubordination, so angered Mountbatten that he sent a message to Marshall requesting Stilwell's dismissal. Marshall urged Mountbatten to reconsider, and then attempted to end the trouble between him and Stilwell for good, writing Mountbatten as follows:

> You will find, if you get below the surface, that he wants merely to get things done without delays ... He will provide tremendous energy, courage and unlimited imagination to any aggressive proposals and operations. His mind is far more alert than almost any of our generals and his training and understanding are on an unusually high level. Impatience with conservatism and slow motion is his weakness—but a damned good one in this emergency.[23]

On March 3, 1944, Marshall sent a message to Stilwell in which he ordered him to reestablish a "working relationship" with Mountbatten and his staff. [24] There is no mention of this flap as such in either Stilwell's or Mountbatten's published diaries for this period. However, Stilwell's unpublished notes are quoted in *Stilwell's Command Problems*.[25] Mountbatten later wrote in his *Report* that "[I]n one of his other capacities, Lieut.-General Stilwell considered it his duty to send his own Mission to Washington, ahead of mine without informing me of the fact."[26] Part of the issue, as Marshall pointed out, was that the AXIOM dispute had been leaked to the press. [27] In fact, that same day John MacCormac wrote in the *New York Times* the following comment:

> General Stilwell is reported to be disappointed at the failure to launch a large-scale campaign to retake Burma. Some younger American officers are said to hold the same view and have spread the report here that Admiral Mountbatten, regarded in the European war as a commander of great initiative and resourcefulness, was proving a disappointment in his new post. It is reported, however, that General Wedemeyer, who, because of his position, knows the difficulties under which Admiral Mountbatten must operate, does not share this view. . . It is known, in fact, that some American observers have asserted to President Roosevelt that Britain is far more likely to regard the recapture of Burma and Malaya as chief objectives in the southeast Asia campaign than the opening up of supply routes into China to facilitate an attack on Japan—which would be the American idea of putting first things first.[28]

One month later Hanson W. Baldwin, the military editor of the *New York Times*, wrote: "The British have never looked with much favor on a Burma campaign. The British regard the Andaman Islands, an amphibious operation against Malaya and the capture of Singapore as the logical objectives."[29]

Stilwell duly "ate crow," as he put it, and told Marshall that he and Mountbatten were now "good personal friends." [30] Although Mountbatten accepted Stilwell's apology, he wrote to Field-Marshal Sir John Dill (1881-1944), head of the British Military Mission in Washington (and a close friend of Marshall's),

> He really is a grand old warrior but only the Trinity could carry out his duties which require him to be in Delhi, Chungking and the Ledo Front simultaneously, and I still think Al Wedemeyer or Sultan [U.S. Lieutenant General Daniel Sultan (1885-1947), Stilwell's deputy in CBI] should be appointed as Commanding

General for the American SEA theater and that Stilwell's command should be confined to China though he could certainly continue with the title of deputy SAC [Supreme Allied Commander], SEA, since he had never really done anything about those duties during the whole time I have been out here.[31]

Only two Allied commanders in SEAC—Stilwell and Slim—were actually fighting the Japanese, and Mountbatten proposed to remove one of them from the field but allow him to stay in a meaningless administrative position.

Mountbatten wrote Stilwell, "I am so glad that we were able to get together again and resolve all our outstanding difficulties, as indeed we always seem to succeed in doing when we meet."[32] Marshall sent Stilwell a coded radio message, which read in part:

> I have now come to the conclusion in the effort to find some man to improve the abnormal command relationships in the South East Asia and in China Theaters: It seems to me that so long as you feel it necessary to exercise command and leadership of the Ledo Road Force, Sultan should have delegated to him authority to act directly with Mountbatten in practically all matters, subject to the policies that you have established.[33]

The fallout over the AXIOM Mission was also exacerbated when Wedemeyer, who had played a minor role in SEAC up to this point, now became one of Stilwell's opponents, which shaped the last period of Stilwell's time in CBI. On June 22, 1944, Stilwell wrote in his diary that "Louis wants me relieved as deputy supreme Allied commander and has approached Marshall. Substitute to be Wedemeyer or Sultan. Good God—to be ousted in favor of Wedemeyer—that would be a disgrace. *Just a feeling of relief if it's done.*"[34] Wedemeyer for his part wrote "I had never accepted the Stilwell premise that an all-weather road should be constructed and maintained through the jungles and rugged terrain of northern Burma."[35] However, what Wedemeyer called "the Stilwell premise" was basic U.S. policy, from FDR on down—to reconnect the old Burma Road. Stilwell agreed with that policy and sought to carry it out. [36] Churchill and Mountbatten disagreed with that policy. That was the conflict in a nutshell.

On February 3, 1944, Mountbatten had written to Lt. General H. L. ("Pug") Ismay (1887-1965), Churchill's chief military assistant and staff officer, and later Mountbatten's Chief of Staff in India in 1947, about Stilwell and the Americans, as follows:

> It is only at the level of the war staff that the American point of view can be put forward, because the CINCs' planners include only a few of Stilwell's representatives. These all have the same mistrust and dislike of the British that Stilwell has. This is illustrated by the fact that Stilwell's and his staff completely disagree with the strategy paper [regarding AXIOM], in spite of the fact that the Americans on Mountbatten's staff agree with it entirely . . .

> In three months the American staff have completely altered the relationship between the British and American forces in SEAC. Wavell and Auchinleck have told him that all of Stilwell's forces have been mistrustful and deceitful. When some of Mountbatten's young American staff officers first arrived, they had to live with General Stilwell's staff because of the shortage of accommodation. The other members of Mountbatten's staff virtually ostracised them. Much of this antagonism has disappeared. Mountbatten is on friendly terms with "Vinegar Joe," and Mountbatten's American staff has improved relations, but Stilwell still harbours anti-British feelings. Mountbatten's American staff has done so much to improve relations. . . [37]

Despite the friction between them, Stilwell and Mountbatten were able to cooperate some of the time. In December 1943, the U.S. Tenth Air Force of the U.S. Army Air Forces (USAAF) and the RAF Bengal Command were combined to create an "integrated" Anglo-American command, similar to Eisenhower combining the USAAF and the RAF for D-Day in Europe.[38] The combined forces were designated Eastern Air Command (EAC), to be commanded by U.S. Major General George Stratemeyer, who in turn would report to RAF Air Chief Marshal Sir Richard Peirse (1892-1970), the SEAC Air Commander in-Chief. "In effect, the British, while retaining the top-ranking position in the air organization, had relinquished operational control of all combat units to Stratemeyer."[39]

In a letter to Lt. General H.H. ("Hap") Arnold (1886-1950), Commanding General of the U.S. Army Air Force (USAAF), Mountbatten wrote:

> Things are going so well that Mountbatten hesitates to report Stilwell's interference in SACSEA's operational orders to 10 USAAF. However, he has the whole matter on record, to produce in defence of the vital need for integration, if ever this is questioned. *He and Stilwell are, in fact, getting on much better now that the matter of 10 USAAF has been settled.*[40] [my italics]

The "matter" was who would control the Tenth Air Force. Mountbatten asserted his authority as Supreme Commander to put it under a unified command and Marshall agreed with him.

On March 16, 1944, Mountbatten wrote to the JCS that:

> After seeing the performance of Stilwell's Chinese forces and hearing of the wonderful show which Wingate and Cochran's No. 1 Air Commando have put up I am becoming convinced that Allied Forces could march all over Burma provided they have adequate air supply and air support and yet more transport aircraft and the rapid formation of further Air Commandos on Cochran's style both in England and America.[41]

This was one strategic area upon which both Stilwell and Mountbatten agreed, even though they were fighting separate campaigns, because aircraft were essential in supplying the army in remote areas of Burma and evacuating the wounded. Mountbatten finally got the first 100 out of a total of 400 transport planes from the U.S. in May 1944, which changed the Allied strategy in Burma for the rest of the war in 1944 and 1945.[42] After the spring of 1944 Allied air power made it easier to conduct long-range operations in Burma, which the Allies had not had been able to do in 1942 and 1943. Ground troops could be supplied by air, the wounded could be evacuated by air, and the Japanese lost control of the airspace over North Burma. As the authors of *Stilwell's Command Problems* put it, "Thus SEAC began to acquire the great fleets of air transports which so changed the nature of war in Burma."[43]

The Japanese attack on the Arakan front in February 1944 once again exposed the major differences in Allied strategy in CBI and SEAC between the U.S. and Britain and between Mountbatten and Stilwell. In particular, Stilwell and Mountbatten did not agree about how many aircraft were needed in the respective British and American theaters in Burma. On February 14, 1944, Mountbatten asked Stilwell to ask the Combined Chiefs of Staff (CCS) for thirty "Hump" planes for the Arakan supply dropping. On February 17, Stilwell wired New Delhi about the situation in the Arakan, saying he did not think that it was serious enough to call for the aircraft. However, Mountbatten persisted and a few days later the CCS approved shifting twenty-five C-46's with crews from the Assam-Yunnan airway. They helped to solve the Arakan supply problem and allowed the British to take the offensive.[44]

Another order came from Mountbatten the following month, directing both Stilwell and Peirse to divert up to 30 C-47 aircraft to assist Slim.[45] On February 21, 1944, the U.S. Joint Chiefs of Staff had asked the British Chiefs of Staff to direct Mountbatten to seize both Myitkyina and Schwebo, a city in north central Burma. [46] London replied that Mountbatten had undertaken the maximum offensive based on his communication lines and also that Stilwell could not take or hold Myitkyina. (As we will see, they were wrong about that!) Although Mountbatten was more concerned about the Arakan offensive, he wanted to speed up the building of the Hump Airway, saying that even if the Ledo Road were opened, the relatively small amount that could be transported would be of little value to China.[47]

Thus, two different Allied campaigns were being fought within the larger Burma Campaign by 1944. Stilwell and Slim were fighting on separate land fronts in Burma, while Mountbatten and Wedemeyer became convinced that a sweeping amphibious operation would be more effective. At odds were two very different strategies. Those strategies were the outcome of the changing situation that unfolded in late 1943 and early 1944. They also reflected how the Burma Campaign fitted into the wider context of Anglo-American relations in World War II. Personalities aside, Stilwell and Mountbatten simply represented two very different national interests, one wishing to go by land, the other wishing to go by sea.

In the spring of 1944, however, the Japanese would force Mountbatten's hand by launching a major offensive across the Chindwin River into India. Mountbatten had a land war in Burma, whether he wanted one or not.

CHAPTER TEN

THE JAPANESE STRIKE BACK —KOHIMA AND IMPHAL

While Mountbatten and Stilwell were overseeing their respective campaigns in Burma, the Japanese were planning a major offensive in Assam in the spring of 1944, to which the Arakan offensive in February 1944 had been the prelude. Mountbatten as Supreme Commander of SEAC was in overall charge of the British operations in the Arakan and in Bengal-Assam, while Stilwell as the U.S. Commanding General in CBI was in charge of the Chinese forces fighting in North Burma. Thus, although Mountbatten did not have direct operational control over Stilwell's forces, Stilwell was supposed to keep Mountbatten informed of what he did. However, by January 1944 Stilwell was operating as an independent commander. In contrast to this unwieldy chain of command, Slim, as General Officer Commanding (G.O.C.) of the 14th Army, reported to Mountbatten, who in turn reported to the British Chiefs of Staff.

Meanwhile, the Japanese considered Assam, not the Arakan, of critical importance. According to Ziegler, "By striking at Assam, the Japanese believed that they would sever communications between the 14th Army and Stilwell's Chinese forces in the north, and prepare a bridgehead from which the British hegemony in India could be destroyed."[1] The goal of the Japanese plan, code-named the *U Go offensive, or Operation C,* was to halt the Allied advance back into Burma. The Japanese saw it as "the final throw in Southeast Asia."[2] It was actually a limited offensive. The Japanese armed forces were still thinking of offensive as opposed to defensive strategy, which they did not use except in the Pacific during their retreat there after 1943. It would have been better for the Japanese to have withdrawn behind the Chindwin or the Irrawaddy and then to have waited for the British, instead of advancing into eastern India, which was at the end of their supply lines. The Japanese, never good at logistics, were about to launch a campaign that would cause them to outrun their lines of supply and be forced back into Burma. They ran into unexpectedly tough resistance: the men of the 14th Army.

The two main components of the Japanese Burma Area Army (1943-1945) in 1944 were the 15th and the 28th Armies with twelve divisions, eight divisions of seasoned Japanese troops and four Thai divisions.[3] On the eve of the operation, General Renya Mutaguchi (1888-1966), who had commanded the Japanese 15th Army since 1943, gave a "pep talk" to his troops on the importance of the Assam campaign:

> The Army has now reached the state of invincibility, and the day when the Rising Sun shall proclaim our definite victory in India is not far off. When we strike we must reach our objectives with the speed of wildfire despite the obstacles of the river, mountain and labyrinthine jungle. We must sweep aside the paltry opposition we encounter and add luster to the Army tradition by achieving a victory of annihilation. Both officers and men must fight to the death for their country and accept the burden of duties that are the lot of a soldier of Japan.[4]

This statement summed up the Japanese determination to fight to the death. However, that determination would lead not to victory, but rather to one of the two greatest land defeats for the Japanese Imperial Army in World War II (along with the Soviet invasion of Manchuria in August 1945).

The Japanese attacked across the Chindwin River in March 1944. When the Imphal campaign began, Slim's three main choices were to advance across the Chindwin to meet the Japanese, defend the western river-bank, or sit tight in the Imphal area, which is what he did. By the spring of 1944, Stilwell was fighting one battle in North Burma and Slim was fighting another in the Arakan, until the Japanese called off their offensive there. Because of the Japanese offensive in Assam, Slim's forces would fight in northeast India for the rest of the spring and early summer of 1944. The Battles of Imphal and Kohima (sometimes called "the Stalingrad of the East," due to the ferocity of the fighting, not the size of the battles) from March to June 1944, soon turned into a series of bloody battles where British and Indian forces held out against a strong Japanese force.

The battles of Kohima and Imphal were Slim's battles; Mountbatten as Supreme Commander did not take direct control, except when he sent the British 2nd Division to relieve the Siege of Kohima in April 1944. After Kohima was relieved in a series of fierce battles, such as the famous "Battle of the Tennis Court" (April-May 1944), the British then focused on relieving Imphal. On June 22, 1944, the British finally linked the Kohima-Imphal Road.[5]

The Japanese Army called off the offensive and began to retreat back into Burma, over the mountains and back across the Chindwin. It was a death-strewn retreat. By July 4, 1944, over 17,000 Japanese troops had been killed and the 15th and 31st Japanese Divisions had been wiped out as combat organizations.[6]

British historian Eric Morris wrote the following comment on the campaign:

> The Battle of Kohima and Imphal falls into two phases. The first was the Japanese offensive, from March 8 until April 5, when they cut off the IV Corps at Imphal and smaller garrisons at Kohima and Jorsoma. It then took the defenders until June 22 to break the encirclement. Imphal has sometimes been mistakenly portrayed as two or even three battles. In fact, Slim conducted the operation

as a single coherent engagement, never losing sight of his original objective: to inflict a crippling defeat on the enemy as a prelude to the invasion of Burma.[7]

The battles of Kohima and Imphal were the high point of the Japanese efforts to stop the British from regaining Burma. They also illustrated the different military priorities between the British and the U.S. in CBI by 1944. Since Kohima and Imphal were British battles, they did not have a direct impact on Anglo-American relations. Almost all of the accounts of the two battles have focused on how they turned the tide against the Japanese in Burma in 1944. There were two separate campaigns going on at the same time, with Stilwell fighting to build the Ledo Road and the British fighting a defensive campaign against the Japanese invasion. Once again, they reflected the American obsession with China and the British obsession with India.

After the end of the Imphal-Kohima campaign, Mountbatten wrote in his report:

> In the third week of June, the situation was critical, and it seemed possible, after all the efforts of the previous two months, that early in June, the IV would finally run out of reserves. But on June 22, with a week and a half in hand, the 2d British and 5th Indian divisions met at a point twenty-nine miles north of Imphal and the road to the plain was open. On the same day the convoys began to roll in. The Japanese bid for India was virtually over, and ahead lay the prospect of the first major victory in Burma.[8]

Mountbatten described Kohima as "[P]robably one of the greatest battles in history ... in effect the Battle of Burma ... naked unparalleled heroism ... the British/Indian Thermopylae. In the annals of military history, this great battle of Kohima is known as The Battle of the Tennis Court, and in this tennis court lie the mortal remains of thousands of Allied soldiers, who could not make it back to their homes and their dear ones."[9] The reference to Thermopylae may appear to be exaggerated, but there is a valid historical parallel between the 300 Spartans in 480

BC[10] and the defenders of Kohima in 1944. As the words of the Kohima Memorial put it, "for your tomorrow we gave our today," which echo the lines of Thermopylae, "Go tell the Spartans, you that passeth by, that here obedient to their word we lie." Just as the Spartans saved Greece, the men at Kohima saved India.

Once again, as in the Arakan, Allied air power played a decisive role, making it possible for British and Indian troops to fight for three months, relying on air supplies. The Japanese lamented their own lack of supplies; one radio broadcast said, "The enemy received food supplies through the air route, while our men continued in battle eating a handful of barley or grain." [11]

When the British-Indian troops advanced to the India-Burma border in July 1944, they found the remaining Japanese forces in Burma were wounded, tired, hungry, on the run, and desperate after their disastrous rout. Following the victories at Kohima and Imphal, Slim began preparing for the final part of the Burma Campaign after mid-1944. He later wrote: "Our problem, therefore, was to get as many divisions and as much armour as possible, and as quickly as possible, into the Shwebo Plain [in central Burma], and there fight an army battle." [12]

On June 27, 1944, General Arnold sent the following message to Mountbatten congratulating him and SEAC for reopening the Imphal Road, which was summarized as follows in the Mountbatten Archives:

> Arnold congratulates Mountbatten and all those concerned in SEAC on the reopening of the Imphal Road. Conditions were very difficult, and this could not have been achieved without "the fine aggressive spirit which I am sure will carry us on to further victories." [13]

During the Imphal and Kohima battles, Slim went to Stilwell's headquarters to discuss the main issues of CBI, which included the Chinese divisions under Stilwell. Later, Slim wrote:

In all these actions Stilwell kept a close hand on the Chinese troops, steadying them when they faltered, prodding them when they hesitated, even finding their battalions for them when they lost them ... Stilwell met me at the airfield looking more like a duck hunter than ever, with his wind jacket, campaign hat, and leggings ... I was struck as I always was when I visited Stilwell's headquarters, how unnecessarily primitive all its arrangements were. There was, compared with my own or other headquarters, no shortage of transport or supplies, yet he delighted in [an] exhibition of rough living, which like his omission of rank badges and the rest was designed to foster the idea of the tough, hard-bitten, plain, fighting general. Goodness knows he was tough and wiry enough to be recognised as such without the play acting ... Stilwell, thank heaven, had a sense of humour and he could and did, not infrequently, laugh at himself.[14]

This statement shows how much Slim admired Stilwell as a soldier's general like himself. Although Stilwell disliked most of the British he met in CBI, he and Slim got along well because they were very similar. Stilwell was an old-line infantry officer and Slim had been a Gurkha officer in the Indian Army after World War I. Both of them personally led and inspired their troops. Back in March 1942, during the British retreat from Burma, Stilwell had praised Slim as a general, writing in his diary "Good old Slim. Maybe he's all right after all. [15]

In the introduction to Slim's memoirs, David W. Hogan described his opinion of Stilwell:

Notwithstanding his disagreements with Stilwell on many points of strategy, Slim actually appears to like the acerbic American. To be sure, he clearly finds Stilwell to be a bit of a caricature with his stubbornness, his unnecessary prejudices, and his efforts to maintain for press and public the image of a rugged foot soldier, uninterested in the trappings of command. But Slim was impressed with Stilwell's mental and physical toughness, determination, sincerity, and courage. He evaluates Stilwell as "not a great soldier in the highest sense, but he was a leader in the field; no one else I know could have made his Chinese do what they did."[16]

Perhaps most importantly, both Stilwell and Slim liked and respected Asian soldiers, unlike many of the British and American officers in the theater.[17] They both wanted to fight a land war in Burma, while Mountbatten was fixated on amphibious operations. Like Mountbatten, and unlike Stilwell, Slim tried to work with his allies and did not criticize them publicly. However, Slim was not as concerned with his historic image as was Mountbatten, and was not a prima donna like Montgomery, who caused problems with Eisenhower in Europe both before and after D-Day.[18] Slim was simply a superb field general. As a modern historian wrote:

> The reason the Japanese faced such tough, disciplined and versatile forces at Kohima-Imphal was that Slim himself had forged a "New Model Army"[19] and had worked for nearly two years on building up equipment, morale, elan and *esprit de corps*. Besides, Slim's personality was ideal for this particular campaign, since he had two great gifts: the ability to turn round a battle that was going in the enemy's favour; and the talent to improvise quickly so that the enemy was soon dancing to his tune. In contrast to the muddled objectives of the Japanese, he knew precisely what his aims were at every hour of every day, and this clarity communicated itself in his lucid and economical strategic briefings, which so impressed all who heard them. A master of timing, he had the art of proceeding neither too fast nor too slow.[20]

CHAPTER ELEVEN

THE SIEGE OF MYITKYINA

Myitkyina in North Burma, with its airfield, was the key to reopening the Burma Road. Its capture by the Japanese in 1942 effectively ended the First Burma Campaign.[1] As long as it remained in Japanese hands, Allied supplies would have to be flown from India into China over the Hump, a long and dangerous journey, and Japanese planes could harass the cargo planes flying that route. Taking it would allow Allied planes to fly a safer, more southerly route. Moreover, taking Myitkyina could also split Japanese forces in North Burma and open the way for the Allies to drive down the Irrawaddy Valley to Mandalay in Central Burma.[2] At the same time, the Siege of Myitkyina, along with the Arakan offensive, highlighted the strategic, political, and personal differences between Mountbatten and Stilwell in CBI and SEAC. Myitkyina was part of the Chinese and American campaign to build the Ledo Road and connect it with the Burma Road as the Allied land route to China through North Burma. The British concentrated on Western Burma, heading for Rangoon, as the way back to Singapore.

The main Japanese force facing Stilwell's Northern Combat Area Command (NCAC) was the crack 18th Division (the *Chrysanthemum Division*), one of the ablest and best-trained divisions of the Imperial

Japanese Army, which had participated in the First Burma Campaign and the capture of Singapore.[3] Defending Myitkyina itself were elements of the 33rd Imperial Japanese Army (1944-1945) under General Masaki Honda.[4] He had even placed the garrison, at first consisting of only about 300 men, under his direct command.[5]

The Japanese Order of Battle under the 33rd IJA was as follows:

2 Division: Okazaki

18 Division: Tanaka

53 Division: Takeda

56 Division: Matsuyama

24 Independent Mixed Brigade: Hayashi

Myitkyina Garrison: Genzo Mizukami[6]

In a message to Marshall on April 16, 1944, U.S. Lieutenant General Daniel Sultan, Stilwell's deputy in CBI, outlined the two phases of Stilwell's Myitkyina operation: taking the airfield there and opening up the link with China. Sultan also suggested how the Burma Campaign should assist the Pacific War campaign for 1944:

> At Supreme Commander's meeting [I] presented the thought that we consider the operation as having two phases. The objective in [the] first phase would be to seize and hold Myitkyina as quickly as possible to permit an increase in air lift to China; the second phase to provide for further movement to the south to open road and pipeline to China . . . Mountbatten's principal British advisors will continue to recommend strongly to him that Southeast Asia Command should go no farther than north Burma to assist Pacific operations . . . if they can possibly avoid it.[7]

By late 1943 and early 1944 Stilwell was totally focused on the drive to Myitkyina. Although he was criticized, then and after, for "disappearing in the jungles," he and the Chinese troops he had personally trained—

and had insisted be properly fed, clothed, and paid—"accomplished a victory which had generally been regarded as impossible.[8] He launched an offensive across the mountains and rivers of North Burma, building roads as he went, across terrain that was inhospitable at best. Supplied by air, he moved with great speed, sending the bulk of his forces across the Kumon Range and down the valley of the Irrawaddy, unbeknownst to the Japanese. His goal was to take the airstrip at Myitkyina and then the town itself.[9]

Although most of Stilwell's forces were Chinese, a significant number were American —the legendary Merrill's Marauders—and an equally significant number were British and Indian, the famous Chindits. Designed to be long-range raiders, they were originally deployed to the south of Myitkyina, with instructions to cut off the Japanese line of supply.[10] He also had 300 Kachins, Burmese hill people and converts to Christianity. They hated the Japanese, who had desecrated their churches. How Stilwell deployed these forces in the attack on Myitkyina, which turned into a bitter and protracted siege from May to August 1944, remains the most controversial episode of his military career.

By late spring both the Marauders and the Chindits were exhausted. On May 17, 1944, Stilwell captured Myitkyina airfield, but not the town, which became his obsession for the rest of the campaign. The failure to take the town was due to a series of causes, including a decision to fly in anti-aircraft units instead of the infantry that Stilwell had requested, the exhausted state of the Marauders, who believed their "hitch" was up, and the panic that occurred in some Chinese units who had never before been in combat. The Japanese dug in and held onto the town.

In the words of the official U.S. Air Force History:

> General Stilwell was then faced with the responsibility of conducting a long siege of Myitkyina while his own armies had no lines of communication other than air supply, the efficiency of which was already threatened by the approaching rainy monsoon. Stilwell was disappointed and ill with worry. Yet in retrospect it

is easy to see that he had won an impressive victory and, what was probably more significant, his faith had been justified in the military qualities of the Chinese soldier when given proper training and equipment.[11]

Just before the capture of the airfield, Stilwell gloated in his diary, writing, "WILL THIS BURN UP THE LIMIES."[12] Ziegler wrote that Mountbatten did not seem to be "decomposed" by this.[13] In fact, according to McLynn, he was furious for not having been told in advance that Stilwell was moving on the town,[14] especially when Churchill cabled him, saying that "The Americans have by a brilliant feat of arms landed us in Myitkyina, . . ."[15] It must have been unbearable for a proud man like Mountbatten to have learned about Myitkyina from his own Prime Minister, rather than the other way round. Although the U.S. Joint Chiefs had agreed on the Myitkyina operation, and Stilwell had told Slim, he had not told Mountbatten, which showed how much Stilwell had come to dislike and even distrust him by 1944. Slim, however, did not seem to be bothered by all this. He later wrote in his memoirs, "After all, everyone knew he [Stilwell] had been ordered to take Myitkyina, and whatever his motives in this secrecy I was prepared to humor him."[16] Eldridge wrote that Stilwell sent daily radio messages to SEAC in Ceylon, giving his position, so that anyone who read the war map could see where he was.[17] At the same time, it was more than a bit disingenuous to suggest that the Supreme Allied Commander be kept informed of important troop movements by having to read the daily situation map.

After Myitkyina airfield was taken, Mountbatten wrote his daughter: "Isn't the news of the capture of Myitkyina airfield great? It is one of my most interesting fronts, commanded by my deputy General Stilwell."[18] The reference to Stilwell as "my deputy" suggests Mountbatten had actually planned the operation himself, as opposed to not knowing about it until it had already happened. It also suggests that Mountbatten, not for the first and certainly not for the last time, was trying to take credit for the actions of one of his subordinates. In any case, although he was angry at not having been informed in advance of the drive to Myitkyina,

Mountbatten congratulated Stilwell (and the Chindits) on having taken the airfield.

Stilwell wrote in his diary for May 19: "MtBatten [*sic*] sent 'Order of Day,' & included Lentaigne's crowd [the Chindits], because they had cut the jap [*sic*] communications! Louis had radioed Dill already, to tell him it was proof of the 'perfect unity' in S.E.A.C. They must horn in and get all the credit. . . Childish Louis—publicity crazy. . .The more I see of limies [the British], the worse I hate them."[19]

By the end of May 1944, the battle for Myitkyina had stalemated. Stilwell had been more concerned with taking the airfield than the town, which was now strongly held. The Japanese forces there were more numerous than he had anticipated, with more than 3,000 soldiers holding onto the town, including reinforcements from the Japanese Army's 56th Division, who were rushed in from the Salween River to the east.[20] The element of surprise had been lost. Moreover, the Japanese still had the 18th Division, whose casualty rate would reach an appalling 50 percent by the end of the siege.[21]

One of the options Stilwell had to take the town was to use the 36th British Indian Division in North Burma, which was experienced in battle and which might have been flown into the Myitkyina airfield.[22] According to Romanus and Sunderland, "Stilwell briefly considered asking that the 36th Division be rushed in to take Myitkyina. Giving no reason in his diary,[23] he decided against this move and instead resolved to order in some U.S. combat engineers from the Ledo Road. 'I will probably have to use some of our engineer units to keep an American flavor in the fight,' he told Marshall."[24]

On May 22, 1944, Sultan sent Stilwell a message, which read in part, "It is unthinkable that we not hold on to Myitkyina with reference to other points raised by General Giffard. None are required beyond the 36 Indian Division as for reinforcement [*sic*] by British/Indian Divisions."[25] On May 28, 1944, General Giffard sent a message to Mountbatten, writing that the "36 Div is being prepared for operations in CAI [Chinese Army in India, *i.e.*, Stilwell] area earliest possible. Every effort will be made to assist CAI to hold Myitkyina."[26]

These comments suggest that the 36th Division was going to be sent to Myitkyina. However, for whatever reason, Stilwell decided not to use it at the outset and instead used the Chinese troops and the Marauders, even having his officers go through the hospitals in India where there were sick Marauders and flying them back to Myitkyina.[27] Stilwell's advance to Myitkyina had driven both the Marauders and the Chindits to the breaking point. By mid-May 1944, the Chindits were almost in open revolt against Stilwell, claiming that his orders were impossible to carry out. However, Stilwell saw the Chindits as complainers, when his Chinese troops were fighting just as hard, and here his Anglophobia may have reached epic proportions. Despite their problems, the Chindits, with support from Chinese troops, fought a fierce battle with the Japanese at Mogaung, just to the southwest of Myitkyina, which was taken by Gurkha Chindit troops on June 26.[28] The Chindits also blocked the southern approaches to Myitkyina before they were forced to withdraw.[29]

The siege of Myitkyina was both Stilwell's most controversial operation and also his finest hour in CBI from 1942-1944. Stilwell had been laying siege to Myitkyina since the spring of 1944, while Slim was still fighting in Assam at Kohima and Imphal. Both of them were in the fight of their lives.

Between May 16 and July 6, 1944, Stilwell or his staff sent a series of increasingly strong messages to the Chindits, at one point accusing them of "apparent disobedience to orders."[30] On May 27, 1944, Stilwell sent a message to Sultan, as follows:

> British withdrawal from Hopin block[31] has opened the door to the japs [sic]. If Louis expects Myitkyina to be held at all costs, will keep hold [sic] it? Suppose weather continues bad and I can't land troops. Will he give me his parachute regiment? [32]

The next day Stilwell sent another message to Sultan, saying that "The British east of Myitkyina have let me down. The British southwest of Mogaung have let me down, and the japs [*sic*] can now use the railway freely."[33]

At this point Mountbatten decided to exercise personal control over the campaign to try to head off a confrontation between Stilwell and General Lentaigne, who commanded the Chindits after Wingate's death. Mountbatten wrote in his *Report to the Combined Chiefs of Staff* the following comment: "[S]ince relations between Lieut-General Stilwell and Major-General Lentaigne were obviously strained, I decided to thrash out this matter with them personally, and met them both at their Headquarters at Shaduzup on the 30th June."[34] Mountbatten's diary entry for June 30, 1944, describes his meeting with Stilwell and Lentaigne in these words:

> After lunch I had a long conference with Joe Stilwell and Joe Lentaigne. It will be remembered that the latter succeeded Wingate in command of the Chindits, who have now been placed under Stilwell's orders. Although Stilwell has always shown himself as quite remarkably friendly to me the meeting was not easy as there were several points of difference to be cleared up. However, he met me very handsomely, more than half way. If only I could see him every day there would never be any difficulties in this Command between the Americans and ourselves. Not that we do have many difficulties, as our relations on the whole are now very good.[35]

This positive statement reflected Mountbatten's diplomatic view of trying to get people to agree on important strategic issues, which Eisenhower was very good at doing in Europe. It also reflected Mountbatten's generally positive outlook in his diaries, which seem to have been written for posterity. Finally, it may have reflected Mountbatten's honest view at the time that when he and Stilwell met face to face, Stilwell was generally agreeable.[36]

Stilwell's comments on the same meeting were, as usual, more direct. On July 2, 1944, he wrote to his wife, "Mountbatten has been up again. He had the nerve to make a speech at our headquarters but he doesn't fool our GIs much. They are getting a look at the British Empah [*sic*] with its pants down and the aspect is not so pretty. You can imagine how popular I am with the Limeys."[37] At the meeting on June 30 Mountbatten had ordered an increase in the number of airdrops to the Chindits and also ordered the medical authorities be instructed immediately to examine the Chindits and airlift out the sick. Stilwell had complained that the Chindits had not followed his orders, and Lentaigne had responded that the orders were unclear, so Mountbatten directed "that in all cases where General Stilwell's orders were not crystal clear to those concerned in their execution, it was for General Lentaigne personally to see General Stilwell and clarify the matter."[38]

On July 15, 1944, Mountbatten sent a message to Stilwell expressing his concern that the Chindits had been overtaxed and that Mountbatten felt he had "broken [his] promise to [them] and am forcing them to stay in long after Wingate, or his successor Lentaigne, considered was either right or feasible."[39] Mountbatten said the 77th and 111th Brigades, and the 14th and West African Brigades, which were supposed to have been withdrawn after May 31 and June 27, because of their operational limit in North Burma, would remain in the field until Myitkyina was taken. He also told Stilwell he was sending 36th Indian Division to Myitkyina to aid in the siege and to relieve the Chindits.[40]

On July 19 Stilwell replied to Mountbatten, saying, "I have never objected to the evacuation of sick and wounded."[41] However, Stilwell set a very high bar for being sick, so this comment was disingenuous at best and downright callous at worst. Stilwell also said Lentaigne had urged him to take the Chindits out of the field for good. Mountbatten replied on July 21, saying that all unfit men should be evacuated "without delay."[42] On July 23 he wrote Stilwell that "I am most anxious that all the remaining LRP Brigades should be relieved at the earliest possible moment by 36 Division."[43]

Stilwell finally allowed the last of the Chindits to withdraw on August 1, 1944, two days before Myitkyina fell to his forces.[44] By August 7, the last Chindit formation was replaced by the Indian 36th Division. The last Chindits left Burma on August 27 and in February 1945 the Chindits were officially disbanded after being in action for two years.[45]

In the summer of 1944, Stilwell also had a meeting with British Lieutenant-Colonel James Michael "Mad Mike" Calvert DSO (1913-1998), a leader in the 1943 and 1944 Chindit operations. Stilwell wanted Calvert court-martialed after Calvert tried to get his Chindits pulled out of the line and back to India. They had the following conversation when they met:

Stilwell: "Well Calvert, I have been waiting to meet you for some time."

Calvert: "I have been waiting to meet you too, sir."

Stilwell: "You send some very strong signals, Calvert."

Calvert: "You should see the ones my brigade-major won't let me send."

Stilwell (laughing): "I have just the same trouble with my own staff officers when I draft signals to Washington."[46]

This broke the ice and there was no more talk of courts-martial.[47] Moreover, Calvert convinced Stilwell that the latter's staff had not kept him fully informed as to just how much the Chindits had been through and how much they had actually accomplished.[48]

Although Stilwell and Calvert were able to patch things up, this brief interlude of cooperation could not hide the fact Stilwell had pushed the Chindits very hard in the Myitkyina offensive, using them as regular infantry, a role for which they were not suited.[49] Stilwell, a regular infantry officer to his bones, had simply never liked the Chindits, with their reputation for commando-style tactics. When one of his officers suggested using them to support the Chinese further north, Stilwell replied: "If you make further use of the word Chindit you will get [a] new job on the Calcutta docks."[50]

Mountbatten later wrote, "I was sorry, but not surprised, when Lieut.-General Stilwell reported to me later that he had had trouble with them [the Chindits and the Marauders]—and, with typical frankness, admitted that this was through their having been overtaxed."[51]

On August 3, 1944, the siege of Myitkyina finally ended after two-and-a half months. Stilwell's Chinese and American forces at last took the town, which had been desperately defended by its Japanese garrison. Most of the Japanese defenders were killed, although almost 200 surrendered, a fact that in itself showed that some Japanese soldiers were losing the will to die for the emperor (Hirohito or Showa [1901-1989], Emperor of Japan from 1926 to1989), which also happened at the Battle of Okinawa in 1945. Some escaped downriver, only to be wiped out by Kachin Rangers, Burmese hill people who had been trained by the American Office of Strategic Services (OSS), and who hated the Japanese. The Japanese garrison commander committed suicide, after having apologized to the emperor.[52]

Slim wrote in his memoirs that the capture of Myitkyina "was the largest seizure of enemy-held territory that had yet occurred ... the success of this northern offensive was in the main due to the Ledo Chinese divisions—and that was Stilwell."[53] Stilwell's ground forces were supported by Allied airpower, which flew in supplies and troops and pounded the Japanese positions with constant sorties. Even Stilwell, the quintessential infantryman, came to rely upon close-in air support. In *The Army Air Forces in World War II*, the official wartime history of the USAAF, the authors wrote about the vital role of close-in air support in the Siege of Myitkyina. After acknowledging the role played by Stilwell's field artillery, which also pounded the Japanese positions, they wrote: "Equally important in the final victory of Stilwell's troops was the close-in ground support provided by the Tenth Air Force."[54] Between May 17 and August 3, 1944, when the town at last was taken, Allied fighters flew a total of 2,515 sorties.[55]

Not only did the taking of Myitkyina open up the land route, but the Hump air route from India to China was no longer as dangerous as it had been in the past.[56] This led to a rapid increase in the Allied deliveries to China by air, which went from 18,000 to 39,000 tons between June and November 1944.[57] The Japanese could no longer use the airstrip at Myitkyina and RAF and USAAF planes could harass them on the ground. It was the beginning of the end for the Japanese in North Burma.

Mountbatten had wanted to use Myitkyina to strengthen the air route, while Stilwell wanted to concentrate on the road and pipeline links. In June 1944 the Combined Chiefs of Staff ordered him to do both, putting the air link first, then the road and pipeline links.[58] Even Wedemeyer said that "[T]he immediate objective of operations during the next dry season should be the securing of the trace of a land route to CHINA."[59] (The capitalization is in the original.)

With the fall of Myitkyina, Stilwell's job in CBI was essentially over after two years, even though he did not realize it at the time. Churchill's reaction was glowing but also realistic. He wrote that "These successes were largely due to Stilwell's leadership, energy, and pertinacity; but his troops were exhausted by their efforts and many had to be withdrawn."[60] Mountbatten and Stilwell had clashed over using the Chindits in major combat roles, and Mountbatten had felt it necessary for him to assert personal control in the field for the first time.[61] Since Mountbatten was a naval officer, not an infantry officer, this was an unusual role for him. Mountbatten wrote that this change of command structure was done at Stilwell's insistence, presumably because Stilwell refused to serve under Giffard and he could no longer serve under Slim once the Chinese troops had reached Kamaing in North Burma.[62]

While Stilwell was fighting to take Myitkyina, Mountbatten wrote to Chiang on July 28, 1944, asking him to keep the Chinese forces in India and Burma up to strength, as previously agreed:

> The Viceroy and the government of India recently agreed to a total strength of 102,000 Chinese troops in India, but General Stilwell reports that there are just under 80,000 in India and Burma. This shortage is probably due to 14 and 50 Chinese Divisions being under strength on their arrival and also to the 4,000 reinforcements

needed to keep the force at maximum strength not having been sent. The Chinese Army has advanced so magnificently in India that Mountbatten is sure that the Generalissimo would agree that the force should be kept up to strength. Such a great military leader must see the need for his troops to carry on with their victorious move southwards, but they may be slowed down if they are under strength. Everything possible must be done to keep the Japanese on the retreat in north Burma.[63]

By the fall of 1944, in Europe and elsewhere, the British were completely stretched militarily and financially, after having fought for five long years. British military historian Sir Michael Howard explained:

The British needed a rapid result because they were virtually running out of resources. They had no more troops. They had virtually no supplies. Their whole economy depended on the war ending at the end of 1944. Eisenhower didn't have any of those problems [in Europe from D-Day to VE Day]. He had vast numbers of men. The resources of the United States were endless. There was no great hurry about finishing the war.[64]

In Southeast Asia the main issue was how to end the war there with two very different priorities, China for the Americans and Singapore for the British. Ironically, it was Chiang in China and not Mountbatten in Southeast Asia who caused the major rift in the fall of 1944 which led to Stilwell's removal from CBI.

CHAPTER TWELVE

THE JAPANESE STRIKE BACK—*ICHIGO!*

Although the Chinese forces in India and Burma were important in those two theaters, the main problem that concerned Chiang in 1944 was the new Japanese offensive in East China codenamed *Ichigo* or Ichi-Go ("Operation Number One"). Also called *Tairiku Datsū Sakusen*, or "Continent Cross-Through Operation" (Chinese: *Battle of Henan-Hunan-Guangxi* or *Yù Xiāng Guì Huìzhàn*), it began in April 1944. The Japanese goal was to cut through East China from north to south and establish a land link down into French Indo-China and Malaya. This would enable them to move supplies by land, because by that time U.S. Navy submarines were sinking Japanese ships bringing raw materials from Southeast Asia to Japan at an alarming rate, so that many of those supplies never reached Japan. Part of the Japanese plan was also to destroy Chennault's airplanes, which had been harassing them with air raids. In May 1944, during the second phase of *Ichigo*, the Japanese overran Chennault's airbases, triggering a refugee crisis.[1] Chiang saw *Ichigo* as a major crisis that threatened China itself, while for him Burma had always been a sideshow.

Figure 9. Map of Operation *Ichigo*

Operation *Ichigo*

This offensive, which was really three separate battles, namely the Battle of Central Henan, the Battles of Changsha and Hengyang, and the Battle of Guilin-Liuzhou, lasted from April to December 1944 and early 1945, when the Japanese forces reached French Indochina from the north. It was the first major Japanese offensive in China since 1941, involving half a million troops, the largest number deployed in Japanese military history before 1945. During the *Ichigo* offensive, the Nationalists lost most the Chinese provinces of Henan, Hunan, Guangxi, Guangdong, Fujian, and a large part of Guizhou to the Japanese. The Nationalists lost over 130,000 killed in action, 10 major airbases, 36 airports and important sources for food and recruits with the loss of Henan, Hunan, and Guangxi.[2]

Ichigo was also the last major Japanese operational victory in World War II. They had effectively lost the naval war in the Pacific at the Battles of Midway (1942) and Guadalcanal (1942-1943), and they were in full retreat across the Pacific by mid-1944. The authors of *Stilwell's Command Problems* noted that, apart from *Ichigo*, "The summer of 1944 was a black one for the Japanese Empire."[3] Although it did not knock China out of the war, the *Ichigo* offensive was a major crisis in China and CBI that also had important effects on Anglo-American strategy among Mountbatten, Stilwell, and Chiang.

The West Point Atlas of American Wars described *Ichigo* as follows:

> In April, 1944, the China stalemate exploded. Apparently fearful that the defeats they had suffered in the Southwest Pacific would endanger their control of the South China Sea, the Japanese launched a series of offensives to consolidate their position on the Asiatic mainland, These offensives . . . swept the Chinese off the principal north-south rail lines in central and southern China, giving the Japanese continuous land communications between northern Manchuria and Singapore. Seven of Chennault's airfields were overrun, forcing him farther into the interior. . . This was the last large-scale Japanese offensive. Elsewhere, it was already obvious that Japan had lost the war.[4]

Some American planners even believed the Japanese were using *Ichigo* in a bid to preserve their empire if the home islands were to be conquered, with the Japanese Army "rooting" itself into the mainland, thereby prolonging the war even further.[5] Like the fear that fanatical Nazi units such as the SS would dig into a "National Redoubt" in the Bavarian Alps before Nazi Germany's surrender in 1945, forcing Allied forces into a bitter guerrilla war in Germany for years to come, this fear would also prove groundless, but it seemed real at the time.

Adding to the confusion was the attitude of Chiang, who distrusted his own generals and feared that American supplies that were sent to Chinese commanders would be used against him. He forbade Chennault to send supplies to his troops. Stilwell also feared that American supplies might end up in the wrong hands. According to the authors of *Stilwell's Command Problems*, Stilwell "was reluctant to give arms to the Chinese without concrete evidence that they would be used against the common foe rather than in domestic squabbles . . ."[6] Partly for this reason, and partly because he thought Chennault would waste any supplies, he refused to release them.[7] That was a mistake. By that time the Stilwell-Chennault feud had reached epic proportions. Ironically, by that time it was Chennault who was urging Stilwell to send supplies to Chiang's commanders in East China, while Chiang was urging Stilwell to send more supplies to Chennault.[8]

Overall, Stilwell remained unconcerned about *Ichigo*, because he thought the Japanese would outrun their lines of communication.[9] That, after all, is what had happened in Burma. But China with its road and rail network was not Burma, and the Japanese managed to cut a swath from north to south, linking up their forces in China with those in Indochina and Malaya. For Stilwell the Japanese offensive made the Burma Campaign all the more important, in order to re-establish a land route from India through North Burma into China. Stilwell wanted to drive from North Burma into Southwest China, combining the Chinese forces under his command into a massive army that would drive the

Japanese back to the coast.[10] Mountbatten was focused on the British finally getting back into Burma, while events in China were beyond his control and China was outside the boundaries of SEAC.

Late in November 1944 the Japanese advance on Kweiyang, to the east of the vital airfield at Kunming, was checked by American-trained Chinese troops who had been flown in from Burma. [11] Ironically, these were the troops whom Stilwell had trained. So, in the end, his insistence on a well-trained and equipped Chinese Army had paid off. However, by that time the damage had been done, and much of East China had been overrun by the Japanese. In his final report to the Joint Chiefs of Staff, USA, which covered the period in CBI from May 21, 1942-October 24, 1944, Stilwell wrote about the loss of the China airfields, which had been built at the cost of 2 billion Chinese dollars, and their intended goal to assist in the completion of the American strategy in the Pacific.[12]

In Europe the Battle of the Bulge—Hitler's last offensive in the west from December 1944 to January 1945—caused a similar but smaller crisis in Anglo-Americans relations between Ike and Monty over how to advance into Germany on a broad front vs. the single thrust after D-Day and the Battle of Normandy.

For Stilwell the main consequence of *Ichigo* was Chiang's total and complete loss of confidence in him, which would be a major factor in his recall from China. Chiang saw in *Ichigo* an existential threat to China, while Stilwell did not. Chennault, who had always been at loggerheads with Stilwell, and who, unlike Stilwell, both respected and was respected by Chiang, also blamed Stilwell, in his case for not providing enough ground troops to protect his airfields. In turn, Stilwell blamed Chennault for provoking the Japanese with repeated air assaults, and for demanding more cargo space that Stilwell wanted to use for equipping the Chinese armies. Chennault, the apostle of airpower, and Stilwell, who believed that only infantry could hold ground, refused to concede that there might be any merit in the other's position. Chennault never wavered from his view that the role of the infantry was to act as security for his airfields, while Stilwell believed that the main task of the air force was to fly in supplies to the ground troops. The gregarious southerner and the acerbic Yankee never saw eye to eye on how to fight the war in China.[13] After the liberation of Rangoon in May 1945, and the transfer of the U.S. Tenth Air Force to China, Chennault was "encouraged" to retire. The "sweetener" was that he would keep the rank of Major General and his retirement pay would not be subject to income tax. He handed in his request for retirement on July 6, 1945, one month before the first atomic bomb was dropped on Japan.[14]

In a final bit of irony, when Stilwell met USAAF General Curtis LeMay (1906-1990) in China in 1944, they stayed up all night arguing about the value of strategic bombing. At the time, LeMay was unable to convince Stilwell that strategic bombing could play a decisive role in the war. Just after the end of the war in 1945, Stilwell visited LeMay at his headquarters on Guam and admitted that he had been mistaken about airpower, especially its devastating impact on Japan: "You have done what you set out to do. I recognize now the terrible military virtues of strategic bombardment."[15] The first B-29 raids on Japan were launched from China. Then the Marianas became the staging area for the all-out air assault on the Japanese Home Islands.[16]

In the end, what made the Japanese victories in Operation *Ichigo* irrelevant was that by the end of 1944 the USAAF, with its bases in the Marianas, was within striking distance of the Japanese Home Islands. The U.S. no longer needed China as a base for its B-29s. At the same time, the China Theater—where the Japanese had the bulk of their forces—was of no use to the Japanese military in protecting Japan. It is ironic that the beginning of the end for the Japanese Empire came not from China, but from a few small islands southeast of Japan which the Japanese had taken from the Germans in 1914 and which the U.S. captured thirty years later in its drive across the Central Pacific. As Professor S.C.M. Paine of the of the U.S. Naval War College put it in her book *The Wars for Asia, 1911-1949,* "Ichigo lost its rationale as the Japanese home islands became the main theater, under air attack not from China, but from the inaccessible Marianas. At the end of 1944, the Japanese called off the Ichigo Campaign in order to redeploy as many troops as possible to defend Japan [against the expected U.S. invasion in 1945]."[17]

It is easy to blame Stilwell in hindsight for having been wrong about strategic bombing, but he did not have a crystal ball. The value of strategic bombing was hotly debated throughout World War II. For Stilwell the value of airpower was to support ground troops, as the RAF and USAAF did in Burma, flying through the monsoon at great personal risk. However, it is fair to say that he was so fixated on Burma that he ignored the far greater importance of *Ichigo*.

Finally, it is important to remember that in the spring and summer of 1944, there were three battles going on at the same time: *Ichigo;* the Japanese drive into India at Kohima and Imphal; and Stilwell's drive to Myitkyina. Chiang rightly saw *Ichigo* as *the* threat to China, while Mountbatten, also rightly, saw Kohima and Imphal as the threat to India. Yet Stilwell still had his orders to take Myitkyina and its strategic airfield, from which the Japanese could menace the flow of air supplies to China over the Hump. The campaign in North Burma, like Burma itself, was caught in between two major Japanese offensives in China and India. Stilwell himself was simply given too many hats to wear at the same time. That would soon change.

CHAPTER THIRTEEN

FAREWELL TO CBI

The last half of 1944 saw the end of the Stilwell-Mountbatten relationship, the reorganization of CBI, and Stilwell's recall from China. After the battles of Kohima, Imphal, and Myitkyina, it was only a matter of time before the Japanese were defeated in Burma once and for all, which would pave the way for the British offensive to liberate Malaya and Singapore. Slim's 14th Army would advance on Mandalay and Rangoon by the end of 1944 or early 1945.

At this point the Allies assumed the Asian-Pacific War would last another year or two. During June and July 1944, Nimitz's forces had captured the Mariana Islands in the Central Pacific and the USAAF was planning to bomb Japan into submission with the new B-29 Superfortresses, which in June 1944 had launched the first raid on Japan since the 1942 Doolittle Raid.[1] MacArthur's forces in the Southwest Pacific were leapfrogging across New Guinea after two years of hard fighting and were preparing to liberate the Philippines.

The situation was still very dire in China. The Japanese offensive had come close to knocking China out of the war in 1944. With the rapid American drive across the Pacific, by 1944 it was clear that China was not going to be the launching point for the Allies' final offensive against Japan, which had been the original U.S. goal in China since 1942. Although Mountbatten and Stilwell were not getting along at this stage of the war, especially on Stilwell's part, it was Stilwell's increasingly hostile relationship with Chiang that was coming to an end after two tumultuous years.[2]

In August 1944, Mountbatten left Ceylon briefly to attend a conference in London. Before he left, he gave a press conference in Kandy about his seven months in SEAC and what he had achieved. He covered a variety of subjects, and he was very complimentary to Stilwell, as reflected in the following remarks:

> [T]he Burma battle front is a single unified front . . .[M]y plans are made in close consultation with my deputy, General Joseph Stilwell. . . General Stilwell, Deputy Supreme Allied Commander and the Commanding General of the American forces in the China, Burma and India theatre, with great gallantry himself commanded the forces on the Ledo front ... It will thus be seen that the capture of Myitkyina and Moguang was the result of a series of closely coordinated operations on the part of British, American, Chinese and West African troops ... I would like to stress in particular the personal help and support I have received from. . .my deputy, General Stilwell, whose long experience of the east has been of signal assistance to me in our common task.[3]

This press conference was part of Mountbatten's diplomatic publicity campaign to put the best light on the Burma Campaign, without mentioning his problems with Stilwell. It was vintage Mountbatten, in particular his repeated references to Stilwell as "my deputy." Despite the veneer of cooperation, by then the two men distrusted each other to a degree that made their working together all but impossible.[4]

In fairness to Mountbatten, although he certainly enjoyed Ceylon as a headquarters, he did a lot of travelling, visiting the Allied troops, British, America, Indian, African, and Chinese, giving a constant round of speeches and exhortations.

HOLIDAY IN KANDY

Stilwell took temporary command of SEAC on August 1, 1944, and used Mountbatten's headquarters as a personal rest stop after the hard campaigning in North Burma during the first half of 1944. In a letter to his wife on the pleasures of Ceylon,[5] Stilwell wrote: "Kandy is 2,000 feet up. Climate like Hawaii. Plenty of fruit. The views are beautiful. In contrast with north Burma, this is a paradise."[6] He needed all the rest he could get, because the early fall of 1944 would prove one of the toughest periods of his entire career.[7]

On August 5, 1944, Stilwell gave his own press conference at Kandy, where he outlined how the war in CBI was progressing after Myitkyina. When he was asked, "What about Japs in Myitkyina?" Stilwell said "They are all cleaned up."[8] On his Chinese forces at Myitkyina, he said that "The Chinese stood up better than either the British or the Americans. The Chinese are tough. The Gurhkas [sic] stood up well, too, but not as well as the Chinese. The Chinese stood up best, the Gurhkas were second and the British and Americans were in last place."[9] When he was asked about Merrill's Marauders, he replied, "They did a very fine job. Very dependable outfit. They were very tough. I was very glad they were not after me."[10] However, when he was asked about the Chindits he went off the record and said, "when it came to active combat in the fight at Myitkyina they were pretty well run down with sickness" and they "did not have the strength remaining to do anything serious."[11] When he was asked, "Is Burma included in the future offensive program," he replied, "Anything south is included in the program till we get to salt water."[12] As far as he was concerned, the road to Rangoon lay through Burma, not by sea from Ceylon.[13]

Finally, when he was asked what he thought of Kandy, he replied, "Wonderful. I think it is the Garden of Eden but I haven't seen the snake yet."[14] Although Stilwell mentioned the Japanese defeats at Kohima and Imphal, and grudgingly acknowledged the role the Chindits played at Myitkyina, he did not mention either Mountbatten or Slim in his interview.

On August 7, 1944, Stilwell was officially promoted to full general, becoming one of only five American officers to attain that rank.[15] However, by the summer of 1944, Mountbatten was becoming frustrated with Stilwell's constant sniping at the British war effort in SEAC and for his insubordination when he told Slim, but not Mountbatten, of the Myitkyina operation. Another major problem was that CBI as a command structure for all of China, Burma, and India, as it had been set up in 1942, was not working. It was time to reorganize the command as the war was entering its final phase. Although China had not been knocked out of the war in 1944, Chiang had lost all patience with Stilwell. For his part, Stilwell had come to detest Chiang even more than Mountbatten did. As already noted, Stilwell had been very critical of Chiang's wartime leadership in general, which Stilwell thought was hindering his ability to fight the Japanese in Burma, and of Chiang's Nationalist government in general for being corrupt and inefficient. This was something FDR only began to see by 1944.

In August 1944, Lt. Col. Dean Rusk, a U.S. Army staff officer (and future U.S. Secretary of State) sent a memorandum to Stilwell about changing the command structure in SEAC: "SAC [Supreme Allied Commander] has a strong and logical case for a land C-in-C [Commander-in-Chief] which will be difficult for the U.S. Chiefs of Staff to resist." The memorandum further recommended that "Integration of U.S. and Chinese forces in SEAC should be held to a minimum ... The HQ Army C-in-C, SEAC, should be British with an all-British staff ... NCAC [Northern Combat Area Command] should come under the operational control of SAC himself."[16] Rusk's memorandum showed there was a lively debate about just how to break up CBI in 1944 that went beyond the personalities of Stilwell and Mountbatten.

In September 1944, Chiang wanted Stilwell to launch a diversionary attack to relieve the Yunnan Force in Burma, which Stilwell refused to do.[17] Chiang threatened to withdraw the Yunnan Force from Burma altogether. Marshall suggested to FDR that he appoint Stilwell commander of all Chinese forces, and not merely serve as Chiang's Chief of Staff. Chiang opposed this and also disagreed with the strategy for the Burma Campaign. Chiang said that FDR had "very good intentions" in nominating Stilwell to command all Chinese troops but that Chiang had lost the "last drop of confidence" he had in Stilwell.[18] Chiang had failed to get rid of Stilwell in 1943 and was determined to do so in 1944. At the same time, and in fairness to Chiang, he could not focus only on North Burma as did Stilwell, who had rarely been in China between January and June 1944. Unlike FDR, Churchill, and Stalin, Chiang was the one major Allied leader who was not securely in power in his own country, which he had helped unify after 1925. Fighting was raging in North China, the Japanese were overrunning Chennault's airfields in East China (as Stilwell had predicted they would if they were pressed hard enough from the air), and perhaps Chiang simply believed that Stilwell did not see the big picture. Chiang wrote an *aide memoire* for transmission to FDR, which said in part, "[W]e have taken Myitkyina but we have lost almost all of east China, and in this General Stilwell cannot be absolved of grave responsibility."[19]

For his part, as noted above, Mountbatten wanted to remove Stilwell from SEAC, but he did not have the authority that Chiang or FDR had. Based upon what he wrote at the time and afterward, Mountbatten apparently would have been happy to have left Stilwell in charge of the China Theater. Mountbatten could only watch from the sidelines in Ceylon after he returned from Britain in early September 1944 as Stilwell's time in CBI came to an end. When Mountbatten returned, Stilwell wrote to his wife that "He was not at ease with me which is not surprising, because his trip had to do with an operation on his deputy's throat. Maybe the fourth star threw a monkey wrench into the machinery."[20]

The authors of *Stilwell's Command Problems* wrote that "Ever since March 1944 Mountbatten had been anxious to see Stilwell transferred from SEAC to the China Theater."[21] However, when Brooke told Marshall in June 1944 that Mountbatten wanted Stilwell removed from SEAC, Marshall refused, saying Stilwell was "the only aggressive and successful commander in chief" Mountbatten had.[22] Even Wedemeyer defended Stilwell, saying he always obeyed Mountbatten's orders promptly once they were given.[23] Yet when Marshall returned to Washington, the Joint Chiefs of Staff began to consider limiting Stilwell to the China Theater.[24] All of this reflected the command problems that Mountbatten wanted to fix so that SEAC could conduct the war in Southeast Asia more efficiently. According to the authors of *Stilwell's Command Problems*, Brooke had somewhat mollified Marshall by saying that all three British senior commanders in SEAC —General Giffard, Admiral Somerville, and Air Chief Marshal Peirse—would also be replaced.[25]

Stilwell wrote in his diary during the Japanese offensive in the summer of 1944 the following entry on FDR's China policy and what might happen after the war: "If we do not take action, our prestige in China will suffer seriously. China will contribute nothing to our efforts against Japan, and the seeds will be planted for chaos in China after the war."[26] Tuchman wrote,

> Militarily China had proved a losing game and by now was not vitally needed except as a holding theater. The strategic aim that took shape at Quebec was to keep China in the war and not much more. No U.S units were planned for CBI; Marshall was definite on that point. Further operations in Burma were to be left as far as possible to the British so that the United States would not be involved in the reconquest of colonial territory—or such was the intention.[27]

Although Burma was not on the main agenda at the Second Quebec Conference, Churchill did review the Allied victories there to date, including Imphal and Kohima. He wrote that "General Stilwell was to be congratulated on his brilliant capture of Myitkyina."[28] However, Churchill also wrote that "In spite of these successes, it was, I continued, most undesirable that the fighting in the Burmese jungles should go on indefinitely."[29] The British plan, codenamed DRACULA, was to take Rangoon before the monsoon in January 1945. However, even after D-Day and the Allied victories in Europe, Mountbatten still did not have the landing craft he needed for an amphibious operation.

By the fall of 1944 it was clear that the war in Europe would not be over by the end of the year and the military forces could not be diverted from Europe to Southeast Asia.[30] During the period leading up to Stilwell's recall, Wedemeyer had been anti-Stilwell but was also critical of Mountbatten's plans. Ziegler wrote, "In Washington in June [1944] Wedemeyer had warned that he would oppose any enterprise of this kind [an amphibious operation] unless satisfied that it would make a '*timely* contribution*' to the opening of the China road." (italics in original) [31] This shows that although Wedemeyer and Stilwell did not get on, they had the same commitment to reopening the land route to China.

In June 1944 Vice President Henry Wallace had gone to China on the Military Observer Mission to try to have Chiang negotiate with the Communists.[32] In September 1944, FDR sent Brigadier General Patrick J. Hurley as his personal envoy in China to work things out between Chiang and Stilwell. Hurley, unlike Stilwell but like Chennault, was pro-Chiang. Hurley and Wallace were two of the many envoys whom FDR sent out to China, as well as to Europe. (Hurley and Wallace had also gone to the Soviet Union.) By this time FDR was getting tired of Chiang's demands but was willing to help him even if it meant that Stilwell had to go. FDR was convinced that China would be a Great Power and did not want to abandon it.[33] FDR was also running for a fourth term, even though he was dying. By that time he was more focused on the war in Europe and the Pacific and planning the postwar world.

STILWELL'S RECALL FROM CHINA

After a series of acrimonious exchanges between FDR and Chiang, in which FDR pushed for Stilwell's appointment as Commander-in-Chief of all Chinese Forces, both Nationalist and Communist, in China as well as in Burma, Stilwell handed Chiang a note from FDR that stretched the limits of diplomacy from one head of state to another. FDR's note to Chiang demanded that he give Stilwell "unrestricted command" of all Chinese forces.[34] No foreigner since the British General Charles "Chinese" Gordon (1833-1885), during the Taiping Rebellion of the 1850s and 1860s, had ever had control of substantial Chinese forces.

Chiang sent a message through Hurley to Marshall and FDR demanding Stilwell's recall.[35] Hurley sent a message to FDR, advising, "If you sustain Stilwell in this controversy you will lose Chiang-Kai-shek and possibly you will lose China with him."[36] This showed how desperate the situation between Chiang and Stilwell had become by late 1944. Chiang believed —not without some justification—that "Stilwell had sacrificed east China for the sake of his campaign in Burma," was indifferent to the fate of East China, and had refused even to consult with Chiang about East China until the beginning of June 1944.[37]

Although Marshall tried to save Stilwell's job, FDR gave "direct and positive" orders to remove Stilwell from CBI. On October 19, 1944, Stilwell's recall became official. That was Chiang's last diplomatic victory in China during the war. Taylor wrote that "Stilwell had won the battle of words, a loss from which the Generalissimo and his regime would never fully recover,"[38] especially after the Chinese civil war resumed in 1946.

In an undated paper, Stilwell wrote that "[M]y relations with Chiang Kai-shek were on an impersonal and official basis, and although we greatly differed often on questions of tactics and strategy, once the decision was made, I did my best to carry it out."[39]

In his diary, Stilwell wrote "THE AX FALLS. Radio from George Marshall. I am 'recalled.' Sultan in temporary command. Wedemeyer to command U.S. troops in China. CBI to split."[40] On October 26, 1944, in his next to last diary entry for CBI, Stilwell wrote: "Thirty-two months of this. Last day in CBI. Radio about split of theater arrived."[41]

Mountbatten recorded his views on Stilwell's recall, writing that "It was a great surprise, however, to hear that General Stilwell was leaving. There had been trouble a year before when I was in Chungking between him and the Generalissimo, which I was able to smooth over personally, which is one reason why I think old Vinegar Joe always appeared to like me."[42] Mountbatten was being disingenuous about his strained relationship with Stilwell and taking credit for having "saved" his job the previous year. An official communication between Mountbatten and General Sultan on October 28, 1944, about Stilwell's position in CBI, was summarized as follows in the Mountbatten Papers:

> It was the previous August that Mountbatten suggested to London that the theatres should be separated and all the Americans be put under Sultan's command. *Mountbatten also recommended that Stilwell be made GOC China and was taken aback when this did not happen.* However, Mountbatten is glad that Wedemeyer has been promoted, though sorry that he will be leaving [HQ SACSEA]. Mountbatten is relying heavily on a renewed spirit of good feeling between the British and American forces. Now that Sultan is in command, Mountbatten is sure that the former's friendly and co-operative spirit will influence the whole of his command. Mountbatten will co-operate with him in any way he can.[43] [italics supplied]

Another official communication between Mountbatten and British General Carton de Wiart, Mountbatten's representative in Chungking, on November 1, was summarized as follows:

> [Mountbatten] thanks Carton de Wiart for his letter of 25 October, concerning the change of command. Lord Mountbatten asks him to thank Hurley for his efforts, although *Hurley seems to think that SACSEA [Mountbatten] wanted Stilwell to leave Asia. In fact, all he wanted was the division of the China and India-Burma Theatres, and has always considered Stilwell the best person for the China Theatre.* He was upset when Wedemeyer left to replace Stilwell,

as was Wedemeyer himself, for the latter thought it impossible to achieve anything with the Generalissimo.[44] [italics supplied]

These two communications give the impression that Mountbatten just wanted Stilwell out of SEAC, but not out of CBI, or at least, that is what he wanted people to believe. In November 1944, Mountbatten wrote FDR that "I was sorry to see Stilwell go, not only because I personally liked him, but because it meant that I lost my beloved Al Wedemeyer."[45] Slim wrote in his memoirs that "The Generalissimo [Chiang] had insisted on it [Stilwell's recall] and, in spite of pressure from Washington and from Admiral Mountbatten, had refused to yield. The only thing that was surprising was that the open breach had not come sooner."[46]

When Stilwell left Chungking, he did not wait for Wedemeyer to replace him or even leave him any of his operational plans, which he had kept secret.[47] Wedemeyer said little at the time, but later wrote that Stilwell had deliberately insulted him.[48] In fact, Marshall had ordered Stilwell back to the U.S. on very short notice, just before the election on November 7, 1944. However, Stilwell at least could have left briefing papers for Wedemeyer.

Stilwell's departure from CBI ended the strategic problems that had plagued his relations with Mountbatten in the Burma Campaign during 1944. Had Stilwell stayed in China into 1945 it is not clear how much more he could have done, because the war was shifting away from China to the Pacific.

Before Stilwell left, he wrote to General Sir Claude Auchinleck (1884-1981), "The Auk," Commander-in-Chief India, the only British general other than Slim and Festing[49] whom Stilwell actually liked. A short and poignant letter, it went as follows:

This is good-bye to you and Lady Auchinleck, with my best wishes for the future. The sheriff has caught up with me, and I have been yanked out, but whatever my glaring deficiencies as a diplomat, I hope you will remember me, as I remember you, as a friend, and that we will meet again, as you have promised, in California.[50]

Apart from Auchinleck, Stilwell also wrote to General Festing of the 36th Division,[51] whose role at Myitkyina remains controversial, to Field Marshal Lord Wavell, by then the Viceroy of India,[52] and to Slim. To Slim he said in part as follows:

> My contact with you has been a refreshing experience, and it is with keen regret that I have to leave, with the job half-done. My hat is off to you as a soldier, and I hope you will think of me as trying to be one, too; my necessary contact with politics was a distasteful phase of my job, and I would have much preferred to stick to my trade in any capacity, however humble . . . Your reputation with our people is very high and deservedly so, and we all wish you the success you are sure to have in your future operations.[53]

Stilwell wrote what Tuchman called "a very decent letter to Chennault taking pride in his achievements and acknowledging the admiration in which he was held by the Chinese."[54] Stilwell also sent farewell letters to several Chinese and American officers with whom he had served in CBI.[55] *Stilwell's Personal File* does not contain any such letter to Mountbatten, nor was the author able to locate one either in the Stilwell or Mountbatten Archives. Stilwell did, however, send a message to Brigadier General Theodore F. Wessels, the U.S. Senior Liaison Officer at SEAC HQ in Kandy, for "eyes alone" delivery to Mountbatten, in which Stilwell offered his "best wishes for a smashing success on your coming operations."[56]

Both British and American newspapers printed Mountbatten's reply, in which he said, "You are leaving behind you the reputation of being a great fighting general . . . I always had the greatest admiration for your fighting qualities."[57]

Mountbatten wrote two final letters to Stilwell. In the first Mountbatten claimed he had saved Stilwell's job in October 1943. The original letter is in the Stilwell Archives at Stanford. Stilwell's handwritten comment at the bottom of the letter reads, "He had nothing whatever to do with it."[58] In the same letter Mountbatten wrote:

> I must take this opportunity of thanking you for the personal friendship which you accorded me and for the invariably loyal and helpful attitude you adopted in dealing with all my requests. Most Englishmen, as you yourself undoubtedly know, find you a difficult man to deal with but, with the exception of the troubles over Lentaigne [i.e., the Chindit controversy], which took such a lot of settling, I can testify that I have found you both easy and helpful in all matters which I raised in person direct with you. [59]

Stilwell's handwritten comment here was "Thank God that I am difficult for limies to deal with." This letter was probably hand-delivered to Stilwell in California, because in his diary for November 24, 1944, he wrote "Special Messenger from Wash.with personal letter from Louis. My God. What stupidity."[60]

The second letter congratulated Stilwell on his appointment as Commanding General, Army Ground Forces in the United States, and expressed regret that Stilwell could not accept a British decoration.[61] Stilwell replied to Mountbatten on February 23, 1945, ending with "My best wishes to you and all members of your command for a most successful campaign."[62]

Thus ended the Stilwell-Mountbatten wartime collaboration. They never saw each other again, nor did they communicate with each other. Ironically, however, Mountbatten's obituary in the *New York Times* after his assassination in 1979 said that "Toward the end of the war, however, Stilwell warmed somewhat toward Lord Mountbatten."[63]

As with the AXIOM controversy in early 1944, Stilwell's recall was widely publicized. Robert Musel, a correspondent for the *Los Angeles Times,* wrote on November 2, 1944:

> Informants said that Stilwell and Mountbatten disagreed sharply regarding strategy in the Far East and that they were not on

speaking terms when Stilwell was recalled... Britain was especially sensitive to criticism of Mountbatten's appointment to the South-east Asia Command when some sections of the American press asserted that the job should have gone to an American....[64]

Hanson W. Baldwin wrote a very perceptive article in the *New York Times* in which he analyzed the reasons for Stilwell's recall, beyond his personality clash with Chiang. He wrote about the difference between the American "land" and the British "sea" strategies:

> General Stilwell was identified with this "overland" strategy; Lord Mountbatten with amphibious strategy. There was probably no major difference between the two, but the former was often openly impatient with the slow-moving and negative attitudes of the New Delhi administration.[65]

Brooks Atkinson, who had recently interviewed Stilwell, wrote in the *New York Times* in November 1944 that his recall "represents the political triumph of a moribund, corrupt regime that is more concerned with maintaining its political supremacy than driving the Japanese out of China."[66]

The *Los Angeles Times* ran an article that said "[*T*]*he Daily Express* [a leading British newspaper] said that Stilwell's recall 'may not be the end of a reshuffle of high-ranking commanders' among British personnel also."[67] In fact, not long after Stilwell's recall, Mountbatten also replaced all three British senior commanders in SEAC in a housecleaning of the command structure at the end of 1944.[68] Stilwell's job was divided into three parts, with Wedemeyer in China, Sultan in North Burma, and Lt.-General Raymond Wheeler (1885-1974), SEAC Chief of Supply, replacing Wedemeyer in Kandy.[69] So, in the end it took three U.S. generals to replace Vinegar Joe, or at least to wear all the hats he had worn.

The media coverage in the U.S. also highlighted the contrasting Anglo-American views on the command structure in CBI and SEAC. The *Los Angeles Times* ran an article on October 29, 1944, which proposed

Whatever the reasons for the removal of Gen. Joseph (Vinegar Joe) Stilwell from his Far Eastern Command, the shift itself does not augur well for the immediate success of further Allied operations in North Burma . . . How successful he has been in [his role as SEAC Deputy Commander] is indicated by the fact that it will take two generals to replace him.[70] [As noted above, it actually took three generals to replace him!]

This book is not about Stilwell and Chiang, or Stilwell and Chennault, but about Stilwell and Mountbatten. Therefore, it makes no judgment about who was "right" and who was "wrong" in China. Perhaps McLynn put it best when he wrote the following comment about Stilwell:

The most accurate criticism of Stilwell was that he was a polarizing figure, who never truckled and therefore never went in for the grubby compromises that are the stock-in-trade of politics. If he really wanted to bring Chiang to heel, he had to make sure that all US political and military personnel presented a united front alongside him. Sadly, he never even attempted such a "coalition of the willing."[71]

In January 1945, the 500-mile Ledo Road was completed after almost three years, costing $37,000,000, with the first convoy reaching China in February. By the end of the war, the Ledo Road had delivered 34,000 tons of supplies to China. Its completion was Stilwell's final accomplishment in CBI, although he was not there to see it. Ironically, Chiang officially renamed the Ledo-Burma Road the "Stilwell Road."[72] That road could only have been built as a result of Stilwell's determination. On January 25, 1945, the U.S. Joint Chiefs of Staff sent Mountbatten the following congratulations on the completion of the road:

The CCS are sending congratulations to Mountbatten and SEAC on the occasion of the reopening of the land route to China. Marshall sends his personal congratulations to Sultan for the part the Americans played in this, and especially for the actions of the Engineers and other service forces who worked in adverse conditions to provide the connecting links and to keep forward areas supplied, enabling them to continue construction and fighting. General Stilwell deserves credit for thinking of the road project in the first place and for making it happen. This achievement is due to allied teamwork and will prove to be a significant point in the history of the Far East.[73]

The West Point Atlas of American Wars put it this way:

Operations in India, Burma, and China represent, above all, a logistical triumph. Supplies, in large part originating in the United States, were moved into remote corners of the Burmese jungle and the hills of China in sufficient quantity to maintain major air and ground offensives. In this, the transport plane and the bulldozer changed the entire concept of transportation in the Far East. Yet, at the same time, pack mules, porters, elephants, and improvised river shipping were frequently invaluable. This was a war fought for extended periods in unhealthy, rain-sodden, insect-ridden areas—probably the loneliest, most alien, and most primitive war Americans have ever faced [along with the Pacific and Vietnam wars].[74]

Stilwell had won his war in North Burma, opening up the Ledo Road and making sure that supplies would get to China. He had done it over the determined opposition of not only the Japanese, but also that of his own allies, who never agreed with his overland strategy. Now he was coming home, at least for a while.

STILWELL COMES HOME

Back home in Carmel, Stilwell was finally allowed to give a press conference, which took place in the garden of his home on November 15, 1944. In his diary, Stilwell described the press conference very briefly: "Press and photographers in P.M. Gang of 25—Carl in a dither. Kept my mouth shut [about China]."[75] Vinegar Joe was always good copy, like MacArthur and Patton. Before Stilwell's recall from China, *Yank:*

The Army Weekly, in its October 6, 1944, issue did an article on Stilwell titled "Stilwell: The GIs' Favorite" and what he planned to do after CBI and the war:

> Uncle Joe's one ambition is to win the war and get the hell home as quickly as possible. He has no personal post-war political or business aspirations. When peace comes, he plans to retire from the Army and settle down with his family in Carmel, Calif. There on the beach he will be able to don his old corduroy trousers and spend his days slogging through the sands with his favorite dog, a soft-eyed giant Schnauzer named Gareth. The little things in life are what Uncle Joe enjoys most.[76]

On November 16, 1944, *The Charlotte News* wrote about Stilwell:

> General Joseph Stilwell, having arrived back in the U.S. after his recall from the command of the China-Burma-India theater, spoke to newsmen in Carmel, CA., but refused to discuss his recall. Instead, he heaped praise on the American fighting men and the excellent training they had received. He found that the Japanese were good soldiers and, as they were started at a young age, well-trained also; but the way the Americans did it, he believed, was a "damned sight better."[77]

The November 23, 1944 issue of *CBI Roundup* had a short article about Stilwell's return to Carmel, entitled " 'UNCLE JOE' CHATS ABOUT GARDEN, FAMILY, WEATHER." [78]

This is what *Time* wrote about Stilwell in its November 27, 1944 edition:

> General Joseph W. ("Vinegar Joe") Stilwell, commandless at his Carmel, Calif, home, shed his ribbonless four-starred khaki for slacks and an old black sweater, met the press informally. Mum on the subject of his removal from China, grizzled Vinegar Joe said his hat was off to this generation of U.S. fighting men . . .[79]

Although *The Stilwell Papers* end with his recall from China, his war-time diaries are available online from the Hoover Institution at Stanford

University. Two entries from 1945 show he was still not enamored of either Mountbatten or Wedemeyer:

> Monday, March 5, 1945: "Lentaigne [Lt. Gen. Walter Lentaigne, Wingate's successor as commander of the Chindits] sent word to me that he had to do some of the things he did. Ordered to by Mountbatten.—(Leese [General Oliver Leese, Commanding Officer, Land Forces, Southeast Asia] & [General Bill] Slim think Louis is a bloody fool.) [80]

Monday, July 27, 1945: "G.C.M [George C. Marshall] has lost confidence in Wedemeyer."[81]

In June 1945 Stilwell took command of the U.S. Tenth Army (the last U.S. Army command established in the Pacific War) at the end of the Battle of Okinawa, which was the Tenth Army's only battle of the war. By the time he took command the battle was almost over and he was scheduled to be part of the invasion of Japan. When some British and Commonwealth units were taken away from SEAC and placed under his command at Okinawa, Stilwell noted in his diary: "Mountbatten has to give up units for this operation! Ain't life funny? [82] According to an article in the *Los Angeles Times* at the time of his death, a year later.

> It was on Okinawa that Stilwell finally lost his famous campaign hat. He was up flying around in an observation plan when the hat blew off, but an eager G.I.—recognizing the headgear—swam out into the ocean and retrieved it. Stilwell gave him six bottles of whiskey as a fitting reward.[83]

Stilwell would only live two more years after his recall from China. After Japan's surrender on August 15, 1945 (VJ Day) following the atomic bombings of Hiroshima and Nagasaki and the Soviet invasion of Manchuria, he attended the official Japanese surrender on the USS *Missouri* in Tokyo Bay on September 2, 1945. On September 7, 1945, Stilwell took the official surrender of all Japanese forces on Okinawa. In November 1945 he was appointed to head a "War Department Equipment

Board" to investigate the modernization of the Army during World War II. In March 1946, Stilwell took command of the Sixth Army at the Presidio of San Francisco. In July 1946, he was an observer at the first postwar nuclear tests at Bikini Atoll in the Marshall Islands (Operation Crossroads).[84]

Early that fall, Stilwell suddenly became ill with liver cancer, after having gone into the hospital for a routine checkup. He died at the Presidio of San Francisco (which he called "Frisco" in his 1939 diary) on Saturday afternoon, October 12, 1946. According to one obituary, "He died in an ordinary ward at Letterman General Hospital—scorning special comforts and privileges to the last as he had ignored personal safety and fatigue in the jungles of Burma."[85] He was sixty-three years old, the same age as FDR when he died. In accordance with his wishes there was no public funeral service and a few days later he was cremated and his ashes were scattered over the Pacific Ocean not far from his beloved Carmel.[86]

On October 14, 1946, *The Times* (London) ran his obituary. It read in part as follows:

> [H]e proved his leadership by his wonderful retreat from Burma in 1942, when the Japanese had reached Mandalay and Lashio and were menacing with envelopment the whole of the allied forces in Burma. Cut off from his troops he successfully led a remarkable jungle march of a miscellaneous party by the only remaining route into India. In the words of one who took part in this appalling trek, "Stilwell alternately performed the services of company commander, mess sergeant, gun-bearer, and guide, bedding down beside us in the jungle, standing in line with us at food time, coaxing others to march when they thought they could not, until we arrived safely... Stilwell, as commander of all United States forces in China, India and Burma, had an important part to play in the discussions which took place in Washington, in Delhi, and in Chungking. When the British Fourteenth Army began to move, Stilwell was impatient with what he considered to be unnecessary quiescence on the part of the Chinese commanders, and his impatience led to an open breach with the Generalissimo,

which in turn led to his recall to the United States. . . It is pleasant to be able to record that Generalissimo Chiang Kai-shek has paid a generous tribute to his memory." [87]

Perhaps the obituary in the *Los Angeles Times* put it best when it said that "Vinegar Joe learned the art of war and the secret of languages but he never mastered diplomacy. He said what he meant, and he meant what he said—so the sparks almost always flew."[88]

Winifred Stilwell died in 1972. Their daughter Alison had a studio in Carmel, where she was a well-known local artist, in the courtyard area of the Pine Inn. She passed away in 1991.[89] Her sister Nancy also lived in Carmel, where she died in 1997.[90] After World War II, Stilwell's older son, Brigadier General Joseph W. Stilwell, Jr. served in Korea and Vietnam, and died when his plane vanished over the Pacific in 1966. The youngest daughter, named Winifred like her mother, passed away in 2005, and the youngest child and second son, Benjamin, died in 2014.

The Stilwell home is still there, overlooking Carmel Beach, with its plaque in front telling the passersby whose home it was.

Figure 10. Plaque at the Stilwell House, Carmel, California.

Photo by author.

CHAPTER FOURTEEN

MOUNTBATTEN AND THE END OF SEAC (1945-1946)

While Stilwell was preparing for his next assignment in 1945, the British 14th Army under Slim advanced into Burma and liberated Mandalay after a fierce battle, where he did a classic and rare double envelopment around the Japanese forces. The British flag flew once again at Fort Dufferin, the city's stronghold, built on the site of the old royal palace. The British then retook Rangoon between March and May 1945, just ahead of the monsoon.[1] When the Japanese tried to make a stand at Toungoo, between Rangoon and Mandalay, they were routed by Karens led by British officers.[2]

By the summer of 1945 most of Burma had been liberated and the next move in SEAC was the invasion of Malaya, Operation Zipper, which was being planned for September 1945. At that point fate—and the U.S. Army Air Forces—intervened, dropping two atomic bombs on Japan. When Japan surrendered on August 15, 1945, the sudden end of the war meant that thousands of Allied soldiers wouldn't have to fight against the Japanese in Malaya.[3]

Mountbatten had first learned about the atomic bomb—"the greatest secret of the war"—from President Harry Truman (1884-1972), Marshall, and Churchill at the Potsdam Conference in July 1945. During a meeting on July 25, 1945, Truman, Marshall, and Mountbatten discussed the operational (*i.e.*, Operation Olympic, the planned American invasion of Kyushu, Japan, in November 1945) and political situation of the Pacific War and the Japanese military buildup on Kyushu, which was based on the latest Ultra radio intelligence Truman received before approving the use of the atomic bombs. (The Ultra intercepts were classified until the late 1970s.) At Potsdam it had been agreed that SEAC would also include southern French Indochina (South Vietnam after 1954), Java, Borneo, and the Celebes, so that Mountbatten would now be responsible for the former French and Dutch colonial possessions.[4]

After Potsdam, Mountbatten returned from Britain to Ceylon via Cairo on August 14, 1945. For Mountbatten, too, the sudden end of the war brought a huge sigh of relief. On VJ Day, the boundaries of SEAC were expanded to include southern French Indochina, Thailand, Java, and Borneo.[5]

Nevertheless, Operation Zipper took place as planned on September 9, 1945, but the landings were unopposed.[6] It is ironic that Operation Zipper was Mountbatten's only major amphibious operation in SEAC, because by 1945 he had both the ships and the landing craft he had not had in 1944.[7]

Between the end of the war and Japan's official surrender, Mountbatten's immediate problem in Southeast Asia was to save Allied POWs in Burma, Thailand, and Singapore, who were dying every day from Japanese maltreatment. Just after Japan's surrender, aid was dropped into many of the POW camps, but that was not enough. In late August 1945, Mountbatten's wife, Edwina (Countess Mountbatten of Burma, 1901-1960), who had been a member of the St. John's Ambulance Brigade since the beginning of World War II, undertook a courageous mission to save Allied POWs before the Allied forces could reach them in the

Japanese-held areas. She had nerves of steel in dealing with the Japanese guards. Unarmed and with only a small escort, she ordered them to treat the surviving POWs humanely, such as giving them desperately needed medical supplies that the Japanese had hoarded. By doing this, she helped save them from certain death and helped arrange for their repatriation after they recovered.

On September 12, 1945, ten days after MacArthur had taken the Japanese surrender on the U.S.S. *Missouri* in Tokyo Bay, Mountbatten took the Japanese surrender at the City Hall in Singapore. That ceremony finally avenged the British defeat there in 1942.[8]

With the war officially over, Mountbatten faced the challenge of handling 700,000 Japanese military personnel before their repatriation back to Japan, restoring law and order—ironically, often with Japanese troops—before the Allied troops arrived in areas under his control, and dealing with the return of the British, French, and the Dutch to their colonies. The chaotic situation the British forces faced in Southeast Asia at the end of the war was summed up by Slim, who wrote that "Appeals from our French and Dutch Allies, cries for help, demands for troops, threats of continued Japanese resistance, apprehensions of wholesale massacre, forebodings of economic collapse, warnings of starvation of the whole population, poured into our headquarters from every quarter."[9]

Four places in particular dominated Mountbatten's postwar operations in SEAC from the fall of 1945 to the spring of 1946: Malaya, Burma, French Indo-China, and the Netherlands East Indies. Each of them presented a particular challenge, often as great as the challenges Mountbatten had faced working with Stilwell and Chiang in defeating the Japanese.

Mountbatten and Malayan Unity

Mountbatten's first immediate postwar problem as Supreme Commander was handling Malaya's complex situation following Japan's surrender. His first problem there was dealing with the bad relationship between the Chinese and Malays that had grown worse during the war, because the Chinese had generally fought against the Japanese in the resistance, while the Malay police had generally cooperated with them.[10] His other problem was dealing with the Chinese Communists of the far-left Malayan People's Anti-Japanese Union (MPAJU); it had led the resistance against the Japanese occupation with Allied help during the war. Mountbatten had backed the MPAJU because of their aid to the Allies, but he underestimated the fact that they were hostile to the return of any colonial government.

Mountbatten also had to deal with the new independence movement in Malaya. Before the war, Malaya had no independence movement as such, because it had been ruled by different sultans under British protection. The war had changed all that, because many Malayans had felt betrayed by the British defeat in 1942. What Mountbatten wanted was a united Malaya: he didn't want the largely Chinese population of Singapore to split with the rest of Malaya. The new Labor Government in Britain wanted to unite Malaya into a federation by abolishing the old sultanates, along with the Straits Settlements of Penang (Georgetown), Malacca, and Singapore.

Along with the problems of unifying Malaya, the end of the war had brought inflation, near-famine, and strikes against SEAC's control. The arrest of Soon Kwong, one of the most militant of Malaya's Chinese leaders, in October 1945, led to the first serious crisis between the colonial government and the Malayan Chinese. Kwong was convicted by a court consisting of British officers, but legally the proceedings were shaky. In January 1946 Mountbatten asked General Messervy, the British Military Governor, to release Kwong because imprisoning him was against Mountbatten's policy in Malaya. He was released two weeks later.[11]

Mountbatten was at heart a socialist and a democrat (despite being the great-grandson of Queen Victoria), who believed that only the rule of law and order would restore peace in Malaya. Although he was criticized by some of his advisors for his liberal tendencies, General Slim thought that Mountbatten was right in his policies. In fact, Malaya later did split along ethnic lines, with Singapore becoming an independent (and mainly Chinese) city-state.

On April 1, 1946, Singapore and the Union of Malaya went from SEAC's control to civil government. In May 1946 Malcolm MacDonald (1901-1981) (the son of Ramsey MacDonald, the first British Labour Prime Minister), took over as Governor-General of Malaya. After that, Mountbatten's job in Malaya was officially over. After he left in the spring of 1946, the British tried to forge a united Malaya while battling the Chinese Communist insurgency that delayed Malaya's independence until 1957. Singapore became an independent nation in 1965 and Malaya (Malaysia after 1965) became a member of the British Commonwealth.

MOUNTBATTEN AND THE PATH TO BURMESE INDEPENDENCE

Burma was another area of difficulty in SEAC's area of control. Like Malaya, it had been under British control before the war, but unlike Malaya, Burma had a growing independence movement when the Japanese invaded in 1941. For Mountbatten, Burma was a particularly hard problem because, apart from restoring order, he had to rebuild Burma's economy as well as the government. To help him rebuild Burma, Mountbatten relied on the Civil Affairs Service (Burma), which had broad powers under SEAC's control, but which had no business making long-term political decisions. Mountbatten used the government in Burma under Governor Sir Reginald Dorman-Smith, GBE (1899-1977), who had spent the war in exile in Simla in India and whom Mountbatten had known since 1944.

While the war raged, Mountbatten and Dorman-Smith got on well because they had similar liberal leanings regarding the postwar government in Burma after liberation. Mountbatten said Dorman-Smith "has first-class ideas on the future of Burma, and we see eye to eye on all

Burma questions."[12] Following Burma's liberation and the end of the war, relations between them changed when disagreements arose over who had real control in Burma. Mountbatten wanted complete independence, while Dorman-Smith was in favor of dominion status. In this power struggle, Mountbatten wrote angrily, "Damn it all, I'm *governing* Burma —not he, whatever his title."[13] The main disagreement was over the Burmese National Army or BNA (similar to India's INA in Burma during the war), which had been set up by the Japanese to fight the British under Burma's independence leader, Aung San (1915-1947). At first they had fought for the Japanese, but realizing that the Japanese occupiers were worse than the British (and were also losing the war), they went over to the Allied side in March 1945 when Burma was being liberated. In the last part of the war, they machine-gunned their former allies "with the greatest cheerfulness" (to borrow a phrase from Sir John Keegan, the late British military historian), killing thousands of Japanese soldiers trying to cross monsoon-swollen rivers.

After Rangoon was liberated in May 1945, Slim met with Aung San at Mountbatten's request and was impressed with him. He later wrote that he "found him a realist, honest and patriotic" and "always felt, that with proper treatment, Aung San would have proved a Burmese Smuts."[14] (Referring to Jan Christiaan Smuts, the Boer commando leader who later cooperated with the British and became Prime Minister of South Africa.) However, in September 1945 Mountbatten took pains to point out to Aung San "the comparatively small share that his forces had had in the liberation of Burma, compared with the Karens, Chins, Kachins and Nagas."[15]

Even before Japan's surrender, Mountbatten had faced opposition for his support of Aung San from Dorman-Smith, from the Civil Affairs Service and from elements in the British government. It's a "what if" question whether things would have been better if Mountbatten had had complete control of the situation in Burma in 1945. In October 1945, Mountbatten turned over Burma from SEAC's control to Dorman-Smith, who retired in 1946 after becoming ill. Mountbatten felt that he had only completed half the job of rebuilding Burma and later said the only mistake in his life was "when he agreed to hand over the government of Burma before the time was ripe."[16]

After the fall of 1945, Mountbatten's job in Burma was over. In September 1946, Aung San became Prime Minister and began negotiations with Britain over Burmese independence. After the transfer of power, things in Burma grew worse as independence neared. In July 1947 Aung San and eight of his colleagues were assassinated, probably on the orders of U Saw, a former prime minister, whom the British had interned during World War II.[17] On January 4, 1948, Burma became independent and cut all ties with Britain, unlike India, which remained in the Commonwealth. In the end, Mountbatten's main goal of having Aung San rebuild Burma was crushed, along with the hope of a united and democratic Burma. Aung San's daughter, Aung San Su Kyi, is now the leader of the pro-democracy movement there.

MOUNTBATTEN AND THE RETURN OF THE FRENCH

While Mountbatten was dealing with Burma's postwar problems, his attention was also focused on what was then called French Indochina, now Vietnam, Laos, and Cambodia. At the Potsdam Conference in July-August 1945, it had been agreed that Indochina would be divided at the 16th parallel into two spheres of influence, Chinese in the north and British in the south, who would each take the Japanese surrender in their respective areas before the French returned. Like the division of Germany and Korea, the 16th parallel in Indochina would go from a temporary postwar boundary to a Cold War frontier in a short period of time.

Chiang sent troops to accept the surrender of Japanese forces in the north. The Chinese troops remained until 1946, when the French returned. Meanwhile, on September 2, 1945, Ho Chi Minh (c.1890-1969), the leader of the Communist Viet Minh, proclaimed the Republic of Vietnam in

Hanoi, quoting liberally from our own Declaration of Independence. On September 11, 1945 (the day before the Japanese surrender in Singapore), Mountbatten's SEAC took over Saigon with Major General Sir Douglas D. Gracey's 20th Indian Division, of 1,600 Gurkhas, Punjabis and Rajputs, as the British occupation force. Gracey overstepped the authority of his mandate by declaring martial law in Southern Indochina in late September 1945, as well as openly siding with the French trying to re-establish control over Saigon by ousting the local Vietnamese leaders. While Ho Chi Minh had established his government in the north, the Viet Minh were sending guerrillas to the south. To maintain order in this tense situation, Mountbatten had to use the Japanese troops who were still there (as well as in Singapore and the Dutch East Indies), since British control was so thin.

When Viet Minh guerrillas killed French civilians in Saigon on September 24, 1945, the Japanese troops did nothing, not because they were reluctant to turn against their fellow Asians, whom they had brutally occupied and killed during the war, but because they did not want to be seen as aiding the British and the French.[18] In October 1945, General Philippe Leclerc (1902-1947),[19] who had led the French 2nd Armored Division during the liberation of Paris in 1944, arrived with 1,000 men to re-establish French control in the south after the British left. After crushing the Viet Minh with the help of Japanese soldiers and air force, the south was "pacified" by early 1946. In January 1946, the British occupation of Saigon ended. In March, Indochina was taken out of SEAC's control. During this period, Mountbatten's policy was to play a minor role before the French returned to all of Indochina. In May 1946, Leclerc occupied Hanoi.

When Mountbatten was interviewed in the television program *The World at War* (1974), he said that before turning over Southern Indochina to the French, he had urged Leclerc to make friends with the local insurgents (Ho's Viet Minh) and the Vietnamese as well, by not restoring France's prewar colonial rule. Leclerc had told him that his instructions were to take over militarily and that's what he did. Leclerc's former A.D.C. told Mountbatten in 1972 that he remembered what Mountbatten had told Leclerc and "Leclerc had given long anxious thought and then had said that he was a soldier and he had come out to fight, and fight he would."[20] It will always be another "what if" question whether Mountbatten could have urged the French to negotiate or if the Viet Minh would have cooperated with them after the war.

Indochina had been an area of American interest during the war but was not a high priority. FDR had several ideas for postwar Indochina, such as making it a trusteeship, since he did not want the French to come back. However, there was no concrete American policy on Indochina in 1945. In January 1945, FDR told the new Secretary of State Edward R. Stettinius, Jr. (1900-1949) "I do not want to get mixed up in any Indochina decision ... Action at this time is premature."[21] Ziegler wrote that "Roosevelt in particular disliked the idea of handing Indochina back to the French, and even at the beginning of 1945 would go no farther than to say that it was a matter to be settled when the war was over."[22] In his book on the subject, modern historian D. Cameron Watt accused FDR of having "abandoned" the French in Vietnam and said he ordered the American commanders in China not to provide arms and ammunition to the French.[23] After FDR's death, President Truman did not consider Indochina a high priority until the Cold War began heating up after 1947.

MOUNTBATTEN AND THE RETURN OF THE DUTCH

The Dutch East Indies—today's Indonesia—presented problems similar to those in Indochina. Like the French, the Dutch were determined to reclaim their empire after the war, but they too needed British help. As in Indochina, the Dutch also faced a strong independence movement, led by Achmed Sukarno (1901-1970). As Ziegler wrote, "The Indonesians however, were more firmly entrenched than the Vietnamese; the Dutch weaker than the French. For both these reasons Mountbatten's problems were to prove more painful and protracted in Indonesia than Indochina."[24]

When the British occupied Java in September 1945 they expected little opposition from Indonesian nationalists. As in Indochina, Mountbatten's instructions were to take the Japanese surrender and liberate Allied POWs held in camps on Java. Although Mountbatten tried to have the Dutch, under Lieutenant-Governor Hubertus van Mook (1894-1965), negotiate with Sukarno, the Dutch refused because they considered Sukarno a traitor for having collaborated with the Japanese. When van Mook finally agreed to do so, his policy was rejected both by the Netherlands government and the Dutch ambassador in London, who considered any negotiation with Sukarno as treason.

During this time, General Sir Philip Christison (1893-1993), the British commander in Indonesia, was ordered to occupy the major cities on Java, but not the whole island, before the Dutch returned. This was met with hostility, both by the Dutch, who saw it as a betrayal, and by the Indonesians, who saw it as a way to thwart independence. Shortly after the British occupied the port of Surabaya, they faced savage, street-to-street fighting from Indonesian nationalists.[25] At Surabaya on October 30, 1945, the British commander, Brigadier Aubertin Mallaby (1899-1945) was assassinated by Indonesian nationalists during his tour of the city.[26] It was both tragic and ironic that a city that had survived World War II unscathed was destroyed immediately after the war. Indonesians later called it "the Hero City."

Mountbatten saw Dutch stubbornness as the cause of the problem, while London thought it was better to support them against Sukarno's nationalists. Edwina Mountbatten, who had helped save dying POWs, tried to raise the matter with the new British Labour government and felt confident that they wouldn't support the Dutch much longer. To the British, Indonesia was a low priority. The Americans were against British involvement in Indonesia; Ziegler wrote that "The Americans added to the pressure by ruling that American vessels not be used to ferry Indian troops from Bangkok to Java."[27] The U.S. did not feel it had to support the Dutch in Indonesia (unlike our support for the French in Indochina), because they were not as important allies as were the French.

In December 1945 the British persuaded the Dutch to agree on semi-dominion status, while the British forces kept most of Java peaceful. By the spring of 1946 things had temporarily settled down, with Sukarno withdrawing in favor of Dr. Sutan Sjahrir (1909-1966), another Indonesian leader. During this period, the Dutch began reoccupying Java without too many incidents. However, by the time Mountbatten left in April 1946, trouble was again brewing between the Dutch and the Indonesians. The war for Indonesian independence would last until 1949, when the Dutch finally admitted defeat in trying to re-establish their colonial empire.

Mountbatten and the End of SEAC

By May 1946, Mountbatten's immediate postwar role in SEAC was over. The end of the war was a frustrating time because of the lack of coordination after the Allied victory over Japan. Although Mountbatten sought to achieve a smooth transition of power in Southeast Asia, local politics and the returning colonial powers ended that immediate postwar hope. On the whole, however, Mountbatten did an excellent job restoring local law and order, maintaining temporary peace in Indochina and Indonesia (before the main conflicts broke out there after 1946), and laying the foundation for independence in Burma and Malaya. He wrote to General Baron Lionel "Pug" Ismay (1887-1965) that "I can honestly say that I shall have cleared up my theatre and completed my tasks, with the exception of what looks like a long-drawn-out but ever decreasing commitment in the Netherlands East Indies."[28] Mountbatten's role was necessarily short-term and he cannot be blamed because those countries went to hell in a handbasket after he departed. Burma became a military dictatorship and is only now slowly coming out of its long, dark night. Malaya went through civil war in the 1950s and Singapore left (or was pushed out) in 1965. Indonesia was also convulsed by civil war and dictatorship, and the sad history of Vietnam for the next thirty years is only too well known. Whether Mountbatten's policy of encouraging independence movements in those countries helped or hindered their development remains an open question.

By mid-1946, with the ending of SEAC, Mountbatten "was itching for a return to England and the Navy,"[29] which he loved. On May 30, 1946, he sailed from Singapore to attend the British Victory Parade in London on June 8. In a farewell signal to Air Chief Marshal Sir Keith Park (1892-1975), Allied Air Commander, South-East Asia (who had helped win the Battle of Britain in 1940), Mountbatten described SEAC's postwar period as "troubled days of peace," which summed it up perfectly.[30] SEAC, a wartime organization, was no longer needed. In November 1946, SEAC was disbanded because there was no longer any need for a joint command in Southeast Asia.

MOUNTBATTEN AFTER SEAC

Mountbatten became the last Viceroy of British India (and the first Governor-General of an independent India),[31] First Sea Lord, Chairman of the NATO Military Committee, and Chief of the Defence Staff (CDS). Along with Slim, he became a patron of the Burma Star Association, comprised of British veterans of the Burma Campaign. In 1968 he did a television series about his life and career that was entitled, not surprisingly, *The Life and Times of Lord Mountbatten*, which was later turned into a book.[32] During the 1970s Mountbatten gave several interviews in which he reminisced about his role in World War II. During one interview he wondered aloud to one American historian about what he called "the unreasonable attitude of Stilwell."[33]

Edwina, Countess Mountbatten of Burma, died suddenly in 1960. Mountbatten lived to a great age, celebrating his seventy-ninth birthday in June 1979. On Monday, August 27, 1979, near his summer home in the west of Ireland, he was assassinated by the Irish Republican Army (IRA) because he was a prominent member of the British Royal Family.

Several others, including one of his grandsons and a young Irish lad, also died when his boat was blown up by the IRA.

Admiral of the Fleet the Earl Mountbatten of Burma was given a state funeral in London on September 5, 1979, and is buried in Romsey Abbey, Hampshire. His most recent biographer Adrian Smith wrote simply that "Lord Louis died before his time was up."[34]

Mountbatten's obituary in *The New York Times* on October 28, 1979, included this reference to Stilwell:

> One of his chief antagonists was the American who served as his deputy commander, Lieut. Gen. Joseph W. Stilwell, widely known as Vinegar Joe, a sobriquet richly earned and maintained. To his face he called Lord Mountbatten "Limey Louis," while behind his back he was "Glamour Boy," "a welcher," a "loathsome limey" and "Curly Lashes." Toward the end of the war, however, Stilwell warmed somewhat toward Lord Mountbatten.[35]

As we have seen, this was not really true, but obituaries are the time to put aside hard feelings.

CHAPTER FIFTEEN

LEGACIES

Both Stilwell and Mountbatten were great leaders who led their forces to victory against the Japanese in World War II. They both had their faults, but that should not obscure their achievements. They were both self-promoters—Mountbatten more so than Stilwell—but just as even paranoids have enemies, even self-promoters have accomplishments.

Mountbatten was a naval officer who wanted to launch a seaborne offensive against the Japanese, which he could not do until after the end of the war because of the lack of landing craft and other naval resources. Despite that, he was able to lead the British back to Burma, Malaya, and Singapore, which was the goal of the whole campaign. However, even if Mountbatten and Stilwell had been the best of friends and had worked together better than they actually did, they still could not have reconciled the different war aims of the U.S. and the British in Southeast Asia before and after Japan's defeat.

Stilwell was an infantryman who fought a land war against overwhelming odds. The main mission of Stilwell and the U.S. in CBI was to help keep China supplied and in the war, which is what he did. Stilwell's main wartime achievement was to help keep China in the war through the Ledo and Burma Roads. He had completed that mission by the time he was recalled in 1944. It is amazing that he lasted as long as he did in CBI when one considers the enormous challenges of dealing with competing allies (the British) and often uncooperative allies (Chiang) and fighting with limited resources between 1942 and 1944. The main problem was that Stilwell in CBI did not have the resources or the strategic priority that the three main U.S. warlords, MacArthur, Eisenhower, and Nimitz, had in the Pacific and Europe. Although China fell to the Communists in 1949, which was after Stilwell's death, he probably could not have done much to change the situation, even had he lived.

Because of Stilwell's untimely death, his story, like Patton's, was written by other people who often had specific postwar agendas, both pro and con, especially as regards American policy towards China. White and Tuchman wrote glowing accounts of Stilwell, while Chennault and Wedemeyer were both very critical of him. A recent critic wrote that the "myth" of Stilwell's war against both the Japanese and Chiang by sympathetic historians has obscured Stilwell's faults until recently.[1] Apart from Tuchman's Pulitzer-prize winning biography in 1970, popular history largely passed Stilwell by. Unlike Patton, Stilwell never had a blockbuster movie made about him.[2] He was portrayed briefly at the beginning of *Objective Burma* (1945), which the British disliked because it showed the Americans retaking Burma almost single-handedly.

The importance of Stilwell's victories in North Burma was forgotten in the acrimonious atmosphere of the "who lost China?" debate in the U.S. after 1949. When *The Stilwell Papers*, which was edited by the journalist Theodore White, was published in 1948, Slim was very critical of it because he believed that it was rushed into print by Stilwell's widow and it did not accurately portray Stilwell's role in the war.[3] Stilwell became the target of harsh criticism after his death during the early Cold War after the Communist victory in China, especially among the China Lobby, which accused him of being "pro-Communist." This was nonsense. Stilwell was a Republican. A recent biographer of FDR wrote that "Stilwell was from a zealously Republican family and was not full of admiration for his own commander in chief, about whom some of his diary references were amusingly acidulous."[4]

After the 1950s, the pro-Stilwell view was revived by, among others, John Paton Davies and Barbara Tuchman, which then became the dominant view in the Stilwell historiography, especially among Americans. British historians such as the late Louis Allen took a decidedly different view, as did some Nationalist Chinese historians. To them Stilwell was simply an irascible Anglophobe who refused to work with Chiang and Chennault (the only American military official who got along with the very difficult Chiang—the only person who really lost China in 1949) to hold the Communists at bay while at the same time fighting off the Japanese. Chiang's recent biographer Jonathan Fenby wrote that "Vinegar Joe was the wrong man at the wrong time."[5] Although there is some truth in this statement as regards Stilwell and Chiang, it completely ignores Stilwell's accomplishments in North Burma.

Perhaps Frank McLynn put it best when he wrote, "Stilwell, a classic love-him-or-hate-him personality, seemed to make new enemies every day."[6] One might add, even in death. However, despite his faults as a diplomat, Stilwell was a fine soldier who served his country well and wanted the U.S. to maintain a strong role in East Asia during and after World War II. That it has certainly done.

Finally, what about Stilwell and his single-minded fixation on North Burma, even when the Japanese were threatening China itself in 1944? Even today, some historians of this period insist the Burma Campaign was a waste of men and resources: Churchill did not want it (apart from defending India), Chiang did not want it, and Mountbatten did not want it. Some claim that Stilwell only fought it to erase the humiliation of having to retreat from Burma in 1942.

With all due respect, this author disagrees. The Burma-Ledo Road from Burma and India to China was the only land supply route left. How else was the U.S. going to supply China and keep it in the war after 1942, if not through India or Burma? The alternative was the dangerous Hump air route over the Himalayas, which did not provide enough supplies. There was no sea supply route due to Japanese control of the coastal areas. Although it is true that Burma's location in the war against Japan was not as significant as that of the Philippines, Iwo Jima or Okinawa, the Allied engagement and defeat of the Japanese Army in Burma was significant for many reasons. It saved India from invasion, opened up a land route to China, destroyed some of the finest divisions in the Japanese Army, and enabled the British to reconquer Burma in 1945.

The authors of *Stilwell's Command Problems* said it best:

> Therefore, with the Assam line of communications bringing up supplies in a great stream, with the Hump airline at an all-time high in efficiency, with a pipeline delivering fuel to Myitkyina, and the Ledo Road soon to reach Myitkyina, the stage was set for the last act in China's wartime drama, in which the blockade would be broken. Thanks to Stilwell, his successors in 1945 would have the means to carry on the work he had almost single-handedly begun in 1942 in compliance with Marshall's order: "Support China!"[7]

Even more than Stilwell, Mountbatten was an important figure in the creation of modern Southeast Asia because he knew that World War II had created a new Southeast Asia, one that would no longer remain part of the European colonial empires. His time in SEAC was also the end of British Asia, even though the British came back in triumph, briefly, in 1945. His main wartime achievement was overseeing the victorious British campaign in Burma. Overall, he was able to smooth the transition from war to peace in Southeast Asia as best he could, with greater success in Burma and Malaya than in Indochina and Indonesia, where the French and the Dutch simply refused to leave. Even Burma and Malaya were wracked by strife, although Mountbatten cannot be blamed for Burma's slide into despotism and for the Malayan Civil War of the 1950s. After all, it was he who had urged a conciliatory policy in Burma. After becoming independent in 1948, it was taken over by a military dictatorship in 1962, and it took half a century for it to begin emerging from the shadows. In November 2012, President Barack Obama made the first state visit of an American President to Burma.

Mountbatten was also part of the larger issues that divided the United States and Great Britain with regards to how they viewed the region during and after the war. Churchill wanted to maintain the British Empire, while FDR did not. Although he was British, Mountbatten was more American in his liberal attitudes, especially in reaching out to nationalist groups in Southeast Asia in the aftermath of the Allied victory there. Most historians of the period after 1945 have concluded that Mountbatten's approach of encouraging a democratic nationalism was correct, but that it often came too late when dealing with the French and the Dutch. However, other historians have argued that many Americans (and by inference more liberal Britons like Mountbatten), both during and after the war, often assumed that Asian independence movements were more liberal and democratic than they actually were.[8]

The period between 1944 and 1946, between Stilwell's recall and death and the end of SEAC, was when World War II became the Cold War between the U.S. and the Soviet Union in Europe and Asia. Most of the American historiography on Southeast Asia after 1945 has focused on the U.S.'s eventual involvement in the Vietnam War and the mistakes that were made there from 1945 to 1975. Those mistakes began in earnest toward the end of the war. The official anti-colonialist policy on the one hand, and support for the French and Dutch on the other, during the early Cold War, sent a mixed message to the people of Southeast Asia. Washington publicly supported the concepts of anti-colonialism and self-determination in theory, but by 1947 growing concerns over the spread of communism led the Truman administration to conclude that "all Stalinists in colonial areas are nationalists."[9]

Mountbatten certainly had his faults, and modesty was never one of his virtues, but he was a charismatic leader who understood which way the winds of change were blowing, both during and after the war. He also understood the value of showmanship. One of his great achievements was to rally British and Commonwealth troops in Burma, which Stilwell did not do for either his Chinese or American troops, because he thought pep rallies for the troops did not really matter.[10] Max Hastings wrote, "Almost every man who saw Mountbatten descend from a plane to visit them, in dazzling naval whites or jungle greens, was cheered by the experience." [11] Also, unlike Stilwell, who opened himself up, perhaps too much so, in his diary, Mountbatten was very circumspect in his diary and in the official report he wrote after the war. It was as if he were writing for posterity. Finally, Stilwell never had a chance to rewrite history in the way Mountbatten attempted to do for the rest of his long life. Stilwell, even more than Mountbatten, died before his time was up.

Because Burma became independent in 1948 and the British Empire in Southeast Asia ended in the 1950s and 1960s, the British gradually forgot about the war in Burma, where they had fought to regain what they had lost in 1942. Perhaps it was easy to forget because, for the British, even victory could not conceal what Bayly and Harper called "this sudden and dramatic humiliation of an old and complacent supremacy—the British Empire in Asia."[12] As Jackson wrote, "By 1945 Britain's capacity to sustain a global imperial role had been greatly diminished. War imperialism worked for the moment but worked against the longer retention of Empire."[13] In *The World at War*, Laurence Olivier described the British victory and return to Southeast Asia in 1945 as "an empty victory."[14] Had Britain's Eastern Empire not ended as suddenly as it did, British and Burmese students today, in both London and Rangoon (Yangon), might be studying Slim's victory over the Japanese on the Mandalay Plain, where he planned and executed a classic double-envelopment of an entire Japanese army.

In the novel *The Division of the Spoils*, the last part of *The Raj Quartet* by the late British novelist Paul Scott, who served in the British Indian Army during the war, British Army Intelligence Sergeant Guy Perron describes the final phase of the British Empire in India, and some of the old prewar British attitudes about it, at the end of the war in 1945: "Can't the fool [British Major, later Lt. Col. Ronald Merrick, the nasty, racist, and social climbing protagonist] see that nobody in the [civil and military British ruling] class he aspires to belong has ever cared a damn about the empire and that all that God-the-Father-God-the-*raj* was a lot of insular middle-and lower-middle-class * * *."[15] (Before 1947, all British residents in India from the Viceroy on down were called the *Rajiv*.) Although this passage refers to India before independence and partition in 1947 (it was an independent nation in all but name by 1945), it also reflects the ending of the British Empire in South Asia and Southeast Asia in the decade after World War II.

Perhaps Wedemeyer, who was both Stilwell's nemesis and his successor, best summed up the Stilwell-Mountbatten wartime relationship when he wrote the following in his memoirs:

> The British had been unco-operative, stuffy, and seemingly resentful of the American Commander who was striving to get on with the fighting. . . Stilwell's unfortunate experience in that complex area was not all of his own making. I think Mountbatten realized this and was sincere, although unsuccessful, in his effort to create mutual trust and friendly cooperation. However, he was by training, experience, and background the exact antithesis of Vinegar Joe, a typical old-fashioned Indian fighter, reveling in the rugged life of a field soldier.[16]

Stilwell was a soldier, not a diplomat, while Mountbatten was a courtier and a diplomat, as well as a naval officer. They were different kinds of men pursuing different and often contradictory national policies. Whatever their differences, both Stilwell and Mountbatten helped to win the war for the Allies in Southeast Asia. Perhaps that is their best legacy.

Epilogue

London, October, 1946

On October 9, 1946, Mountbatten addressed the Royal United Services Institution in London, making his first overall statement on his role in SEAC. Field-Marshal Alanbrooke was the chairman of the meeting. In his remarks Mountbatten paid tribute to Stilwell, saying in part:

> The American Commanding General in China, Burma and India was that great character Lieut.-General Joseph W. Stilwell, popularly known as "Vinegar Joe." In addition to commanding the American land and air forces in China, Burma and India, he was the Chief of Staff to the Supreme Commander of the China Theatre, Generalissimo Chiang-Kai-Shek. He was now to receive a third appointment as Deputy Supreme Allied Commander, South-East Asia. I wondered how he would solve the problem of filling three such high level posts, but he did so in his usual unexpected manner by filling none of them himself. He appointed deputies and asked to be allowed to do a fourth job which was much neared his heart, namely, to command the Northern Combat Area in Burma. I should like to pay tribute to him as a Corps Commander and, later, as the equivalent of an Army Commander in the field.[1]

Stilwell died three days later.

APPENDIX A

STILWELL AND THE SIEGE OF MYITKYINA:
A HISTORIOGRAPHICAL DEBATE

For more than seventy years, there has been a historiographical debate over Stilwell's strategy during the siege of Myitkyina in the Burma Campaign. According to Tuchman, Stilwell wanted the honor of capturing Myitkyina to go to the Chinese before the monsoon, and errors in decision-making made the situation worse for three months.[1] Other historians, including Romanus, Sunderland, and Nathan Prefer, said it was national pride that made Stilwell reject the 36th Division in the campaign to take Myitkyina during the spring and summer of 1944.[2] However, these views are disputed by British historian and Stilwell biographer David Rooney:

> It was Stilwell's paranoia about Myitkyina that coloured the decision. It was not national pride but his own pride and Anglophobia which dictated it. He was not going to see his great prize captured by any Limey unit. This disgraceful decision led to eleven weeks of vicious fighting and countless deaths.[3]

British historian Frank McLynn concurs, writing that "Worst of all, Stilwell was offered the fresh troops of the British 36th Division, but pigheadedly turned down the offer, as he did not want to be beholden to the Limeys; Myitkyina, in his view, had to be an all-American operation."[4] British historian Louis Allen, himself a veteran of the Burma Campaign, wrote that "The British 36th Division (Festing) was ready to fly in— as it later did, to take the Railway Corridor—and could have been put into Myitkyina airfield at short notice. The men were fit and ready for battle . . . [but] it was unthinkable for Stilwell to call on the British to pick his chestnuts out of the fire." [5]

According to a Central Intelligence Agency (CIA) Historical Review comment in 1993: "At this time Stilwell could probably have got the 36th British division to take Myitkyina, but having, in his own words, 'burned up the Limeys' by his coup in seizing the airfield, he insisted on keeping it an American-Chinese show."[6]

However, other accounts call into question whether Stilwell rejected the 36th Division out of hand or whether it simply was not ready. U.S. Army Colonel (later General) Ernest F. Easterbrook (1908-1989), Stilwell's executive assistant (and also his son-in-law), who was at Myitkyina, wrote in his diary entry for May 23, 1944, "Plan for 36th to come in about July."[7] On June 9, 1944, at a staff conference in Assam, plans were made for the 36th Division to be sent by road and rail to Ledo and then to Myitkyina. According to the conference minutes, "It was agreed that 36 Ind Div could not be supplied by air until aircraft could be released from IMPHAL operations."[8] The next day, June 10, 1944, Stilwell wrote in his diary "Arranged with Festing for 36th [Division].[9] In fact, Mountbatten ordered the 36th Division to Myitkyina *after it had rested and refitted,* and it arrived at Mogaung, southwest of Myitkyina, on July 7, 1944, to relieve the Chindits. This suggested that the division was not ready to jump into the Myitkyina fight on short notice. [10]

When it finally arrived, U.S. Army Major Fred Eldridge, who was Stilwell's public relations officer, wrote that "The Boss [Stilwell] was very pleased with both the division and Major General Francis Wogan Festing."[11] According to Festing's biographer, British historian Lyall Wilkes, ["T]he Division represented an international team effort skillfully held together by Festing. Not only was he directly under the command of General Stilwell, but his air supplies and his tactical air support was solely in the hands of the USA 10th Air Force."[12]

General Stilwell's grandson, John Easterbrook, recounts the following tale of when Stilwell finally met Festing:

> David Quaid [a U.S. Army combat photographer] was on his way to JWS' [Stilwell's] headquarters at Shaduzup when COL Cannon

gave him a ride in a jeep. David ended up in the back with Brigadier Francis Festing, commanding the British 36th Division. Festing was 6'4" or thereabouts, so it was cozy in the jeep. When they arrived at Shaduzup David saw Festing approach JWS who was very intent while doing some paperwork. Festing drew himself up to his full height, snapped to attention, complete with stomping of a foot and almost knocking himself out with a salute to his right temple. Then, in a loud voice: "Brigadier Festing, 36th Division! At your service. Suh! What are your orders, Suh?" JWS looked up at him and simply said "Take Taungni."[13]

Festing's biographer wrote that "[T]he Chindits would remain in the area only until 36th Division, refitting at Shillong in Assam, would arrive in the area and be placed under Stilwell's command when the over-exhausted Chindits would be flown out." [14]

All of this suggests that Stilwell may have decided to use the 36th Division after all, perhaps when he realized he was in for a long siege, or that the division could not have been airlifted into Myitkyina any sooner. It is important to remember that the siege of Myitkyina was taking place at almost the same time as the British were fighting for their lives at Kohima and Imphal and were stretched thin in supplying Stilwell's forces. There were only so many aircraft available to fly in the 36th Division—thousands of men—and Slim desperately needed aircraft to resupply his men at Kohima and Imphal.

In any event, the sources noted above—either primary source records from the time or the recollections of field officers who were actually there—are entitled to as much if not more weight than the opinions of historians long after the fact. Those sources call into question McLynn's, Rooney's, and Allen's claim that the sole reason Stilwell did not use the 36th Division at the beginning of the siege was due to his Anglophobia. However, regardless of why it happened, according to McLynn, "the failure to take Myitkyina town after the walkover victory at the airfield turned into one of Stilwell's greatest humiliations ... Fighting in the monsoon with demoralised troops against a determined and well-entrenched enemy, Stilwell had to endure weeks of mental turmoil."[15]

Ziegler wrote in the same vein: "The feat was a remarkable one, though made less useful by his [Stilwell's] failure to complete the job by taking the town."[16] Slim wrote that "The long-drawn-out siege of Myitkyina was a great disappointment to Stilwell, and it was at this period that he really lived up to his nickname, Vinegar Joe."[17]

Perhaps we should give Slim the last word on this, because he, better than most, understood the demands of being a field soldier and a field commander. He wrote that:

> Actually it would have been wiser to take the whole of the Chindits out then; they had shot their bolt. So, too, for that matter had the Marauders, who a little later packed in completely. Both forces, Chindits and Marauders, had been subjected to intense strain, both had unwisely been promised that their ordeal would be short, and both were asked to do more than was possible.[18]

APPENDIX B

JOSEPH W. STILWELL, "THE BRITISH" (1935), STILWELL PAPERS, HOOVER INSTITUTION, STANFORD UNIVERSITY "THE BRITISH"

The British are smugly complacent about their own superiority. They have such "healthy" interests—like riding horses. All other people's interests are stupid or "unhealthy" or queer. (If they are different, they MUST be queer.) They make such a noise about it too. "Just imagine – he doesn't dress for dinner. Why a Britisher* dresses for dinner even in Uganda." It's supposed to maintain the prestige of the Superior Man and shows his superiority concretely. They can't realize that it makes an impression only on the shallowest of minds and that anyone with any brains at all can see through them. The Britisher can't be himself—he must be, or rather appear to be, one of the Clives or Rhodes who helped build that grandest work of man, the British Empire. Granted that they have integrity, are more or less incorruptible and coldly business-like for Jolly Old England, they spoil it all for anyone else by making such a blare about it. They have a monopoly on all the virtues and they carry this critical attitude into the smallest details of life. Imagine so and so not having a tubbing in the morning! O, you don't ride? My God, what a bounder! Swimming? Handball? What excruciatingly stupid things to do. What, no tea? Imagine not serving tea! Why all Britishers do it.

If you wonder why Americans are not hot for the grand old British Empire, you should listen to anyone of a thousand British lecturers who make tours through the U.S., taking our money, and in return make the most biting and acid criticism of everything American. Money-lovers, provincials, unpolished, crude, uneducated, lawless, Different from the British. Enough to damn anyone. And most of them are so stupid that they believe they get away with it,—that they thus stamp their superiority on us all. They can't realize that they are meeting with true politeness,— he and his opinions are really of so little consequence to the average American that they listen merely out of curiosity and pay no more attention than to perhaps a joke of it on the [golf] links.

If Great Britain had sense enough to send around a few people who were modest, had a sense of humor, and could see just a little good in someone else, what a hit she would make in the United States. And what a lot of concrete good it would do her.

* In the 1930s and 1940s, the term *Britisher* was used for both British natives or any British subjects. Today it is mainly used in India, where it become popular during the British Raj period.

Figure 11. Chart of South-East Asia Command Structure

Appendix C

South-East Asia Command Structure, 1943-1944

(Key Figures are highlighted)

COMBINED CHIEFS OF STAFF

BRITISH CHIEFS OF STAFF   AMERICAN CHIEFS OF STAFF

SACSEA (Supreme Allied Commander South-East Asia)

(Mountbatten)

DEPUTY SACSEA----------COMMANDING GENERAL------ CHIEF OF STAFF TO
(Stilwell)   CBI THEATER   CHIANG KAI-SHEK

(Stilwell)   (Stilwell)

CHIEF OF STAFF

DEPUTY CHIEF OF STAFF

(Wedemeyer)

CINC EASTERN FLEET------CINC ALLIED LAND FORCES----ALLIED AIR CINC

(Giffard)

CINC EAST INDIES FLEET

GENERAL OFFICER COMMANDING

14TH ARMY

(Slim)

A Note on the Sources

There have been fewer books on the Burma Campaign than on the other more famous theaters in World War II such as the European and Pacific, but the amount that has been written is still voluminous. Fortunately, both historians and general readers have the benefit of Stilwell's and Mountbatten's own diaries, *The Stilwell Papers* (1948), edited by the late American journalist Theodore White, and *The Personal Diary of Admiral the Lord Louis Mountbatten, 1943-1946* (1988), edited by Mountbatten's official biographer, the British historian Philip Ziegler. These are the places to start for an understanding of the Stilwell-Mountbatten relationship. However, while Stilwell's diary entries suffer from being too acerbic, Mountbatten's are often rather bland, and give the impression they were written very much with an eye for the future. Both diaries refer only briefly to or omit entirely descriptions of key events.

The best complete biographies of Stilwell and Mountbatten, respectively, are *Stilwell and the American Experience in China, 1911-1945* (1970) by Barbara Tuchman, and *Mountbatten* (1985) by Philip Ziegler. Tuchman in particular was very pro-Stilwell and reflected his critical attitude toward Chiang. Recent scholarship has taken a more nuanced view of their relationship and of Chiang himself. However, in fairness to her, she wrote during the Vietnam War, before the full horror of Mao's Cultural Revolution became widely known in the West. Tuchman is kinder to Mountbatten than Ziegler is to Stilwell, who wrote that he "despised every race except his own" (Ziegler, 243), which, given Stilwell's repeated and documented praise of Chinese soldiers, is untrue.

Stilwell's Command Problems (1956) by Charles F. Romanus and Riley Sunderland, the second volume in an official U.S. Army three-volume series on Stilwell's mission to China and on the U.S. Army in CBI, is a solid account. *Stilwell's Personal File* (1976), by the same authors, is a collection of Stilwell's wartime papers in five volumes. The American historian Nathan Prefer contributed to the discussion with *Vinegar Joe's War: Stilwell's Campaigns for Burma* (2000). Donovan Webster's *The Burma Road* (2003) is a highly readable account by a journalist who actually went there to see for himself what it was like. More recently the British historian David Rooney wrote a short book with the provocative title *Stilwell the Patriot: Vinegar Joe, the Brits and Chiang Kai-Shek* (2005), which gives a generally favorable portrayal.

Most of the literature about Stilwell discusses his complex and antagonistic relationship with Chiang. These include the following: *Way of a Fighter: The Memoirs of Claire Lee Chennault* (1949); *General Stillwell in China, 1942-1944: The Full Story* (1972), by Chin-tung Liang; and *The Generalissimo: Chiang Kai-shek and the Struggle for Modern China* (2009), by Jay Taylor. These books are highly critical of Stilwell and favorable towards Chiang. Also very critical are *The Wars for Asia, 1911-1949* (2012) by S.C.M. Paine and *Chiang Kai-shek: China's Generalissimo and the Nation He Lost* (2003) by Jonathan Fenby. Paine is the more highly critical—her Stilwell is the exact opposite of Tuchman's heroic figure—while Fenby's critique seems more in sorrow than in anger: in his view, Stilwell, whatever his other virtues, was simply the wrong man for the job.

A notable exception to the barrage of criticism is John Paton Davies's *Dragon by the Tail: American, British, Japanese, and Russian Encounters with China and One Another* (1972), a memoir by Stilwell's chief political advisor, who was there at the time and was able to observe what was actually happening.

Mountbatten lived much longer than did Stilwell, so he was able to give a full account of his stewardship in SEAC, starting with his address to the Royal United Services Institution on October 9, 1946, published the following month as "The Strategy of the South-East Asia Campaign" (*Journal of the Royal United Services Institution*, November 1946). His *Report to the Combined Chiefs of Staff by the Supreme Allied Commander, South-East Asia* (1951) is a detailed account of the campaign.

In 1968 Mountbatten, always the consummate showman, did a television series about his life and career, which was entitled (not surprisingly) *The Life and Times of Lord Mountbatten*, and which was adapted into a book in 1970.

Richard Hough's *Mountbatten: A Biography* (1981) is a solid, readable account of Mountbatten's life, but gives only a cursory treatment of his wartime relationship with Stilwell, implying that they were closer than they actually were. The most recent treatment, *Mountbatten: Apprentice War Lord* (2010) by Adrian Smith, recounts Mountbatten's life up to his appointment as Supreme Allied Commander Southeast Asia and provides valuable insights into his character. Also of great value is the late Sir Ian McGeoch's biography of Mountbatten, entitled *The Princely Sailor: Mountbatten of Burma* (1996). Like Mountbatten himself, McGeoch was a serving officer in the Royal Navy who rose to the rank of admiral. (Surprisingly, among all these fine works, there is no published partial biography of Mountbatten that is devoted exclusively to his role as Supreme Allied Commander.)

Defeat into Victory (1956) by Slim is one of the great military memoirs and a good introduction to the Burma Campaign. *Allies of a Kind: The United States, Britain and the War against Japan, 1941-1945* (1978) by Christopher Thorne, is an excellent discussion of the wartime Anglo-American relationship in East Asia and Southeast Asia. *Burma: The Longest War, 1941-45* (1984) by Louis Allen, is an overall look at the Burma Campaign from the British and Japanese perspectives. More recently, *Forgotten Armies: The Fall of British Asia, 1941-1945* (2005), by Christopher Bayly and Tim Harper, looks at the Burma Campaign in the larger context of the end of British Asia. The most recent major work is *The Burma Campaign: Disaster into Triumph, 1942-1945* (2011), by Frank McLynn, which focuses on the foursome of Slim, Mountbatten, Stilwell, and Wingate. That book is the closest there is to a dual biography of Stilwell and Mountbatten.

Two excellent summaries of the relevant literature were done by Eugene L. Rasor, an American historian and bibliographer, in 1998: *The China-Burma-India Campaign, 1931-1945: Historiography and Annotated Bibliography,* and *Earl Mountbatten of Burma, 1900-1979: Historiography and Annotated Bibliography.*

Finally, the two main archival sources are the Stilwell Papers, Hoover Institution, Stanford University, and the Mountbatten Papers, Special Collections, Hartley Library, University of Southampton, UK. Although the Stilwell Papers have not been digitized, an excellent finding aid has been digitized and it is available online for general public access. Stilwell's complete diaries are also available online. The Mountbatten Papers have been digitized and are available online upon registration with the Special Collections, Hartley Library.

ENDNOTES

NOTES TO PROLOGUE

1. Adrian Smith, "Mountbatten Goes to the Movies: Promoting the Heroic Myth Through Cinema," *Historical Journal of Film, Radio, and Television* 26, no. 3 (2006): 395-416.

2. Philip Ziegler, ed., *Personal Diary of Admiral the Lord Louis Mountbatten* (London: Collins, 1988), 21.

3. Stilwell Diary, October 27, 1943, Hoover Institution Archives: The World War II Diaries of General Joseph W. Stilwell (1941-1945), 155. Neither Stilwell nor Mountbatten gave the name of the movie. http://media.hoover.org/sites/default/files/documents/1943Stilwell20120515.pdf

The Hoover Archives also has Stilwell's Diaries online from 1900-1939 and 1945-1946.

4. Theodore H. White, ed., *The Stilwell Papers* (1948; repr., New York: Da Capo Press, 1991), 236. His close friends called Mountbatten "Dickie." Stilwell referred to him as "Louis" (when they were on friendly terms).

5. Ibid.

NOTES TO INTRODUCTION

1. British military historian Alex Danchev wrote a paper titled "Very Special Relationship: Field Marshal Sir John Dill and General George Marshall," which explored the wartime bond between them and how it shaped the Anglo-American relationship during World War II. (Paper read by Professor Danchev at the Tenth Annual Meeting of the Society for Historians of American Foreign Relations, George Washington University, Washington, D.C., August 2-4, 1984.)

2. When the author visited Britain with his family in 2010, and cleared British immigration, the customs officer, seeing that we were Americans, declined to inspect our luggage and remarked "Come right in—special relationship!"

3. Andrew Roberts, *A History of the English-Speaking Peoples Since 1900* (New York: Harper Collins Publishers, 2006), 1.

4. Martin Gilbert, *Churchill and America* (New York: Free Press, 2005), 436. Churchill's mother, Lady Randolph Churchill, nee Jennie Jerome, (1854-1921) was American, born in Brooklyn.

5. During the war, the Allies used the term *War against Japan* and the *Pacific Theater* in the U.S. vs. "The Pacific War." After 1941, the Japanese used the term *Greater East Asia War.*

6. Some Americans joked that SEAC stood for "Save England's Asian Colonies." Adrian Smith, *Mountbatten: Apprentice War Lord* (London: I.B.Tauris, 2010), 3.

7. Stilwell despised Chiang. Almost the only thing they had in common, apart from the war against Japan, was their dislike of the British. Stilwell's dislike appears to have been mostly personal, while Chiang's was political. For Chiang, Britain was the great imperialist power that had seized Hong Kong in 1841, demanded and received trade concessions from China, and which had generally humiliated the Chinese for over 100 years.

8. The country has been called "Myanmar" since 1989, but throughout this book it is referred to as "Burma," which was its name in the 1940s.

9. Rangoon is now called Yangon, and is no longer the capital, which was moved to a new location at Naypyidaw in 2005.

10. "He was in fact as fragile as steel wire." See Barbara Tuchman, *Stilwell and the American Experience in China 1911-1945* (New York: Macmillan Company, 1970), 4.

11. Theodore White, ed., *The Stilwell Papers* (New York: Da Capo Press, 1991), 230. References to "*Stilwell Papers*" refer to General Stilwell's

wartime diaries and letters, which were edited by the late Theodore White, and which were originally published in 1948, while references to "Stilwell Papers, Hoover Institution" refer to the General Joseph W. Stilwell Archives at the Hoover Institution, Stanford University, Stanford, California.

12. Tuchman, *Stilwell*, 38, 50.

13. Frank McLynn, *The Burma Campaign: Disaster into Triumph, 1942-1945* (New Haven: Yale University Press, 2011), 47.

14. Generals Dwight D. Eisenhower (1890-1969) and George C. Marshall (1880-1959), the U.S. Army Chief of Staff, were the main exceptions, happily as it turned out for the joint Anglo-American war effort.

15. Ian Kikuchi, "Far-Flung and Forgotten: Britain and the War in Burma," *Despatches: The Magazine of the Imperial War Museum* (Summer 2010).

16. Ashley Jackson, *The British Empire and the Second World War* (London: Continuum International Publishing Group, 2006), 7.

NOTES TO CHAPTER ONE

1. Tuchman, *Stilwell*, 12.

2. Ibid., 15.

3. Tuchman, *Stilwell*, 42, 140. The house is named "Llanfair," which means "Church of St. Mary" in Welsh.

4. Ibid., 24-25.

5. Ibid., 38.

6. Ibid., 99.

7. Tuchman, *Stilwell*, 58. Tuchman mentioned Stilwell's attitudes during World War I about British officers, but little about his attitudes toward the British Empire and British imperialism.

8. Ibid., 52.

9. Ibid.

10. David Reynolds, *Rich Relations: The American Occupation of Britain, 1942-1945* (London: HarperCollins, 1995), 31-43. This fine book covers the development of the Anglo-American alliance during and after World War II.

11. Kathleen Burk, *Old World, New World: Great Britain and America from the Beginning* (New York: Grove Press, 2007), 465-466; Alexander De Conde, *A History of American Foreign Policy* (New York: Charles Scribner's Sons, 1963), 498-500; J. Bartlett Brebner, "Canada, The Anglo-Japanese Alliance and the Washington Conference," *Political Science Quarterly* 50, no. 1 (March 1935): 45-58.

12. De Conde, *A History of American Foreign Policy*, 499.

13. Ibid.

14. De Conde, *A History of American Foreign Policy*, 514-515.

15. Burk, *Old World*, 461.

16. Ibid., 440. Burk is an American historian who teaches in Britain.

17. De Conde, *A History of American Foreign Policy*, 497.

18. Alistair Horne, "In Defense of Montgomery," *No End Save Victory: Perspectives on World War II* (New York: Berkeley Books, 2001), 478. This was also pointed out by the British historian David Reynolds in *Rich Relations: The American Occupation of Britain, 1942-1945*.

19. Edward M. Coffman, *The Regulars: The American Army, 1898-1941* (Cambridge: The Belknap Press of Harvard University Press, 2004), 414.

20. Ibid., 268-269.

21. Tuchman, *Stilwell*, 61.

22. "The British," Stilwell Papers, Hoover Institution, Box/Folder 91: 11. Stilwell's grandson, John Easterbrook, told the author "those exact words

appear in Stilwell's handwriting in his unnumbered 1935 diary" (E-mail from John Easterbrook to the author, August 21, 2012). A retyped version with corrections of that paper is attached as Appendix B. The text of that paper appears in Stilwell's online diary dated May 11, 1935 (Stilwell Diary, Hoover Institution, 1935-6-7, Unnumbered). To the best of the author's knowledge, that paper has never been cited in any previously published work.

23. Tuchman, *Stilwell*, 158.

24. Tuchman, *Stilwell*, 198. He tallied up six good qualities, including courage, and 26 bad ones!

25. Tuchman, *Stilwell*, 204.

26. David Rooney, *Stilwell the Patriot: Vinegar Joe, the Brits and Chiang Kai-shek*(London: Greenhill Books/ Pennsylvania: Stackpole Books, 2005), 37.

27. Ibid.

28. Jay Taylor, *The Generalissimo: Chiang Kai-shek and the Struggle for Modern China* (Cambridge, MA: Belknap Press of Harvard University Press, 2009), 191.

29. Tuchman, *Stilwell*, 225.

30. Ibid., 125; Stilwell Papers, 4-5.

31. *Stilwell Papers*, 2.

32. John Keegan, *Six Armies in Normandy: From D-Day to the Liberation of Paris* (New York: Penguin Books, 1982), 23.

33. Ibid.

34. Eisenhower supported that strategy very strongly in 1942. See Dwight D. Eisenhower, *Crusade in Europe* (Garden City, N.Y.: Doubleday & Company, Inc., 1948), 27-28.

35. According to both Stilwell's diary and Tuchman, Drum hemmed and hawed so much that Secretary of War Henry Stimson (1867-1950) decided he would not be the right man for the job (*Stilwell Papers*, 26; Tuchman, 242).

36. *Stilwell Papers*, 25.

37. Tuchman, *Stilwell*, 153.

38. Taylor, *The Generalissimo*, 192.

39. Ibid.

40. Jonathan Fenby, *Chiang Kai-shek: China's Generalissimo and the Nation He Lost* (New York: Carroll & Graf Publishers 2003), 370.

41. Tuchman, *Stilwell*, 173.

42. *Stilwell Papers*, 44, 50.

43. Ibid., 62.

44. Eric Larrabee, *Commander in Chief: Franklin Delano Roosevelt, His Lieutenants, and Their War* (New York: Harper & Row, 1987), 517.

45. Alan Warren, *Burma 1942: The Road from Rangoon to Mandalay* (London: Continuum International Publishing Group, 2011), 169.

46. Ibid., 168.

47. *Stilwell Papers*, 31. Sir Archibald Wavell was Commander-in-Chief, India, from 1941 to 1943, and later the next to last Viceroy of India before Mountbatten from 1943 to 1947.

48. Ibid., 32.

49. Frank McLynn, *The Burma Campaign: Disaster into Triumph, 1942-1945* (New Haven: Yale University Press, 2011), 7-8.

50. Ibid., 6-8.

51. Christopher Bayly and Tim Harper, *Forgotten Armies: The Fall of British Asia, 1941-1945* (Cambridge: The Belknap Press of Harvard University Press, 2005), 13, 310, 170, 180. Aung San was also the father of Aung San Suu Kyi (b. 1945), the Burmese Nobel Peace Prize laureate and leader of the National League for Democracy (NLD).

52. Christopher Thorne, *Allies of a Kind: The United States, Britain, and the War against Japan, 1941-1945* (New York: Oxford University Press, 1978), 6. FDR might have reflected that it was the Burmese who had had "a terrible time" under British rule since 1885.

53. Richard Overy, *Why the Allies Won* (New York: W.W. Norton & Company, Inc., 1995), 325.

54. Field Marshal Viscount Slim, *Defeat into Victory: Battling Japan in Burma and India, 1942-1945* (1956; repr. with new Introduction, New York: Cooper Square Press, 2000), 118-119.

55. Rooney, 63.

56. S.C.M. Paine, *The Wars for Asia, 1911-1949* (Cambridge: Cambridge University Press, 2012), 199.

57. Warren, *Burma 1942*, 215.

58. Ibid., 219, 233.

59. Donovan Webster, *The Burma Road: The Epic Story of the China-Burma-India Theater in World War II* (New York: Harper Perennial, 2004), 39.

60. Warren, *Burma 1942*, 224.

61. Tuchman, *Stilwell*, 300; Warren, *Burma 1942*, 224.

62. *Stilwell Papers*, 106.

63. Slim, 120.

64. In December 1942, there were 17,000 American personnel in the CBI Theater (Warren, *Burma 1942*, 238).

65. Paine, *The Wars for Asia, 1911-1949*, 198.

66. Warren, *Burma 1942*, 245.

67. Winston S. Churchill, *The Second World War: The Hinge of Fate*, *The Second World War: Closing the Ring*, and *The Second World War: Triumph and Tragedy*, 3 vols. (Boston: Houghton Mifflin Company, 1950, 1951, 1953), *passim*.

Notes to Chapter Two

1. Adrian Smith, *Mountbatten: Apprentice War Lord* (London: I.B. Tauris & Co. Ltd, 2010), 29.

2. Ibid.

3. Philip Ziegler, *Mountbatten: A Biography* (New York: Alfred A. Knopf, 1985), 36.

4. Giles MacDonogh, *The Last Kaiser: The Life of Wilhelm II* (New York: St. Martin's Press, 2000), 392.

5. Ziegler, *Mountbatten, passim*; Richard Hough, *Edwina: Countess Mountbatten of Burma*(New York: William Murrow and Company, Inc., 1984).

6. Ibid., 72.

7. Richard Hough, *Mountbatten: A Biography* (New York: Random House, 1981), 61.

8. Reynolds, *Rich Relations*, 35.

9. Ziegler, 229, 338; Philip Ziegler, ed., *Personal Diary of Admiral the Lord Louis Mountbatten* (London: Collins, 1988), 226-227.

10. William Manchester, *The Last Lion: Winston Spencer Churchill: Vol. II, Alone, 1932-1940* (Boston: Little, Brown and Company, 1988), 639-40, 654-55.

11. Quoted in Ziegler, *Mountbatten*, 135.

12. Quoted in Ziegler, *Mountbatten*, 135-136.

13. "The British," Stilwell Papers, Hoover Institution, Stanford, Box/ Folder 91: 11. Mountbatten, although he had a sense of humor and could see the good in others, was not "modest."

14. Ziegler, *Mountbatten, passim*.

15. *Personal Diary of Admiral the Lord Louis Mountbatten*, 111, fn. 1. (Hereafter cited as "Mountbatten Diary")

16. For a good description of American policy in this period, see Conrad Black, *Franklin Delano Roosevelt: Champion of Freedom* (New York: Public Affairs, 2003), 601-648.

17. According to John Paton Davies, Jr., Stilwell's political advisor, FDR's comment to Davies and Stilwell in December 1943 was "Dickie Mountbatten, impulsive kid." John Paton Davies, Jr., *Dragon by the Tail: American, British, Japanese and Russian Encounters with China and One Another* (New York: W.W. Norton & Company, Inc., 1972), 310.

18. Ziegler, *Mountbatten*, 150. This visit took place in September 1941, three months before the Japanese attack on December 7.

19. Ziegler, *Mountbatten*, 176-77. Mountbatten finally became First Sea Lord—his late father's post—in 1955.

20. Ziegler, *Mountbatten*, 155.

21. Ziegler, *Mountbatten*, 156.

22. Mountbatten conversation with Richard Hough, circa 1972-1978, quoted in Hough, 150.

23. Ibid.

24. Eisenhower, *Crusade in Europe*, 67.

25. Ibid.

26. See Ziegler, Chapter 14.

27. Reynolds, *Rich Relations,* 128.

28. Reynolds, *Rich Relations, passim.*

29. Reynolds, *Rich Relations,* 129-130.

30. Sir Ian McGeoch, *The Princely Sailor: Mountbatten of Burma* (London: Brassey's Ltd, 1996), 259.

31. Ziegler, *Mountbatten,* 221.

32. McLynn, *Burma Campaign,* 164.

NOTES TO CHAPTER THREE

1. Burk, *Old World, New World,* 485.

2. Ibid., 497

3. Reynolds, *Rich Relations,* 43.

4. Jonathan Dimbleby, *Destiny in the Desert: The Road to El Alamein —The Battle That Turned The Tide* (Profile Books, 2012), 176. This was Churchill's second meeting with FDR from December 1941-January 1942 to decide Allied strategy after Pearl Harbor.

5. Quoted in Burk, *Old World, New World,* 504. The complete "Open Letter" is contained in the *Life* Archives.

6. Roy Jenkins, *Churchill: A Biography* (New York: Plume, 2001), 702.

7. Ibid.

8. Dimbleby, xvi.

9. In *General Ike: A Personal Reminiscence* (New York: Free Press, 2003), Eisenhower's son, the late historian John Eisenhower, wrote that although Monty was a brilliant British general, his tactlessness caused

more damage in Anglo-American relations in Europe than any other major Allied figure in 1944-1945 (142).

10. Jackson, *The British Empire and the Second World War*, 4, 5-6.

11. Tuchman, *Stilwell*, 309; McLynn, *Burma Campaign*, 440-442, 446.

12. John Masters, *The Road Past Mandalay: A Personal Narrative* (New York: Harper & Brothers, 1961), 153-154. Masters was a former Gurkha officer serving with the Chindits.

13. Quoted in Thorne, *Allies of a Kind*, 221.

14. Ibid. Most of his governorship was spent in exile in India.

15. Quoted in Paul M. Angle, ed., *By These Words* (New York: Rand McNally & Co., 1954), 510.

16. Thorne, *Allies of a Kind*, 61. Atlee became prime minister in 1945.

17. Ibid., 102.

18. Quoted in Jackson, *The British Empire in the Second World War*, 9-10.

19. Memorandum from Davies to Gauss, "The China and South Asia Theaters: Some Political Considerations," November 22, 1943. Stilwell Papers, Hoover Institution, Box/Folder 35:9.

20. Davies, "American Policy in Asia," February 19, 1944, Stilwell Papers, Hoover Institution, Box/Folder 35:16.

21. Memorandum from Davies to Cordell Hull, "Memorandum for the Secretary of State," March 10, 1944, Stilwell Papers, Hoover Institution, Box/Folder 35:19.

22. Davies, "Anglo-American Cooperation in East Asia," November 15, 1943, Stilwell Papers, Hoover Institution, Box/Folder 35:8.

23. Davies, *Dragon by the Tail*, 310.

24. *Mountbatten Diary*, 104.

25. *Mountbatten Diary*, 104.

26. E. Bruce Reynolds, *Thailand's Secret War: The Free Thai, OSS and SOE during World War II* (Cambridge: Cambridge University Press, 2005), 237.

27. Entry for June 15, 1944. Stilwell Papers, Hoover Institution, Box/Folder 38:3. Other entries on the same date suggest the words "my own people smack me down" refer to General Claire Chennault, who commanded the USAAF in China, whom Stilwell detested.

28. Letter from Eldridge to Col. Stanley Grogan, February 22, 1944, Stilwell Papers, Hoover Institution.

29. Thorne, *Allies of a Kind,* 715. Thorne described it as a "Pax Americana . . . with the help of China."

30. Memo from Eldridge to Stilwell, March 19, 1944, in Riley Sunderland and Charles F. Romanus, eds., *Stilwell's Personal File: China-Burma-India 1942-1944* (Washington, D.C.: Scholarly Resources Inc., 1976), 1535. (Hereafter cited as *Stilwell's Personal File*)

31. Ibid. That statement could have been the epitaph for the Stilwell-Mountbatten relationship.

32. Hanson Baldwin, "Confusion Over Burma Warfare: American and British Differences Over Strategy and Chinese Backwardness Are Among Factors," *New York Times*, April 12, 1944.

33. Edmond Taylor, *Richer by Asia* (Boston: Houghton Mifflin Company, 1964), 29-33, 34, 38.

34. *Mountbatten Diary*, 215. That is precisely what happened when Burma became independent in 1948.

35. *Mountbatten Diary*, 215.

36. Ronald H. Spector, *In the Ruins of Empire: The Japanese Surrender and the Battle for Postwar Asia* (New York: Random House Trade Paperbacks), 2008, 73-74.

37. Masters, *The Road Past Mandalay*, 146-47. Masters served in the British commando force known as the "Chindits." Stilwell, as will be discussed below, did not like the Chindits and the feeling was mutual. (Masters moved to America after the war and became a well-known writer.)

38. Thorne, *Allies of a Kind*, 452.

NOTES TO CHAPTER FOUR

1. Eisenhower took a particular liking to Mountbatten (McLynn, 191-192; Ziegler, 247-248; Eisenhower, *Crusade in Europe*, 67). Mountbatten reciprocated Ike's friendship, even inviting him to his country estate at Broadlands. See Norman Gelb, *Ike and Monty: Generals at War* (New York: William Morrow and Company, 1994), 103.

2. Drafts of "Campaign in Burma," March 10- June 1, 1942, Stilwell Papers, Hoover Institution, Box/Folder 21:9.

3. "Notes from Somervell-Arnold-Dill Mission, 1943," Stilwell Papers, Hoover Institution, Box/Folder 19:6.

4. Charles F. Romanus and Riley Sunderland, *Stilwell's Command Problems* (Washington, D.C.: Officer of the Chief of Military History, Department of the Army, 1956), 5. (Hereafter cited as *Stilwell's Command Problems*)

5. "Report of the Combined Chiefs of Staff Relating to the Implementation of Assumed Basic Undertakings and Specific Operations for the Conduct of the War, 1943-1944," May 25, 1943, Stilwell Papers, Hoover Institution, Box/Folder: 25: 25. Chiang renamed the Ledo Road the "Stilwell Road" in 1945.

6. *Stilwell Papers*, 205.

7. Lord Moran, *Churchill at War 1940-45* (New York: Carroll & Graf, 2002), 116-117. First published in the UK as *Churchill: The Struggle for*

Survival 1940-1965. Although in the form of a diary, the book was really a compilation of notes made at the time and later added to.

8. "Final Report of the Combined Chiefs of Staff to the President and Prime Minister," May 25, 1943, Stilwell Papers, Hoover Institution, Box/Folder: 25: 23.

9. Winston S. Churchill, *Memoirs of the Second World War: Closing the Ring* (Boston: Houghton Mifflin Company, 1951), 92-93.

10. McLynn, *Burma Campaign,* 191.

11. Smith, *Mountbatten: Apprentice War Lord,* 292.

12. Churchill, *Closing the Ring,* 89.

13. Mountbatten, "The Strategy of the South-East Asia Campaign." *Journal of the Royal United Services Institution* 91 (November 1946): 482.

14. Vice-Admiral the Earl Mountbatten of Burma, *Report to the Combined Chiefs of Staff by the Supreme Allied Commander South-East Asia, 1943-1945* (New York: Philosophical Library, 1951), 3.

15. Edmond Taylor, *Richer by Asia,* 2nd ed. (Boston: Houghton Mifflin Company, 1964), 31.

16. Stephen R. Taaffe, *MacArthur's Jungle War: The 1944 New Guinea Campaign* (Lawrence: University Press of Kansas, 1998), *passim.*

17. Ziegler, *Mountbatten,* 231.

18. *Mountbatten Diary,* 54.

19. Ziegler described the reaction of the British Chiefs of Staff as "acquiescent if unenthusiastic" (Ziegler, 220).

20. Max Hastings, *Retribution: The Battle for Japan, 1944-45.* New York: Alfred A. Knopf, 2008, 65.

21. Ibid., 66.

22. Ibid.

23. Ibid., 220.

24. Dennis, *Troubled Days of Peace*, 27.

25. Smith, *Apprentice War Lord*, 4, 308.

26. A chart of the SEAC command structure is attached as Appendix C.

27. Wesley Frank Craven and James Lea Cate, eds., *The Army Air Forces in World War II: Volume Four: The Pacific, August 1942 to July 1944* (Washington, D.C.: Office of Air Force History, 1953), 453.

28. Churchill, *Closing the Ring*, 560-1.

29. *The Good Earth* (1937) and *Dragon Seed* (1942). Given the times, the main roles were played by Caucasian actors, including Katharine Hepburn.

30. From 1939-1944, the Clippers took off from Treasure Island in San Francisco Bay, the site of the 1939-1940 World's Fair, the Golden Gate International Exposition, and then a Navy base from 1941-1997. Ironically, the pre-Pearl Harbor themes of the Fair were the "Pageant of the Pacific" and "Pacific Unity." The Japanese pavilion was a public relations, *i.e.,* propaganda, exercise by Japan, and was the largest of the Pacific and foreign pavilions at the Fair. The local Chinese community represented China at the Fair because the Chinese government could not participate due to the war with Japan.

31. For a discussion of British policy toward China, see Thorne, *Allies of a Kind*, 554-563. Thorne noted that, over Chiang's protest, the Japanese surrendered Hong Kong to the British, not the Chinese, in 1945 (558). Ibid., 293; *Mountbatten Diary*, 291.

32. Churchill, *Closing the Ring*, 560-1.

33. Thorne, 332. Thorne also noted there was some British support for China, based in part upon "considerable commercial opportunities for Britain in China after the war" (196).

34. Ziegler, *Mountbatten,* xiii.

35. Eric Morris, "Uncommon Commoner," *No End Save Victory: Perspectives on World War II* (New York: Berkeley Books, 2001), 605.

36. "Chapter XII: Plans and Events, Fall 1943," page 869, *Stilwell's Personal File: China-Burma-India 1942-1944.* This plan is recited in detail because it lays out exactly what the Americans, British, and Chinese hoped to accomplish in 1944.

37. Tuchman, *Stilwell,* 340. He came to CBI to serve as Theater G-2 (Intelligence Officer) in his father's headquarters in November 1942. He was promoted to full colonel in 1944.

38. Letter dated August 17, 1943, Mountbatten Papers, South East Asia Command, 1943-6, Special Collections, Hartley Library, University of Southampton, UK. Docref=MB1/C137/4/2. http://www.southampton.ac.uk/archives/cataloguedatabases/mbintro.html

39. E. Bruce Reynolds, *Thailand's Secret War: The Free Thai, OSS and SOE During World War II* (Cambridge: Cambridge University Press, 2005), 57.

40. Stilwell Papers, Hoover Institution, Box/Folder: 35:15; Memorandum dated October 27, 1943, Stilwell Papers, Hoover Institution, Box/Folder 36:16.

41. *Stilwell's Personal File,* "Chapter XII: Plans and Events," Fall 1943, 870.

42. Stilwell Papers, Hoover Institution, Box/Folder 35:15.

43. Memorandum dated October 27, 1943, Stilwell Papers, Hoover Institution, Box/Folder 36:16.

44. Ibid.

45. The Y-Force was so designated because it was being formed in China's southwestern Yunnan Province (*Stilwell's Command Problems,* 4-5).

46. Ibid., 57.

47. However, American troops had also fought in the Philippines from 1899-1902.

48. His grandfather Warren Delano had made a fortune in the opium trade, both importing it into China in the 1840s and exporting it to the U.S. during the Civil War. See Geoffrey C. Ward, *Before the Trumpet: Young Franklin Roosevelt, 1882-1905* (New York: Harper & Row, 1985), 87-89.

49. Eric Larrabee, *Commander in Chief: Franklin Delano Roosevelt, His Lieutenants, and Their War* (New York: Harper & Row, 1987), 568.

50. Ibid., 541

NOTES TO CHAPTER FIVE

1. *Stilwell Papers*, 230.

2. Ibid., 235.

3. *Mountbatten Diary*, 12. Ziegler added a footnote that "Presumably because he thought it [*i.e.*, the photo op] would strengthen his credit with Chiang Kai-shek."

4. *Stilwell Papers*, 234.

5. *Mountbatten Diary*, 13.

6. "Peanut" was Stilwell's derisive term for Chiang, which he used throughout his diaries. Stilwell later wrote that Marshall told him FDR didn't like Stilwell calling Chiang "Peanut" (*Stilwell Papers*, 245).

7. *Stilwell Papers*, 234.

8. Mountbatten, *Report to the Combined Chiefs of Staff*, 5.

9. Hough, *Mountbatten: A Biography*, 176-177. Hough's source for this rather colorful statement, complete with the American slang expression "you bet," was a conversation with Mountbatten sometime during the 1970s, some thirty years after the events took place.

10. *Stilwell Papers*, 234.

11. Letter from Mountbatten to Stilwell, October 26, 1944, Stilwell Papers, Hoover Institution.

12. Tuchman, *Stilwell*, 394.

13. Ziegler, *Mountbatten*, 244.

14. Hough was a British naval historian who also wrote a biography of Edwina Mountbatten.

15. *Stilwell Papers*, 233-234; Tuchman, 394-395.

16. Fenby, *Chiang Kai-shek*, 405.

17. *Stilwell's Personal File*, vol. 3, 879.

18. *Stilwell's Personal File*, 1262.

19. Ibid., 1131.

20. Letter to Stilwell from Major General Thomas T. Handy, Assistant Chief of Staff, U.S. Army, December 23, 1943, *Stilwell's Personal File*, vol. 3, 1230

21. *Stilwell Papers*, 238-239. Stilwell's diary, as always, was more colorful in its language than was Mountbatten's, who wrote very much with an eye for posterity.

22. Stilwell to Hearn, undated, probably December 1943, *Stilwell's Personal File*, vol. 3, 1234.

23. Keegan, *Six Armies in Normandy*, 31.

24. *Stilwell Papers*, 237.

25. Wedemeyer was a very able man, but it did not hurt his career in the slightest that his father-in-law, General Stanley Embick, was a close associate of General Marshall. John J. McLaughlin, *General Albert C. Wedemeyer: America's Unsung Strategist in World War II* (Philadelphia: Casemate Publishers, 2012), 19-20.

26. See Thomas J. Fleming, "Chapter 1: The Big Leak," *The New Dealers' War: FDR and the War within World War II* (New York: Basic Books, 2001).

27. Keith E. Eiler, "The Man Who Planned the Victory: An Interview with Gen. Albert C. Wedemeyer," *American Heritage* Magazine 34, no. 6 (October/November 1983).

28. Smith, *Apprentice War Lord*, 195-202; Ziegler, *Mountbatten*, 179-184. In his own memoirs Wedemeyer described Mountbatten as "John the Baptist laying the groundwork for the great strategic evangelist, Winston Churchill." Albert C. Wedemeyer, *Wedemeyer Reports!* (New York: Henry Holt & Company, 1958), 139.

29. Wedemeyer, *Wedemeyer Reports!*, 248.

30. Ibid., Chapter 19.

31. Ibid., 254.

32. Wedmeyer, *Wedemeyer Reports!*, 250.

33. *American Heritage, op. cit.*

34. Wedemeyer, *Wedemeyer Reports!*, 108; Smith, *Apprentice War Lord*, 195.

35. Wedemeyer, *Wedemeyer Reports!*, 108.

36. Letter from Mountbatten to Beaverbrook, February 4, 1944, Mountbatten Papers, University of Southampton, #Docref=MB1/C20/7.

NOTES TO CHAPTER SIX

1. Stalin did not attend because the Soviet Union was not at war with Japan until 1945.

2. *The Army Air Forces in World War II*, vol. 4, 495.

3. *Stilwell Papers*, 245.

4. Ibid., 246.

5. *Mountbatten Diary*, 34. He wrote "how impossible the Chinese are to deal with" (36).

6. Ibid., 32-33.

7. *Stilwell Papers*, 247. Another dig at Wedemeyer's comparative youth.

8. Churchill, *Closing the Ring*, 328.

9. *Stilwell's Personal File*, 1046.

10. Ibid.

11. "Part I, North Burma Campaign, October 1943-August 1944," Stilwell Papers, Hoover Institution, Box/Folder: 17: 2.

12. Larrabee, *Commander in Chief,* 554.

13. In his diary Stilwell recounted a conversation with FDR at Cairo, in which FDR said, "You know *I* have a China history" (*Stilwell Papers*, 251) (italics in original).

14. Ibid., 511.

15. Tuchman, *Stilwell,*241.

16. David B. Woolner, Warren F. Kimball, David Reynolds, eds., *FDR's World: War, Peace, and Legacies* (New York: Palgrave Macmillan, 2008), 70.

17. Larrabee, *Commander in Chief,* 578. Larrabee was a Stilwell fan, as both his book *Commander in Chief* and his introduction to the 1991 edition of *The Stilwell Papers* show, but he also quotes Secretary of War Henry Stimson in support of this argument.

18. Churchill, *Closing the Ring*, 328. Stilwell wrote in his diary after Cairo that, as far as Chiang was concerned, "Nothing is possible without a big amphibious operation. He [Chiang] doesn't know what a big amphibious operation is, but unfortunately Mountbatten was honest about it. So now

that it is on a reduced scale, he [Chiang] screams. It is fatal to promise anything" (*Stilwell Papers*, 265).

19. Taylor, *The Generalissimo*, 261; *Mountbatten Diary*, 39, fn. 1; *Stilwell's Command Problems*, 65-66; McLynn, *Burma Campaign*, 224-225; Chin-tung Liang, *General Stilwell in China, 1942-1944: The Full Story* (St. Jamaica, N.Y.: John's University Press, 1972), 161.

20. *Stilwell Papers*, 265.

21. Taylor, *The Generalissimo*, 253.

22. Tuchman, *Stilwell*, 407.

23. Taylor, *The Generalissimo*, 254.

24. *Stilwell's Personal File*, vol. 3, 1047.

25. *Stilwell Papers*, 340.

26. "File 109, Letters, lists, memoranda, notes, printed matter, and reports relating to the general administration of the China-Burma-India Theatre, 1942-1944," Stilwell Papers, Hoover Institution, Box/Folder: 28:25-29.

27. *Stilwell's Personal File*, 1321.

NOTES TO CHAPTER SEVEN

1. Wesley Frank Craven and James Lea Cate, eds. *The Army Air Forces in World War II: Volume IV: The Pacific: Guadalcanal to Saipan, August 1942 to July 1944* (Chicago: University of Chicago Press, 1983), 514.

2. Tuchman, *Stilwell*, 488-89; *The Army Air Forces in World War II: Volume Five: The Pacific: Matterhorn to Nagasaki, June 1944 to August 1945*, 79-80.

3. Ziegler, *Mountbatten*, 251.

4. See *The World at War*.

5. Slim, *Defeat into Victory,* 178.

6. Ziegler, *Mountbatten,* 252.

7. Richard Frank, *Downfall: The End of the Imperial Japanese Empire* (New York: Penguin Books, 1999), 163. These Indians became indirect victims of the Japanese, among the roughly 17 million Asians who died under Japanese rule from 1931 to 1945.

8. The INA also fought a civil war in Burma against the Indian Army, so the term is appropriate, and Ziegler used it to describe the INA in his biography of Mountbatten (Ziegler, 257).

9. Ibid., 52; Thorne, *Allies of a Kind,* 233. Regarding Bose and the INA, see Leonard Gordon, *Brothers Against the Raj,* and Marshall J, Getz, *Subhas Chandra Bose.*

10. Letter from Christianson to Mountbatten, February 26, 1944, Mountbatten Archives, #Docref=MB1/C49/1

11. National Archives of Singapore, on-line archives, http://www.s1942.org.sg/s1942/indian_national_army/memorial.htm

12. Mountbatten, *Report to the Combined Chiefs of Staff,* 5.

13. Bill Henry, "By the Way," *Los Angeles Times,* April 20, 1944.

14. It is hard to understand today just how scarred the British commanders were by their heavy losses in World War I.

15. Napoleon at Rochefort, July 15, 1815, quoted in John Bartlett, *Familiar Quotations* (Boston: Little, Brown and Company, 1955), 400.

16. Winston S. Churchill, *The Second World War: The Hinge of Fate,* 94.

17. Ziegler, *Mountbatten,* 278. Ziegler also notes that the British Chiefs of Staff had recommended a Ceylon HQ for SEAC in June 1943, before SEAC was formally established.

18. Bayly and Harper, *Forgotten Armies,* 376.

19. McLynn, *Burma Campaign*, 338-39; *Mountbatten Diary*, 99-103.

20. Ibid.

21. WRNS, or "WRENS," was the acronym for "Women's Royal Naval Service." Mountbatten's daughter Patricia, now Countess Mountbatten of Burma, was a WREN during the war.

22. *Mountbatten Diary*, 99-103.

23. Letter from Mountbatten to Alan Brooke, December 6, 1943, Mountbatten Papers, University of Southampton, #Docref=MB1/C50/9.

24. Quoted in Fred Eldridge, *Wrath in Burma: The Uncensored Story of General Stilwell and International Maneuvers in the Far East* (Garden City, N.Y.: Doubleday, 1946), 263. Eldridge was an officer on Stilwell's public relations staff.

25. Even Slim, another field soldier who did not indulge in creature comforts for himself, thought Stilwell's manner of living was too primitive (Slim, *Defeat into Victory*, 256).

26. http://www.tcm.com/tcmdb/title/576919/The-Battle-of-China/notes.html

27. Stilwell Diary, Hoover Institution, January 15, 1945, p. 270.

28. *Objective Burma!* starred Errol Flynn, who at least was Australian by birth.

29. *Roundup*, September 24, 1942.

30. *Roundup*, April 11, 1946.

31. Field-Marshal, Viscount William Slim, *Defeat into Victory* (New York: Cooper Square Press, 2000), 190.

32. *Mountbatten Diary*, 176.

33. *Mountbatten Diary*, 241.

34. Ibid.

35. http://www.colonialfilm.org.uk

36. Ian Kikuchi, "Far-Flung and Forgotten: Britain and the War in Burma," *Despatches* (Summer 2010), 25. *Objective Burma!* was banned in Britain in 1945 and was not generally released until 1952.

NOTES TO CHAPTER EIGHT

1. Burma, which was a separate British colony after 1937, had the misfortune to be located between the warring powers, and next to Thailand, which was officially a Japanese ally. In that way Thailand was similar to Hungary, Romania, and Bulgaria, German Axis allies in the Balkans."

2. Ziegler, *Mountbatten*, 250.

3. "It's a Lovely Day Tomorrow: Burma 1942-1944," *The World at War* (Thames Television, 1973, 1974). The jungle war in Burma and India "made up in ferocity what it lacked in scale." This was the only episode of the 26-part series devoted to the Burma Campaign.

4. Ziegler, *Mountbatten*, 268.

5. Thorne said the Japanese planned "autonomy for Burma" (Thorne, *Allies of a Kind*, 52).

6. Ibid.

7. "Burma: The Richest of Poor Countries," *National Geographic* (July 1995) map, 78.

8. Ibid.

9. *Stilwell Papers*, 267.

10. Tuchman, *Stilwell*, 416.

11. McLynn, *The Burma Campaign*, 234.

12. Warren, *Burma 1942*, 213.

13. Brig. Gen. Vincent J. Esposito, ed., *The West Point Atlas of American Wars: Vol. II, 1900-1953* (New York: Frederick A. Praeger, Publishers, 1959), Map 142.

14. *The Pacific War Online Encyclopedia*, "Arakan," 1.

15. Stilwell Papers, Hoover Institution, Box/Folder: 28:1.

16. McLynn, 350; *The West Point Atlas of American Wars*, Map 142. Lungling had been taken by the Japanese, retaken by the Chinese, taken again by the Japanese, and finally retaken once and for all by the Chinese in 1944.

17. *Forgotten Armies: The Fall of British Asia, 1941-1945*, 379.

18. *The Army Air Forces in World War II*, vol. 4, 500-501.

19. Ibid., 502-503.

20. *The Pacific War Online Encyclopedia*, Arakan, 3.

21. *The Pacific War Online Encyclopedia*, Arakan, 3.

22. *Personal Diary of Admiral the Lord Louis Mountbatten*, 66.

23. Slim, *Defeat into Victory*, 246-47.

NOTES TO CHAPTER NINE

1. *Stilwell Papers*, 275-276.

2. Ibid., 290.

3. *Mountbatten Diary*, 80.

4. *Mountbatten Diary*, 114.

5. *Mountbatten Diary*, 54.

6. *Stilwell Papers*, 275. "Walla-walla" means "meeting or conference" in Hindi (Ibid., 278).

7. Tuchman, *Stilwell*, 424; Message from Stilwell to Major General Daniel Sultan, U.S. Deputy Commander, CBI, May 27, 1944, *Stilwell's Personal File*, vol. 4, 1747.

8. Slim, 205-207; Mountbatten, *Report to the Combined Chiefs of Staff*, 8.

9. Moser, 119; McLynn, 244. Neither Stilwell, Mountbatten, nor Slim recount this conversation in their respective diaries or memoirs, or give the exact date it took place, but it was probably in January 1944. Tuchman suggests it took place in early January 1944 (Tuchman, 427-428).

10. *Mountbatten*, 58. Ziegler was Mountbatten's "official" historian and edited his diary.

11. Mountbatten, *Report to the Combined Chiefs of Staff*, 31.

12. This comment was another shot at Wedemeyer, who was known as a strategic planner.

13. *Stilwell*, 278-279. Robert Clive, "Clive of India," 1st Baron Clive (1725-1774), established British control over Bengal in 1757, with a relatively small force, although more than 123 men.

14. Wedemeyer, *Wedemeyer Reports!*, 258.

15. McLynn, *Burma Campaign*, 245-246.

16. Wedemeyer, *Wedemeyer Reports!*, 258; McLynn, *Burma Campaign*, 244-245.

17. Ibid. This dispute caused the flare-up at the January 31, 1944, conference. However, Mountbatten later wrote he told Stilwell to "occupy Northern Burma, up to and including the Mogaung-Myitkyina area" (Mountbatten, *Report to the Combined Chiefs of Staff*, 34).

18. *Stilwell Papers*, 239, 258, 277.

19. Wedemeyer, *Wedemeyer Reports!*, 258; Mountbatten called Wedemeyer "one of the originators of the 'sea' as opposed to the 'road' strategy. . .," Mountbatten, *Report to the Combined Chiefs of Staff*, 31.

20. McLynn, *Burma Campaign*, 246. Also, see Thorne, *Allies of a Kind*, at 409-410 for a discussion of AXIOM.

21. Churchill, *Closing the Ring*, 569-575. Radio messages to and from Stilwell around this time reflected U.S. concerns that Mountbatten should move quickly in North Burma. See *Stilwell's Personal File*, vol. 4, 1387, 1393, 1413-1420.

22. Churchill, *Closing the Ring*, 573. Of course he liked it—he had sent Mountbatten out to Southeast Asia to retake Singapore by sea, not to retake Burma by land.

23. McLynn, *Burma Campaign*, 246-247. This was yet another instance of Marshall protecting Stilwell.

24. *Stilwell's Command Problems*, 169; Radio from Marshall to Stilwell, March 3, 1944, *Stilwell's Personal File*, vol. 4, 1444-1445.

25. *Stilwell's Command Problems*, 169.

26. Mountbatten, *Report to the Combined Chiefs of Staff*, 31.

27. Thorne, *Allies of a Kind*, 453-454; McLynn, *Burma Campaign*, 248-249.

28. John MacCormac, "A Rift Over Burma Put to Roosevelt: Stilwell and Mountbatten Are Divided on Method and Speed in Operations," *New York Times*, March 3, 1944.

29. Hanson W. Baldwin, "Confusion over Burma Warfare: American and British Differences over Strategy and Chinese Backwardness are Among Factors," *New York Times*, April 12, 1944.

30. *Stilwell's Command Problems*, 170. This was not true, as later events demonstrated.

31. Quoted in *Stilwell's Command Problems*, 170.

32. Letter from Mountbatten to Stilwell, March 18, 1944, *Stilwell's Personal File*, vol. 4, 1525.

33. Radio from Marshall to Stilwell, March 25, 1944, Ibid., 1546, 1554. U.S. Lieut. General Daniel Sultan was Stilwell's deputy theater commander.

34. *Stilwell Papers*, 305 (italics supplied).

35. Wedemeyer, *Wedemeyer Reports!*, 257. According to Thorne, Wedemeyer changed his mind later and actually supported the land route to China (Thorne, 452). Even at the time Wedemeyer wrote Churchill that "[T]he most realistic justification for a land route across Upper Burma is the fact that such a route would clearly facilitate the installation, maintenance, and protection of vital pipelines to support our air effort from bases in China" (June 15, 1944, quoted in Wedemeyer, *Wedemeyer Reports!*, 265).

36. Radio from Sultan to Stilwell, February 21, 1944, *Stilwell's Personal File*, vol. 4, 1413-1414. Marshall wanted a road, a pipeline, and a "buffer zone" in North Burma to protect the Hump airway (*Stilwell's Command Problems*, 200-201).

37. Letter from Mountbatten to Ismay, February 3, 1944, Mountbatten Papers, #Docref=MB1/C147/27.

38. Wesley Frank Craven and James Lea Cate, eds., *The Army Air Forces in World War II: Volume Five: The Pacific, June 1944 to August 1945* (Washington, D.C.: Office of Air Force History, 1953), 204.

39. *The Army Air Forces in World War II: Volume Four*, 458.

40. Letter dated January 3, 1944 from Mountbatten to Arnold, Mountbatten Papers, #Docref=MB1/C11/17. (The Mountbatten Papers sometimes refer to him in the third person.); *Stilwell's Command Problems*, 83-84.

41. *Stilwell's Command Problems*, 99.

42. Ibid.

43. Ibid.

44. "The Arakan-Imphal Problems in 1944 (Draft monographs relating to British operations)," Stilwell Papers, Hoover Institution, Box/Folder 28:1.

45. *Stilwell Personal File*, 1503.

46. Radio from Sultan to Stilwell, February 21, 1944, *Stilwell's Personal File*, vol. 4, 1413-1414; *The West Point Atlas of American Wars: Vol. II, 1900-1953*, Map 142.

47. "The Tactical Picture in 1944 (Draft monographs relating to British operations)," Stilwell Papers, Hoover Institution, Box/Folder: 28:1.

NOTES TO CHAPTER TEN

1. Ziegler, *Mountbatten*, 269.

2. Bayly and Harper, *Forgotten Armies*, 371.

3. Draft monograph relating to British operations, "The Tactical Picture in 1944," Stilwell Papers, Box/Folder: 28:1.

4. Francis Pike, *Hirohito's War: The Pacific War, 1941-1945* (London: Bloomsbury Publishing, 2015), 692.

5. Ian Kikuchi, "Far-Flung and Forgotten: Britain and the War in Burma," *Despatches* (Summer 2010), 22-26. The article said the famous Kohima Epitaph memorializes an important battle in a campaign that has been largely forgotten in Britain. (*Despatches* is the magazine of the Imperial War Museum in London.)

6. Draft monograph relating to British operations, "The Arakan-Imphal Problems in 1944," Stilwell Papers, Hoover Institution, Box/Folder: 28:1.

7. Morris, "Uncommon Commoner," 609-610.

8. Churchill, *Closing the Ring*, 570.

9. https://nagalandjournal.wordpress.com/2013/03/16

10. In 1941 during the German invasion of Greece, ANZAC forces of the British Commonwealth forces held off the German forces at Thermopylae before they retreated and were evacuated.

11. *The Army Air Forces in World War II: Volume Four*, 509-510.

12. Webster, *The Burma Road*, 293.

13. Message from Arnold to Mountbatten, July 27, 1944, Mountbatten Papers, #Docref=MB1/C62/26. The portion in quotation marks is Arnold's own words.

14. Slim, 256; David Rooney, *Stilwell the Patriot: Vinegar Joe, the Brits and Chiang Kai-Shek*. (London and Pennsylvania: Greenhill Books and Stackpole Books, 2005), 182.

15. *Stilwell Papers*, 75. This was high praise from Stilwell, who was not lavish with it.

16. Slim, *Defeat into Victory*, xii. The Chinese called Stilwell "the old gentleman" (*Stilwell Papers*, 274).

17. Slim, *Defeat into Victory*, 29, 103; *Stilwell Diary*, 274-275. Stilwell told Mountbatten that "Chinese troops can stand up under conditions that would stop white troops" (Memorandum from Stilwell to Mountbatten, October 27, 1943. Stilwell Papers, Hoover Institution, Box/Folder 36:16).

18. At the same time, Slim, in common with most generals, did write his memoirs after the war. Military historians have ranked his book, *Defeat into Victory*, with the *Personal Memoirs of Ulysses S. Grant*, as the two best memoirs ever written by generals in English.

19. This was the name of Oliver Cromwell's army during the English Civil War.

20. McLynn, *Burma Campaign*, 327.

NOTES TO CHAPTER ELEVEN

1. Wesley Frank Craven and James Lea Cate, eds., *The Army Air Forces in World War II: Volume One: Plans and Early Operations, January 1939 to August 1942* (Washington, D.C.: Office of Air Force History, 1953), 500.

2. Peattie, Mark, Edward Drea, and Hans van der Ven, eds. *The Battle for China: Essays on the Military History of the Sino-Japanese War of 1937-1945* (Stanford, CA: Stanford University Press, 2011), 372.

3. Tuchman, *Stilwell*, 416.

4. *The West Point Atlas of American Wars: Vol. II, 1900-1953*, Map 142.

5. *The Battle for China*, 373.

6. *The Pacific War Online Encyclopedia*, http://pwencycl.kgbudge.com/M/y/Myitkyina.htm

7. Message from Sultan to Marshall, April 16, 1944, Stilwell Papers, Hoover Institution.

8. *The Army Air Forces in World War II*, vol. 4, 500-501.

9. Ibid.

10. McLynn, *The Burma Campaign*, 350-351.

11. *The Army Air Forces in World War II*, vol. 4, 517.

12. *Stilwell Papers*, 296, Diary entry for May 17, 1944. The capitalization is in the original.

13. *Mountbatten Diary*, 111.

14. McLynn, *Burma Campaign*, 348.

15. Churchill, *Closing the Ring*, 570.

16. Slim, *Defeat into Victory*, 273.

17. Eldridge, *Wrath in Burma*, 264-265.

18. Quoted in Ziegler, *Mountbatten*, 274-275.

19. Stilwell Diaries, Hoover Institution, http://www.hoover.org/library-and-archives/collections/east-asia/featured-collections/joseph-stilwell

20. McLynn, *Burma Campaign*, 348.

21. Tuchman, *Stilwell*, 416-418; 453.

22. The 36th Division, which was part of the British Indian Army, was commanded by Major General Francis Festing, whom Stilwell had earlier complimented as "the only Limey who wants to fight!" (Ziegler, *Mountbatten*, 247; Wedemeyer, *Wedemeyer Reports!*, 257; Eldridge, *Wrath in Burma*, 269-270). Stilwell had also paid the same compliment to both Slim and Mountbatten.

23. Stilwell's original diary has the following entry for May 22: "Q: Ask of 36th Br. Div? No." (Stilwell Diaries, Hoover Institution, http://www.hoover.org/library-and-archives/collections/east-asia/featured-collections/joseph-stilwell)

24. *Stilwell's Command Problems*, 233.

25. *Stilwell's Personal File*, vol. 4, 1728.

26. Message from Giffard to Mountbatten, May 28, 1944, Stilwell Papers, Hoover Institution.

27. *Stilwell's Command Problems*, 240. The Appendix contains a detailed discussion of the controversy over Stilwell's decision not to use the 36th Division at Myitkyina until much later in the siege.

28. http://ww2db.com/battle_spec.php?battle_id=286

29. *The West Point Atlas of American Wars: Vol. II, 1900-1953*, Map 142.

30. "Memorandum from Stilwell's Chief of Staff to Commanding General, Third Indian Division, May 27, 1944," Stilwell Papers, Hoover Institution Box/Folder 21:4. ("Third Indian Division" was the "cover" name for the Chindits.)

31. This was a rail-and-road blockade of the Japanese at Hopin, south-west of Myitkyina, by the Chindits (Mountbatten, *Report to the Combined Chiefs of Staff*, 62).

32. Handwritten message from Stilwell to Sultan, May 27, 1944, *Stilwell's Personal File*, vol. 4, 1743.

33. Handwritten message from Stilwell to Sultan, May 28, 1944, Ibid., 1748. The Chindits were supposed to have cut the rail lines.

34. Mountbatten, *Report to the Combined Chiefs of Staff*, 63.

35. *Mountbatten Diary*, 114. Ziegler says in a footnote that "The point of dispute was Stilwell's handling of Lentaigne's Special Forces."

36. This was before Stilwell's diaries were published in 1948.

37. *Stilwell Papers*, 306.

38. "Notes on Meeting held at General Stilwell's Headquarters on 30 June, 1944," Stilwell Papers, Hoover Institution Box/Folder 34:16.

39. Message from Mountbatten to Stilwell, July 15, 1944, Stilwell Papers, Hoover Institution Box/Folder 25:16.

40. Ibid. The Chindits' official name was the 77th Indian Infantry Brigade.

41. Message from Stilwell to Mountbatten, July 19, 1944, Stilwell Papers, Hoover Institution Box/Folder 23:24. This was not quite true—Stilwell seemed to believe that anyone who went on the sick list was malingering (McGeoch, 126). Stilwell also said the Chindits should remain until the 36th Division had arrived.

42. Letter from Mountbatten to Stilwell, July 21, 1944, Stilwell Papers, Hoover Institution Box/Folder .25:16.

43. Letter from Mountbatten to Stilwell, July 23, 1944, Stilwell Papers, Hoover Institution Box/Folder 25:16.

44. McLynn, *Burma Campaign*, 360.

45. http://www.chindits.info/Thursday/FinalBattles.htm

46. McLynn, *Burma Campaign*, 357.

47. Ibid.

48. Ibid.

49. See McGeoch, *Princely Sailor*, 125.

50. Stilwell to [Commander] Ferris, June 2, 1944, *Stilwell's Personal File*, 1752.

51. Mountbatten, *Report to the Combined Chiefs of Staff*, 63.

52. David Rooney, *Stilwell the Patriot: Vinegar Joe, the Brits and Chiang Kai-Shek*, 208.

53. Slim, *Defeat into Victory*, 281.

54. *The Army Air Forces in World War II*, vol. 5, 209.

55. Ibid., 211.

56. "Activity Accelerates in Burma," *Stilwell's Personal File*, vol. 4, 1255.

57. Tuchman, *Stilwell*, 484. She wrote that "The capture of Myitkyina had enabled the ATC [Air Transport Command] to fly a more southerly route without fear of Japanese fighters."

58. Mountbatten, *Report to the Combined Chiefs of Staff*, 64-65.

59. "Minutes of 134th SAC Meeting," 24 July 1944, page 7, "Operations in Burma-General Stilwell's Plan," Stilwell Papers, Hoover Institution Box/Folder 33:24 (capitalization in original).

60. Churchill, *Closing the Ring*, Chapter 14, "Burma and Beyond," 569-70.

61. Mountbatten, *Report to the Combined Chiefs of Staff*, 62.

62. Ibid.

63. Letter from Mountbatten to Chiang Kai-Shek, July 28, 1944, Mountbatten Papers, #DocrefMB1/C53/42.

64. *Eisenhower: American Experience* videocassette, 1993.

Notes to Chapter Twelve

1. Tuchman, *Stilwell*, 472.

2. Paine, 201-202.

3. Romanus and Sunderland, *Stillwell's Command Problems*, 405.

4. *The West Point Atlas of American Wars: Vol. II, 1900-1953*, Maps 141, 152.

5. Tuchman, *Stilwell*, 467.

6. *Stilwell's Command Problems*, 413.

7. Tuchman, *Stilwell*, 472.

8. *Stilwell's Command Problems*, 413.

9. McLynn, *Burma Campaign*, 391.

10. Ibid.

11. *The West Point Atlas of American Wars: Vol. II, 1900-1953*, Map 141.

12. *The Army Air Forces in World War II*, vol. 5, 225.

13. *The Army Air Forces in World War II*, vol. 5, 270-271.

14. Ibid., 271.

15. Warren Kozak, *Curtis LeMay: The Life and Wars of General Curtis LeMay* (Washington D.C.: Regnery Publishing, 2014), 258. LeMay became famous for the B-29 firebombing raids on Japan in 1945. There is a photo of Stilwell and LeMay meeting in China with the headline "'BOSSES' GET TOGETHER" in the October 26, 1944 issue of *CBI Roundup*.

16. The author's grandfather, a U.S. Navy engineer and one of the celebrated "Sea Bees," helped build one of the airfields on Tinian in the Mariana Islands in the fall of 1944.

17. S.C.M. Paine, *The Wars for Asia, 1911-1949* (Cambridge: Cambridge University Press, 2012), 202.

NOTES TO CHAPTER THIRTEEN

1. The first B-29 raids on Japan were launched from China. Then the Marianas became the staging area for the all-out air assault on Japan in 1944-1945.

2. Stilwell wrote in his diary on July 21, 1944, that "SAC [Supreme Allied Commander—Mountbatten] leaving August 2. He is working to abolish the China-Burma-India [theater]" (*Stilwell Papers*, 307).

3. "Admiral Lord Louis Mountbatten's Address to the Press, August 1944: SEVEN MONTHS' BATTLE," Burma Star Association, http:// www.burmastar.org.uk/aug44mountbatten.htm.

The Burma Star Association is the main organization for British and Commonwealth veterans of the Burma Campaign. Its rules were drawn up by Mountbatten and Slim.

4. On September 12, 1944, Mountbatten wrote in his diary that he believed Stilwell had gone to the Second Quebec Conference without having informed him; Mountbatten discovered that Stilwell had actually gone to Chungking (*Mountbatten Diary*, 132-133).

5. See "The Move to Ceylon," at pages 92-96.

6. *Stilwell Papers*, 310.

7. Bruce Reynolds wrote, "Stilwell arrived in Kandy at the beginning of August 1944 well aware that Mountbatten had been attempting to oust him as deputy commander of SEAC" (Reynolds, *Thailand's Secret War*, 237).

8. "Interview of General Stilwell by the Press at Kandy, Ceylon, 5 August 1944," Stilwell Papers, Hoover Institution, Box/Folder: 34:17, page 2.

9. Ibid., 5.

10. Ibid., 7. In fact, by the end of the siege the Marauders hated Stilwell (McLynn, 355).

11. Ibid., 4.

12. Ibid., 2.

13. Stilwell urged Mountbatten to launch "a vigorous attack across the Chindwin." Handwritten note to Mountbatten, August 14, 1944, Stilwell Papers, Hoover Institution, Box/Folder: 37:4.

14. Ibid., 9.

15. *Stilwell Papers,* 309-310; Tuchman, 475.

16. Lt. Col. Dean Rusk, "Memorandum to General Stilwell, 23 August, 1944," Stilwell Papers, Hoover Institution, Box/Folder 37:3. Rusk (1909-1994) would become the Secretary of State for Presidents John F. Kennedy and Lyndon B. Johnson.

17. Hans van de Ven, "Stilwell in the Stocks: The Chinese Nationalists and the Allied Powers in the Second World War," *Asian Affairs* (November 2003).

18. Taylor, *The Generalissimo,* 292.

19. *Aide memoire* dated October 11, 1944. Quoted in Liang, 269, and in Stilwell's Command Problems, 460-462

20. *The Stilwell Papers,* 313.

21. *Stilwell's Command Problems,* 377. Since Stilwell had always been in the China Theater, it was more a case of limiting his activities to that theater, rather than "transferring" him there.

22. Ibid., 378.

23. Ibid., 377.

24. Ibid., 378.

25. Ibid., 378.

26. *Stilwell Papers*, 322.

27. Tuchman, *Stilwell*, 419-492.

28. Churchill, *Triumph and Tragedy*, 151.

29. Ibid.

30. Ziegler, *Mountbatten*, 282.

31. Ibid.

32. Tuchman, *Stilwell*, 464. This was known as the "DIXIE" Mission, so named because the Communists were the "rebels" in China (Taylor, 383).

33. Black, *FDR: Champion of Freedom*, 1008.

34. Tuchman, *Stilwell*, 493.

35. Stilwell Papers, 331-345; Taylor, 277-295; Tuchman, 499-509; Liang, Chapter X.

36. Tuchman, *Stilwell*, 501.

37. *The Army Air Forces in World War II*, vol. 5, 209.

38. Taylor, *The Generalissimo*, 295.

39. Ibid., 295-96.

40. *Stilwell Papers*, 345.

41. Ibid., 349.

42. *Mountbatten Diary*, 147-148.

43. Communication from Mountbatten to Sultan, October 28, 1944, Mountbatten Papers, Docref-MB1/C62/92.

44. Message from Mountbatten to Carton de Wiart, November 1, 1944, Mountbatten Papers, #Docref=MB1/C42/50.

45. Quoted in Ziegler, *Mountbatten*, 285.

46. Slim, *Defeat into Victory*, 383.

47. Wedemeyer, 303-304. Wedemeyer wrote that Stilwell could at least have waited a day or two.

48. John J. McLaughlin, *General Albert C. Wedemeyer: America's Unsung Strategist in World War II* (Philadelphia: Casemate, 2012), 125, fn. 18.

49. Major General Francis Festing (1902-1976), later Field Marshal Sir Francis Festing, Commanding Officer of the British-Indian 36th Division.

50. Letter from Stilwell to Auchinleck, 20 October 1944, *Stilwell's Personal File*, vol. 5, 2537. Auchlinleck never saw Stilwell in Carmel, because Stilwell died in 1946.

51. Letter from Stilwell to Festing, 20 October 1944, *Stilwell's Personal File*, 2544.

52. Letter from Stilwell to Wavell, 20 October 1944, *Stilwell's Personal File*, 2566.

53. Letter from Stilwell to Slim, 20 October 1944, *Stilwell's Personal File*, 2559. McLynn overlooked this letter and says Stilwell did not write Slim, suspecting they fell out over the Chindits (407).

54. Tuchman, *Stilwell*, 503.

55. Taylor claims Stilwell did not write any farewell letters to Chinese generals at the time of his recall (Taylor, 295). In fact, he wrote several such letters. See *Stilwell's Personal File*: China-Burma-India 1942-1944, vol. 5, 2546-2564.

56. Message 20 October 1944, Stilwell to Wessels for Mountbatten, *Stilwell's Personal File*, vol. 5, 2522.

57. "General Stilwell and S.E.A.C —Farewell Messages," *The Times* (London), November 3, 1944.

58. Letter dated October 26, 1944, Mountbatten to Stilwell, Stilwell Papers, Hoover Institution.

59. Ibid.

60. Stilwell Diary, Hoover Institution, November 24, 1944, page 263.

61. Letter dated January 27, 1945, Mountbatten to Stilwell, Stilwell Papers, Hoover Institution.

62. Letter dated February 23, 1945, Stilwell to Mountbatten, Stilwell Papers, Hoover Institution, Box/Folder 59:2.

63. "Earl Mountbatten of Burma, 79, Military Strategist and Statesman," *New York Times*, August 28, 1979.

64. Robert Musel, "British May Shift Asia Commands: Increasing Evidence of Reshuffle Expected to Include Mountbatten," *Los Angeles Times*, November 2, 1944. The "not on speaking terms" comment was also reported in the *New York Times* in an article entitled "Mountbatten Shift Expected" (*New York Times*, November 1, 1944).

65. Hansen Baldwin, "Behind the Removal of Gen. Stilwell," *New York Times*, October 30, 1944.

66. Quoted in Taylor, 295. According to Taylor, Atkinson did not ask Hurley or anyone else about the complex situation in China, which could have balanced Stilwell's account.

67. "Reshuffle of Mountbatten Command Forecast in London," *Los Angeles Times*, October 30, 1944.

68. Ziegler, *Mountbatten*, 284; see also *The Army Air Forces in World War II*, vol. 5, 232. The authors say that Mountbatten was "pleased" by Stilwell's recall because he had had "his own difficulties with Stilwell regarding proposals for reorganization within SEAC."

69. Mountbatten, *Report to the Combined Chiefs of Staff,* 85.

70. "Gen. Stilwell Is Recalled from Command in Burma," *Los Angeles Times,*October 29, 1944.

71. McLynn, *Burma Campaign,* 230-231.

72. The U.S. Army produced a documentary titled *The Stilwell Road* (1945), which is now at the National Archives. The film was narrated by Ronald Reagan. After VJ Day, the Stilwell Road closed on November 1, 1945.

http://www.youtube.com/watch?v=7eR-fzhSguU

73. Communication dated January 25, 1945, between the U.S. Chiefs of Staff and Mountbatten. Mountbatten Papers, #Docref=MBI/C63/2/16.

74. *West Point Atlas of American Wars,* Map 152.

75. Stilwell Diary 1944, Hoover Institution, 262.

76. "Stilwell: The GIs' Favorite," *Yank: The Army Weekly,* October 6, 1944.

77. *The Charlotte News,* November 16, 1944.

78. "UNCLE JOE" CHATS ABOUT GARDEN, FAMILY, WEATHER," *CBI Roundup,* November 23, 1944. *CBI Roundup* also covered Stilwell's final homecoming from the war in its November 8, 1945, issue.

79. *Time,* November 27, 1944.

80. Stilwell Diary, Hoover Institution, page 279.

81. Stilwell Diary, Hoover Institution, page 314.

82. Ibid.

83. "Gen. Joe Stilwell Dies at Bay City," *Los Angeles Times,* October 13, 1946, 6.

84. Operation Crossroads involved approximately 40,000-42,000 military personnel, mostly Navy. A 1996 article in *The Argus-Press* said that

no increased cancer deaths were found among sailors in the 1946 test. (https://news.google.com/newspapers)

85. "Gen. Joe Stilwell Dies at Bay City," *Los Angeles Times*, October 13, 1946.

86. "Gen. Stilwell Dies; China-Burma Hero Headed Sixth Army," *New York Times*, October 12, 1946 and "Gen. Joe Stilwell Dies at Bay City," *Los Angeles Times*, October 13, 1946.

87. GEN. J. W. STILWELL, THE FAR EASTERN WAR (*The Times*, October 14, 1946).

88. "Gen. Joe Stilwell Dies at Bay City," *Los Angeles Times*, October 13, 1946, 6.

89. http://www.nytimes.com/1991/05/25/obituaries/alison-stil-well-cameron-author-70.html

90. Her son John S. Easterbrook has graciously assisted the author on several occasions by answering questions about General Stilwell and about the Burma Campaign, in which his father, Colonel Ernest Easterbrook, also served.

NOTES TO CHAPTER FOURTEEN

1. "Far-Flung and Forgotten: Britain and the War in Burma," *Despatches* (Summer 2010), 22-26.

2. *West Point Atlas*, Map 151.

3. Ziegler, *Mountbatten*, 299; Richard Frank, *Downfall: The End of the Imperial Japanese Empire* (New York: Penguin Books, 1999), 243-44, 244.

4. *Mountbatten Diary*, 238.

5. http://books.stonebooks.com/record/1001915

6. Ziegler, *Mountbatten*, 301. According to Ziegler the Allies might have suffered a costly setback if the Japanese had resisted, because the

beaches did not support the weight of the British armored vehicles, but the Japanese would have been too weak to actually stop the landings.

7. Ibid., 300.

8. Ibid., 303.

9. Spector, *Ruins of Empire*, 74.

10. Ziegler, 324. Ziegler used the word "collaborated," which in the context of the Axis Powers in World War II is tantamount to an accusation of treason.

11. *Mountbatten Diary*, 288-289.

12. Ziegler, *Mountbatten,*317.

13. Ibid., 318.

14. Slim, *Defeat into Victory*, 520.

15. *Mountbatten Diary*, 241.

16. Ziegler, 322.

17. This internment was mentioned in Chapter 2, at page 25. U Saw was later tried for murder and hanged.

18. See Stanley Karnow, *Vietnam: A History* (New York: Penguin Books, 1984), 165.

19. Leclerc was the French representative when the Japanese surrendered on the USS *Missouri*.

20. Ziegler, *Mountbatten*, 333.

21. Karnow, *Vietnam: A History*, 148.

22. Ziegler, *Mountbatten*, 330.

23. D. Cameron Watt, *Succeeding John Bull: America in Britain's Place 1900-1975* (Cambridge: Cambridge University Press, 1984), 239. On p. 252

he uses the term "moral imperialism" to describe the U.S. as the new superpower in the Cold War after 1945.

24. Ziegler, *Mountbatten,* 333.

25. This is where soldiers of the Indian Army fought under British command for the last time before independence in 1947.

26. Mallaby is buried in the Commonwealth War Graves Commission Cemetery in Menteng Pulo, Jakarta.

27. Ziegler, *Mountbatten,* 335.

28. Quoted in Ziegler, *Mountbatten,* 338.

29. Ibid.

30. Peter Dennis, *Troubled Days of Peace: Mountbatten and South East Asia Command, 1945-46* (New York: St. Martin's Press, 1987), 2.

31. Mountbatten helped to broker the transition to Indian and Pakistani independence and partition in 1947, which was probably his most notable (and controversial) achievement, and which has been the subject of several books and at least one television series, *Mountbatten: The Last Viceroy* (ITV, 1986).

32. See Noble Frankland, *History at War: The Campaigns of an Historian* (London: Giles de la Mare Publishers Limited, 1998), 183, for a shrewd and generally favorable assessment of Mountbatten's character. Frankland, the former director of the Imperial War Museum, wrote, "I admired Mountbatten and saw him as a major figure in the history of the twentieth century."

33. John J. Sbrega, *Anglo-American Relations and Colonialism in East Asia* (New York: Garland Publishing, Inc., 1983), 236, fn. 30.

34. Smith, *Apprentice War Lord,* 27.

35. "Earl Mountbatten of Burma, 79, Military Strategist and Statesman," *The New York Times,* October 28, 1979, p. A 10.

Notes to Chapter Fifteen

1. Hans Van de Ven, "Stilwell in the Stocks: The Chinese Nationalists and the Allied Powers in the Second World War," *Asian Affairs* 39, no. 3 (November 2003). A critical essay about what that author called the "Stilwell myth."

2. Patton was put in charge of Operation Fortitude before D-Day to deceive the Germans about the landings in Normandy, making them think they were a diversion.

3. McLynn, *Burma Campaign,* 407.

4. Conrad Black, *Franklin Delano Roosevelt: Champion of Freedom,* 720. In fact, Stilwell's diary entry for November 7, 1944, Election Day, when he was back home in Carmel, read in part "Girls voted. No use. The Jackass [FDR] won ---," Stilwell Diaries, Hoover Institution, http://media.hoover.org/sites/default/files/documents/1944Stilwell20120516.pdf. (This entry is not contained in *The Stilwell Papers* edited by Theodore White.)

5. Jonathan Fenby, *Chiang Kai-shek: China's Generalissimo and the Nation He Lost* (New York: Carroll & Graf Publishers, 2003), 431.

6. McLynn, *Burma Campaign,* 230-231.

7. Sunderland and Romanus, eds., *Stilwell's Command Problems,* 472.

8. See, for example, D.C. Watt, *Succeeding John Bull: America in Britain's Place 1900-1975* (Cambridge: Cambridge University Press, 1984), *passim.* Even Ziegler suggested that Mountbatten was "naive" in his favorable assessment of the Malayan Communists after the war (Ziegler, 314).

9. Karnow, *Vietnam: A History,* 175, quoting Secretary of State Dean Acheson.

10. However, there were some Americans other than Stilwell who thought Mountbatten was an "extremely popular and capable commander skillful at smoothing Anglo-American relations" (Rasor, *Earl Mountbatten*

of Burma, 1900-1979: Historiography and Annotated Bibliography, 119, citing Thurzal Q. Terry, *Strangers in Their Land: C-B-I- Bombardier, 1939-1945,* 65-71).

11. Hastings, *Retribution,* 66.

12. Bayly and Harper, *Forgotten Armies,* xxix.

13. Jackson, *The British Empire and the Second World War,* 531.

14. "Reckoning" 1945 and after, *The World at War* (Thames Television, 1974).

15. Paul Scott, *The Raj Quartet: The Division of the Spoils* (Chicago: University of Chicago Press, 1975), 208. The books were adapted into the British TV miniseries *The Jewel in the Crown* (1984) on *Masterpiece Theater* (now *Masterpiece*) on PBS.

16. Wedemeyer, 257-258. Although Stilwell had never been an "Indian fighter" he was certainly "old-fashioned" and was, from first to last, a "field soldier." Shortly before his death he was awarded the Combat Infantryman Badge, one of only three general officers in the history of the U.S. Army to be so honored (Tuchman, 528).

NOTES TO EPILOGUE

1. Viscount Mountbatten of Burma, "The Strategy of the South-East Asia Campaign," *Journal of the Royal United Services Institution* 91, no. 564 (November 1946). The editor noted that "General Stilwell's death was reported three days after this lecture was given" (470-471, fn. 1).

NOTES TO APPENDIX A

1. Tuchman, *Stilwell,* 449.

2. *Stilwell's Command Problems,* 233; Nathan Prefer, *Vinegar Joe's War: Stilwell's Campaigns for Burma* (Novato, CA: Presidio Press, 2000), 148.

3. Rooney, *Stilwell the Patriot*, 206. Rooney is generally favorable towards Stilwell, so this criticism should not be lightly dismissed.

4. McLynn, *Burma Campaign*, 348. McLynn, like Rooney, is generally supportive of Stilwell.

5. Louis Allen, *Burma: The Longest War, 1941-1945* (London: J.M. Dent & Sons Ltd., 1984), 367. Allen was a Burma Campaign veteran whose book was highly critical of Stilwell.

6. Central Intelligence Agency Historical Review Program, "Gallahad: Intelligence Aspects," 22 September 1993, https://www.cia.gov/library/center-for-the-study-of-intelligence/kent-csi/vol5no1/html/v05i1a04p_0001.htm. The CIA is the successor to the wartime Office of Strategic Services (OSS), which had armed and trained the Kachin Rangers in North Burma (Moser, 131).

7. The World War II Diaries of Ernest F. Easterbrook (1944-45), Ernest Fred Easterbrook Papers, Hoover Institution. The diaries were transcribed and are available on line in digital form, http://www.hoover.org/library-and-archives/collections/east-asia/featured-collections/ernest-easterbrook

8. "Minutes of an Administrative Staff Conference held at Chabua, on Friday, 9 June 1944," 2-3. Stilwell Papers, Hoover Institute, Box/Folder 33:24. The fight for Imphal was still going on in early June 1944 and aircraft were needed to support the British defense there.

9. Stilwell Diaries, Hoover Institution, http://www.hoover.org/library-and-archives/collections/east-asia/featured-collections/joseph-stilwell

10. Mountbatten, *Report to the Combined Chiefs of Staff*, 65, 74.

11. Eldridge, *Wrath in Burma*, 270. Stilwell wrote in his diary for July 8, "Haslett of 36 Div. in. Good looking egg." (Stilwell Diaries, Hoover Institution, http://www.hoover.org/library-and-archives/collections/east-asia/featured-collections/joseph-stilwell)

12. Lyall Wilkes, *Festing-Field Marshal: A Study of Front Line Frankie, GCB., KBE., DSO* (Sussex, England: The Book Guild Ltd., 1991), 43.

13. David Quaid, conversation with John Easterbrook, March 21, 2002, described in an email from John Easterbrook to the author, October 12, 2012.

14. Lyall Wilkes, *Festing-Field Marshal,* 42.

15. McLynn, *Burma Campaign,* 348, 355.

16. Ziegler, *Mountbatten,* 274.

17. Slim, *Defeat into Victory,* 279.

18. Ibid., 280.

Annotated Bibliography

Books

Allen, Louis. *Burma: The Longest War, 1941-45*. London and Melbourne: J.M. Dent & Sons Ltd, 1984. A good overall look at the Burma Campaign from the British and Japanese perspectives by the late British historian who served in the Burma Campaign. Allen did not like Stilwell and his book makes that very clear.

Angle, Paul M., ed. *By These Words*. New York: Rand McNally & Co., 1954.

Bayley, Christopher, and Tim Harper. *Forgotten Armies: The Fall of British Asia, 1941-1945*. Cambridge, MA: The Belknap Press of Harvard University Press, 2005; originally published in UK in 2004 by Penguin Books Ltd. A new political, military and social history of how British Asia collapsed during World War II, and its aftermath. This book looks at the Burma Campaign in the larger context of the end of British Asia during World War II.

Black, Conrad. *Franklin Delano Roosevelt: Champion of Freedom*. New York: Public Affairs, 2003. A one-volume biography of FDR, full of shrewd insights. Several passages about the Stilwell-FDR relationship.

Burk, Kathleen. *Old World, New World: Great Britain and America from the Beginning*. New York: Grove Press, 2007. A recent history of the Anglo-American relationship by an American professor of history who lives and teaches in Britain.

Churchill, Winston S. *The Second World War: The Hinge of Fate*. Boston: Houghton Mifflin Company, 1950.

———. *Closing the Ring*. Boston: Houghton Mifflin Company, 1951. Volume five.

———. *Triumph and Tragedy*. Boston: Houghton Mifflin Company, 1953. Volume six.

Coffman, Edward M. *The Regulars: The American Army, 1898-1941.* Cambridge: The Belknap Press of Harvard University Press, 2004. A fine history of the U.S. Army from the Spanish-American War to World War II.

Craven, Wesley Frank, and James Lea Cate, eds., *The Army Air Forces in World War II: Volume One: Plans and Early Operations, January 1939 to August 1942.* Washington, D.C.: Office of Air Force History, 1948, 1983.

Craven, Wesley Frank, and James Lea Cate, eds., *The Army Air Forces in World War II: Volume Five: The Pacific, June 1944 to August 1945.* Washington, D.C.: Office of Air Force History, 1953, 1983.

Davies, John Paton, Jr. *Dragon by the Tail: American, British, Japanese, and Russian Encounters With China and One Another.* New York: W.W. Norton & Company, Inc., 1972. A memoir by Stilwell's Chinese chief political advisor in CBI.

De Conde, Alexander. *A History of American Foreign Policy.* New York: Charles Scribner's Sons, 1963.

Dennis, Peter. *Troubled Days of Peace: Mountbatten and South East Asia Command, 1945-46.* New York: St. Martin's Press, 1987. Covers SEAC in the period from VJ Day to 1946.

Dimbleby, Jonathan. *Destiny in the Desert: The Road to El Alamein – The Battle That Turned The Tide.* London: Profile Books Ltd, 2012. Mentions Stilwell and his role during Churchill's meeting with FDR in Washington in 1941-1942.

Eisenhower, Dwight D. *Crusade in Europe.* New York: Doubleday and Company, Inc., 1948. Eisenhower's memoir of the European war mentions his relationship with Mountbatten in 1942.

Eldridge, Fred. *Wrath in Burma: The Uncensored Story of General Stilwell and International Maneuvers in the Far East.* New York: Doubleday & Company, Inc., 1946. Eldridge was an American major in CBI and Stilwell's public relations officer. His memoir, which was published while Stilwell was still living, took a very favorable view of Stilwell.

Esposito, Brig. Gen. Vincent J., Chief Ed. *The West Point Atlas of American Wars: Vol. II, 1900-1953.* New York: Frederick A. Praeger, Publishers,

1959, 1964. The classic account of U.S. military campaigns, this book has excellent maps of the Asian-Pacific War, including the Burma Campaign.

Fenby, Jonathan. *Chiang Kai-shek: China's Generalissimo and the Nation He Lost.* New York: Carroll & Graf Publishers, 2003. A recent biography of Chiang.

Frank, Richard. *Downfall: The End of the Imperial Japanese Empire.* New York: Penguin Books, 1999. A history of the end of Pacific War, which briefly mentions Burma.

———."Why Truman Dropped the Bomb." *The Weekly Standard*, August 8, 2005.

Frankland, Noble. *History at War: The Campaigns of an Historian.* London: Giles de la Mare Publishers Limited, 1998. A memoir by the former director of the Imperial War Museums who worked with Mountbatten on *The Life and Times of Lord Mountbatten* and *The World at War.*

Gilbert, Martin. *Churchill and America.* New York: Free Press, 2005. Churchill's late official historian on the great leader's American roots.

Graham, Gordon. "BROWSING THROUGH A TREASURE HOUSE: The Literature of the Burma Campaign." http://eprints.soas.ac.uk/11668 /1/BCML-W.G.Graham2011.pdf. A list of the major books about the Burma Campaign.

Hastings, Max. *Retribution: The Battle for Japan, 1944-45.* New York: Alfred A. Knopf, 2008. (Published in the UK as *Nemesis*) Excellent short commentaries on Mountbatten and Stilwell in a recent book by one of the great modern British military historians.

Horne, Alistair. "In Defense of Montgomery." *No End Save Victory: Perspectives on World War II.* New York: Berkeley Books, 2001. Essay on Montgomery.

Hough, Richard. *Mountbatten: A Biography.* New York: Random House, 1981. Early biography of Mountbatten. Solid, readable account of Mountbatten's life, but only a cursory treatment of the Stilwell-Mountbatten relationship, implying that they were closer than they actually were.

———. *Edwina: Countess Mountbatten of Burma.* New York: William Murrow and Company, Inc., 1984. A companion biography of Mountbatten's wife by the same author.

Imperial War Museum. The Trustees of the Imperial War Museum, 2000, 2014. The Imperial War Museum guidebook, which mentions the Burma Campaign as part of the War in the Far East.

Iriye, Akira. *Japan and the Wider World: From the Mid-nineteenth Century to the Present.* London and New York: Longman, 1997. Overview of modern Japan since 1850.

Jackson, Ashley. *The British Empire and the Second World War.* Continuum International Publishing Group, 2006. A recent history of the British Empire in World War II, emphasizing that for the British, World War II was an imperial, not just a European, conflict.

James, Robert Rhodes. *Anthony Eden: A Biography.* McGraw-Hill Book Company, 1986. There is a moving account of the death of Eden's older son in an aircrash in Burma near the end of the war and Mountbatten's kindness toward Eden at the time.

Jenkins, Roy. *Churchill: A Biography.* New York: Plume, 2001. A one-volume biography of Churchill by the late British historian and Labor peer.

Karnow, Stanley. *Vietnam: A History.* New York: Penguin Books, 1984.

Keegan, John. *Six Armies in Normandy: From D-Day to the Liberation of Paris.* New York: Penguin Books, 1994; originally published 1982. A look at the U.S. strategy in Europe and Asia along with character studies of Stilwell and Wedemeyer, by the late British military historian.

Kozak, Warren. *Curtis LeMay: The Life and Wars of General Curtis LeMay.* Washington, D.C.: Regnery Publishing, 2014. (https://books.google.com)

Larrabee, Eric. *Commander in Chief: Franklin Delano Roosevelt, His Lieutenants, and Their War.* New York: Harper & Row, 1987. A study of FDR's wartime leadership with his generals and admirals during World War II. Very favorable towards Stilwell.

Liang, Chin-tung. *General Stilwell in China, 1942-1944: the full story* (Asia in the Modern World Series, no. 12). St. John's University Press, 1972. A study of Stilwell's role in CBI. Not favorable to Stilwell, although in fairness Liang says that readers should read both sides.

Manchester, William. *The Last Lion: Winston Spencer Churchill: Vil. II, Alone, 1932-1940.* Boston, Toronto, London: Little, Brown and Company, 1988. One of the best- written biographies of Churchill. Manchester, a World War II U.S. Marine veteran, also wrote a classic biography of Douglas MacArthur: *American Caesar* (1978).

McGeoch, Sir Ian, Vice-Admiral. *The Princely Sailor: Mountbatten of Burma.* London: Brassey's (UK) Ltd., 1996. Solid, readable biography by a retired vice-admiral of the Royal Navy.

McLaughlin, John J. *General Albert C. Wedemeyer: America's Unsung Strategist in World War II.* Philadelphia: Casemate Publishers, 2012. Recent biography of Wedemeyer and his largely forgotten role as the main military strategist in World War II. McLaughlin clearly admires Wedemeyer and is critical of Stilwell, while granting him his due as a field commander.

McLynn, Frank. *The Burma Campaign: Disaster into Triumph, 1942-1945.* New Haven: Yale University Press, 2011. The most recent book on the Burma Campaign focuses on Slim, Mountbatten, Stilwell, and Wingate. Slim comes off the best, Wingate the worst. Balanced views of both Stilwell and Mountbatten. McLynn is highly critical of Taylor's recent biography of Chiang, but he makes a similar mistake regarding Stilwell's farewell letters. McLynn says Stilwell did not write Slim a farewell letter, when in fact he did (McLynn, 407).

Mitter, Rana. *Forgotten Ally: China's World War II, 1937-1945.* New York: Houghton Mifflin Harcourt, 2013. Covers China's often forgotten role in the war.

Moran, Lord. (Charles McMoran Wilson 1st Baron Moran of Manton) *Churchill at War 1940-45.* (New York, Carroll & Graf, 2002), 116-117. First published in the UK as *Churchill: The Struggle for Survival*

1940-1965. Although in the form of a diary, the book was really a compilation of notes made at the time and later added to.

Morris, Eric. "Uncommon Commoner." *No End Save Victory: Perspectives on World War II.* New York: Berkeley Books, 2001. Essay on Slim and the Burma Campaign.

Mountbatten, Admiral the Earl Mountbatten of Burma. *Report to the Combined Chiefs of Staff by Supreme Allied Commander South-East Asia, 1943-1945.* London: His Britannic Majesty's Stationery Office, 1951. This is the official report. A detailed account of Mountbatten's SEAC command and the Burma Campaign from his perspective.

Overy, Richard. *Why the Allies Won.* New York: W.W. Norton & Company, 1995. A study of how the Allies won the war after 1942.

Paine, S.C.M. *The Wars For Asia, 1911-1949.* Cambridge: Cambridge University Press, 2012. A recent history of the Second Sino-Japanese War and the Chinese Civil War, which places it in the wider context of World War II.

Peattie, Mark, Edward Drea, and Hans van der Ven, eds. *The Battle for China: Essays on the Military History of the Sino-Japanese War of 1937-1945.* Stanford, CA: University of Stanford Press, 2011. A recent anthology of the Sino-Japanese War and its role in World War II.

Pike, Francis. *Hirohito's War: The Pacific War, 1941-1945.* London: Bloomsbury Publishing, 2015.

Prefer, Nathan. *Vinegar Joe's War: Stilwell's Campaigns for Burma.* Novato, CA: Presidio Press, 2000.

Rasor, Eugene L. *The China-Burma-India Campaign, 1931-1945: Historiography and Annotated Bibliography.* Westport, CT: Greenwood Press, 1998.

———. *Earl Mountbatten of Burma, 1900-1979: Historiography and Annotated Bibliography.* Westport, Conn and London: Greenwood Press, 1998. An excellent source that lists all of the relevant literature about Mountbatten and contains a thorough discussion of that literature, interwoven with a chronology of his life and career.

Raugh, Jr., Harold E. *Fort Ord* (Images of America series). Charleston, SC: Arcadia Publishing, 2004. Briefly mentions Stilwell in command at Fort Ord, Monterey, California, in 1940-1941.

Reynolds, David. *Rich Relations: The American Occupation of Britain, 1942-1945*. London: Phoenix Press, 2000; originally published 1995. The classic account of the creation of the Anglo-American relationship during World War II.

Reynolds, E. Bruce. *Thailand's Secret War: The Free Thai, OSS and SOE during World War II*. Cambridge: Cambridge University Press, 2005. This book is an excellent account of special operations in Thailand and Southeast Asia during the war. Page 237, especially footnote 122, contains a capsule summary of the Stilwell-Mountbatten relationship.

Ritter, James R., Capt., CEC, USNR. *The War Years 1941-1946*. The author's grandfather's unpublished memoirs of his wartime experiences in the Pacific from 1942-1945, which were written in the 1980s.

Roberts, Andrew. *A History of the English-Speaking Peoples Since 1900*. New York: HarperCollins*Publishers*, 2006; first published in Great Britain by Weidenfeld and Nicolson. Overview of the Anglo-American relationship in the twentieth century and early twenty-first century. Roberts is very critical of Mountbatten.

Rooney, David. *Stilwell the Patriot: Vinegar Joe, the Brits and Chiang Kai-Shek*. London: Greenhill Books, 2005. Recent biography of Stilwell, which is generally quite favorable.

Sbrega, John J. *Anglo-American Relations and Colonialism in East Asia*. New York: Garland Publishing, Inc., 1983.

Slim, William J., Field Marshal Viscount. *Defeat into Victory: Battling Japan in Burma and India, 1942-1945*. New York: Cooper Square Press, 2000; originally published 1956. One of the great military memoirs and a good introduction to the Burma Campaign.

Smith, Adrian. *Mountbatten: Apprentice War Lord*. London: I.B. Tauris & Co Ltd., 2010. Recent biography of Mountbatten's life up to 1943, by a British historian with access to the Mountbatten Archives.

Spector, Ronald H. *In the Ruins of Empire: The Japanese Surrender and the Battle for Postwar Asia*. New York: Random House Trade Paperbacks, 2008. Groundbreaking survey history of the beginning of the Cold War in East Asia and Southeast Asia after 1945.

Sunderland, Riley, and Charles F. Romanus, ed. *Stilwell's Personal File: China-Burma-India 1942-1944*. Washington, D.C.: Scholarly Resources Inc., 1976. An excellent collection of Stilwell's wartime papers in five volumes.

———. *Stilwell's Command Problems*. Washington, D.C.: Office of the Chief of Military History, Department of the Army, 1955. Volume Two of the official U.S. Army three-volume series on Stilwell's mission to China and on the U.S. Army in CBI.

Taaffe, Stephen R. *MacArthur's Jungle War: The 1944 New Guinea Campaign*. Lawrence: University Press of Kansas, 1998. A history of MacArthur's largely forgotten New Guinea Campaign.

Taylor, Jay. *The Generalissimo: Chiang Kai-shek and the Struggle for Modern China*. Belknap Press of Harvard University Press, 2011. Sympathetic towards Chiang, highly critical of Stilwell. Contains factual errors, *e.g.*, Taylor says Stilwell did not write any farewell letters to Chinese generals at the time of his recall in 1944, when in fact he wrote several. (See *Stilwell's Personal File: China-Burma-India 1942-1944, Vol. 5*, 2546-2564)

Terraine, John. *The Life and Times of Lord Mountbatten*. New York: Holt, Rinehart and Winston, 1968, 1980. Based on the TV series about Mountbatten's life and career.

Terry, Thurzal Q. *Strangers in Their Land: C-B-I Bombardier, 1939-1945*. Manhattan, KS: Sunflower Press, 1992.

Thompson, Julian. *The Lifeblood of War: Logistics in Armed Conflict*. London: Brassey Books, 1991.

Thorne, Christopher. *Allies of a Kind: The United States, Britain, and the War against Japan*. New York: Oxford University Press, 1978. Excellent, detailed discussion of the wartime Anglo-American relationship in East Asia and Southeast Asia.

Tuchman, Barbara W. *Stilwell and the American Experience in China 1911-1945*. New York: Macmillan, 1971. The classic biography of Stilwell, for which Tuchman won a Pulitzer Prize. The focus is on Stilwell and China, not Mountbatten and Southeast Asia. However, the book does discuss their relationship, which went from Stilwell's description of Mountbatten as a "good egg" to that of a "glamour boy." Even Tuchman admits that Stilwell's acerbic tongue and Anglophobia sometimes went too far.

Tunzelmann, Alex Von. *Indian Summer: The Secret History of the End of an Empire*. New York: Henry Holt and Company, 2007. A recent history of India's independence and partition, which includes good biographies of Mountbatten and his wife.

Warren, Alan. *Burma 1942: The Road from Rangoon to Mandalay*. London: Continuum International Publishing Group, 2011. A recent history of the 1942 Burma Campaign and how it shaped the war in Southeast Asia.

Watt, D. Cameron. *Succeeding John Bull: America in Britain's Place 1900-1975*. Cambridge: Cambridge University Press, 1984. Good overall survey of Anglo-American relations, with two essays on point, "Britain, America and Indo-China, 1942-1945," and "American anti-colonialist policies and the end of the European colonial empires, 1941-1962." Concludes the U.S, and FDR in particular, went overboard in their anti-colonialism.

Webster, Donovan. *The Burma Road: The Epic Story of the China-Burma-India Theater in World War II*. New York: Harper Perennial, 2003, 2004. A recent history of the Burma Road and its key role in CBI.

Wedemeyer, Albert C. *Wedemeyer Reports!* New York: Henry Holt & Company, 1958. Wedemeyer's own account of CBI and his uneasy relationship with Stilwell.

White, Theodore H., ed. *The Stilwell Papers*. New York: Da Capo Press, 1991; originally published 1948. Good introduction to Stilwell in CBI from his wartime diary. Unfortunately, it perpetuated the "Vinegar Joe" image of Stilwell for almost 60 years after Stilwell's death.

Wilkes, Lyall. *Festing-Field Marshal: A Study of Front Line Frankie, GCB., KBE., DSO* (Sussex, England: The Book Guild Ltd.), 1991, 42. A good short biography of the Commanding General of the British-Indian 36th Division.

Woolner, David B., Warren F. Kimball, and David Reynolds, eds. *FDR's World: War, Peace, and Legacies.* New York: Palgrave Macmillan, 2008.

Ziegler, Philip. *Mountbatten: A Biography.* New York: Alfred A. Knopf, 1985. The official biography, which shows Mountbatten as a great and complex leader, while not ignoring his vanity and egotism. (Rasor calls Ziegler's book "a model for official biography.") (Rasor, *Earl Mountbatten of Burma, 1900-1979: Historiography and Annotated Bibliography*, p.126) _____*Personal Diary of Admiral the Lord Louis Mountbatten.* London: Collins, 1988. Edited by Philip Ziegler. Good introduction to Mountbatten and SEAC, but, unlike Stilwell's acerbic diary entries, these were written with an eye to posterity.

Articles (Authored)

Babb, J.G.D. "Double Victory: Minorities and Women During World War II: Arakan, Second Campaign (December 1943-July 1944)." http://www.historyandheadlines.abc-clio.com

Baldwin, Hansen. "Confusion over Burma Warfare: American and British Differences over Strategy and Chinese Backwardness are Among Factors." *New York Times,* April 12, 1944.

_____."Behind the Removal of Gen. Stilwell." *New York Times,* October 30, 1944.

Brebner, J. Bartlett. "Canada, The Anglo-Japanese Alliance and the Washington Conference." *Political Science Quarterly* 50, no. 1 (March 1935): 45-58.

Kikuchi, Ian. "Far-Flung and forgotten: Britain and the war in Burma." *Despatches* (Summer 2010). Why the Burma Campaign and its aftermath has been largely forgotten in the British view of World War II.

MacCormac, John. "A Rift Over Burma Put To Roosevelt: Stilwell and Mountbatten Are Divided on Method and Speed in Operations." *New York Times,* March 3, 1944.

Mountbatten, Admiral the Viscount Mountbatten of Burma. "The Strategy of the South-East Asia Campaign." *Journal of the Royal United Services Institution* 91 (November 1946): 469-484.

Musel, Robert. "British May Shift Asia Commands: Increasing Evidence of Reshuffle Expected to Include Mountbatten." *Los Angeles Times,* November 2, 1944.

Ritter, Jonathan. "Mountbatten, Anglo-American Policy, and the Creation of Modern Southeast Asia after World War II." *Stanford Journal of East Asian Affairs* 10, no. 2 (Summer 2010).

Sbrega, John J. "Anglo-American Relations and the Selection of Mountbatten as Supreme Allied Commander, South East Asia." *Military Affairs* 46 (October 1982): 139-145.

Smith, Adrian. "Mountbatten Goes to the Movies: Promoting the Heroic Myth Through Cinema." *Historical Journal of Film, Radio, and Television* 26, no. 3 (2006): 395-416.

Van de Ven, Hans. "Stilwell in the Stocks: The Chinese Nationalists and the Allied Powers in the Second World War." *Asian Affairs* 39, no. 3 (November 2003). A critical essay about what that author called the "Stilwell myth."

ARTICLES (UNATTRIBUTED)

"Open Letter" to the "People of England." *Life,* October 12, 1942.

"Gen Stilwell Is Recalled From Command in Burma." *Los Angeles Times,* October 29, 1944.

"Reshuffle of Mountbatten Forecast in London," "Censors Cut Stilwell Dispatch to a Few Words." *Los Angeles Times,* October 30, 1944.

"Unfinished Job Disappointing to Stilwell." *The Washington Post,* November 3, 1944.

"Stilwell, Mountbatten Exchange Best Wishes." *New York Times,* November 3, 1944.

"'UNCLE JOE' CHATS ABOUT GARDEN, FAMILY, WEATHER." *CBI Roundup,* November 23, 1944.

"The Last Viceroy of India: Remembering Lord Louis Mountbatten." *Royal Life* (*Royal Britain*), 2014. Illustrated article on Mountbatten.

"U.S. Department of State Office of the Historian: MILESTONES: 1937-1945," "1937-1945: Diplomacy and the Road to Another War: Introduction," "Japan, China, the United States and the Road to Pearl Harbor, 1937-41," "Wartime Conferences, 1941-1945." https://history. state.gov

Videocassettes and On-Line Sources

"It's a Lovely Day Tomorrow: Burma 1942-1944," *The World at War* (Thames Television, 1973, 1974). A good visual introduction to the Burma Campaign with interviews of the key participants, including Mountbatten. Also interviewed about SEAC after VJ Day in "Reckoning—1945 and after." Also includes period footage of the war in Burma and the aftermath of war in Southeast Asia, with interviews of the veterans and leading military figures, including Mountbatten, who justified his use of Japanese troops to maintain order and described his advice to Leclerc to try and work with the Vietnamese.

The Pacific War Online Encyclopedia, http://pwencycl.kgbudge.com/M/ y/Myitkyina.htm

"General Stilwell Takes Over New Command." (*United News*, 1945). http:// video.google.com/videoplay?docid=3077885841127534029

"General Joseph Stilwell Museum – Chongqing." http://www.youtube. com/watch?v=8Urpi0mklts

C. Peter Chen. "Joseph Stilwell," http://ww2db.com/person_bio.php? person_id=18

*Stilwell Road,*U.S. Army documentary, 1945 (Narrated by Ronald Reagan)

Archives Consulted

Stilwell Papers, Hoover Institution, Stanford University, California.

The World War II Diaries of General Joseph W. Stilwell (1941-1945).

The World War II Diaries of Ernest F. Easterbrook (1944-45).

Papers of Earl Mountbatten of Burma, South East Asia Command, 1943-6, Mountbatten Papers Database, Special Collections, Hartley Library, University of Southampton, UK

The War in the Far East: The Burma Campaign 1941-1945, Imperial War Museum Collections and Research, London, UK.

The National Archives of Singapore, online archives.

Life Magazine Archives http://books.google.com/books?id=TUEEAAAAMBAJ&pg=PA34&source=gbs_toc_r&cad=2#v=onepage&q&f=false

INDEX